IDENTITY, RIGHTS AND CONSTITUTIONAL TRANSFORMATION

Identity, Rights and Constitutional Transformation

Edited by
PATRICK J. HANAFIN
University of Sussex

MELISSA S. WILLIAMS
University of Toronto

Routledge
Taylor & Francis Group
LONDON AND NEW YORK

First published 1999 by Ashgate Publishing

Reissued 2018 by Routledge
2 Park Square, Milton Park, Abingdon, Oxon OX14 4RN
711 Third Avenue, New York, NY 10017, USA

Routledge is an imprint of the Taylor & Francis Group, an informa business

Publisher's Note
The publisher has gone to great lengths to ensure the quality of this reprint but points out that some imperfections in the original copies may be apparent.

Disclaimer
The publisher has made every effort to trace copyright holders and welcomes correspondence from those they have been unable to contact.

A Library of Congress record exists under LC control number: 98037430

ISBN 13: 978-1-138-31484-9 (hbk)
ISBN 13: 978-1-138-31488-7 (pbk)
ISBN 13: 978-0-429-45667-1 (ebk)

Contents

Contributors

Alan C. Cairns taught in the Political Science Department at the University of British Columbia from 1960 until his retirement in 1995. Since then he has taught at the University of Toronto and the University of Saskatchewan. In recent years his research has focused on constitutional politics in Canada, including the Charter of Rights and Freedoms, Aboriginal rights, and constitutional reform. His numerous publications include *Disruptions: Constitutional Struggles From the Charter to Meech* (1991) (McClelland and Stewart), *Charter versus Federalism: The Dilemmas of Constitutional Reform* (1992) (McGill-Queen's), and *Reconfigurations: Canadian Citizenship and Constitutional Change* (1995) (McClelland and Stewart).

Patrick Hanafin is Lecturer in Law at the University of Sussex. His research interests lie in the areas of law and literature, law and postmodernity, constitutional interpretation, law and psychoanalysis, representations of death and dying in cultural and legal discourse, and law and sexual difference. His publications include *Irish Medical Law* (with David Tomkin) (1995) (Round Hall/Sweet and Maxwell), and *Last Rights: Death, Dying and the Law in Ireland* (1997) (Cork University Press).

Vivien Hart is Professor of Politics at the University of Sussex. Her research interests include gender, law and social policy, 20th century issues of women and state, and constitutionalism and political culture. Her publications include *Bound by Our Constitution: Women Workers and the Minimum Wage* (1994) (Princeton University Press) and *Writing a National Identity: Political, Economic, and Cultural Perspectives on the Written Constitution* (co-edited with Shannon Stimson) (1993) (Manchester University Press).

Richard Iton is Assistant Professor of Political Science at the University of Toronto. His research interests include American politics, African-American politics, comparative politics, and the interaction of nationalist thought, class and race. He is the author of *Gateway Blues: Comparative Political Cultures and the Search for the Missing American Left* (forthcoming).

Robert O'Brien is Lecturer in International Relations at the University of Sussex. His research interests include global political economy, OECD trade and monetary relations, North American/EU/East Asian regional integration, and globalisation and democracy. His publications include *Subsidy Regulation and State Transformation in North America, GATT and the EU* (1997) (Macmillan), and "North American integration and international relations theory", *Canadian Journal of Political Science* (December 1995): 693-724.

Damian O'Leary is a Commonwealth Scholar and doctoral candidate at the University of Toronto. His research interests include moral and political philosophy, theories of justice, and problems of political community. His doctoral thesis is titled "Between Unity and Diversity: The Politics of Community in Northern Ireland".

Jan Aart Scholte is Reader in International Studies at Warwick University. His research interests include globalisation and social change, global trade and finance, and the geography of collective identities. His publications include *Globalisation: A Critical Introduction* (Forthcoming 1999) (Macmillan), and "Beyond the Buzzword: Towards a Critical Theory of Globalisation", in E. Kofman and G. Youngs (eds) *Globalisation: Theory and Practice* (1996) (Pinter).

Robert Vipond is Chair of the Department of Political Science at the University of Toronto. His current research centres on constitutional development in Canada and the United States with special reference to the emergence of 'rights talk' in Canada. His publications include *Liberty and Community: Canadian Federalism and the Failure of the Constitution* (1991) (State University of New York Press) as well as articles in the *Canadian Journal of Political Science*, the *Journal of Canadian Studies*, the *University of New Brunswick Law Journal*, *Publius*, and *Intergovernmental Perspectives*.

Melissa S. Williams is Associate Professor of Political Science at the University of Toronto. Her current research interests lie at the intersection of democratic theory and social diversity, and include multiculturalism, the theory of toleration, feminist theory, and legal theory. Her publications include *Voice, Trust, and Memory: Marginalized Groups and the Failings of Liberal Representation* (1998), and articles in *Political Theory*, the *Canadian Journal of Political Science*, and *Citizenship Studies*.

Acknowledgements

We would like to thank Professor Peter Russell and Professor Vivien Hart for their constant support of this project, and all the contributors for their essays and their patience and understanding. Our warm thanks as well to Ms. Hyla Levy of the Department of Political Science, University of Toronto, for her painstaking work on the manuscript. We would also like to thank both the University of Toronto and the Cunliffe Centre for the Study of Constitutionalism at the University of Sussex for funding the initial colloquium from which these essays are drawn and for continued financial assistance during the editing process. In addition we would like to extend our thanks to the Canadian High Commission for assistance with travel funds.

1 Introduction

PATRICK HANAFIN AND MELISSA S. WILLIAMS

These essays grew out of a joint University of Toronto-Sussex University Workshop on Comparative Constitutionalism, held in Toronto in April 1996. The volume, like the workshop itself, bears the clear stamp of Peter Russell from the University of Toronto and of Vivien Hart from Sussex University. Although we have taken up the role of editing the collection, Professors Russell and Hart are ultimately responsible for its existence, as they jointly organised the Workshop as part of an ongoing co-operation between the two universities in the comparative study of constitutional democracy. (They should not, of course, be held responsible for any errors we may have overlooked in the editing process.) Both have contributed extensively to the field of comparative constitutionalism, and particularly to the place of identity in constitutional formation and transformation. We are grateful for their initiative in starting the wide-ranging and, we believe, illuminating conversation that is reflected in these essays.

As we complete our work on this collection, its themes are being played out on the front pages of the newspapers. President Suharto of Indonesia has just resigned his position in favour of his Vice-President, B.J. Habibie, who has indicated an intention of holding binding democratic elections in the coming months. It appears that Suharto, who had maintained tight one-party rule, was ultimately defeated by the constitution that he himself had designed to give the flavour of legitimacy to his regime. What had been a mere paper constitution insinuated itself into the consciousness of the Indonesian people and Suharto's cabinet members, and when Suharto violated the most basic principles of constitutionally limited government he lost the support of even his closest friends and advisors (See Mydans, 1998). Constitutionalism exerts an independent force in politics, even where its progenitors do not intend for it to limit governmental power. The very existence of a constitution may help to transform the identity of individuals who live under it from subjects to rights-bearing citizens.

Ireland, meanwhile, is teaching us some further lessons about constitutions, identity and rights. In the Republic of Ireland, a sweeping 94 percent majority has approved a change to those constitutional provisions which implicitly assert an irredentist claim to the counties of Northern

Ireland. In Northern Ireland itself, a majority of both Catholics and Protestants has voted in favour of the recent Anglo-Irish agreement. In the coming months we will witness elections to a new parliamentary assembly in which neither sector will be able to out-vote the other. These changes in the constitutional provisions of the Republic and of Northern Ireland both reflect and portend transformations in the political identity of Catholics and Protestants.

Taken as a whole, these essays explore the relationship between political and cultural identity, on the one hand, and the form and content of a constitutional order, on the other hand. Constitutions are often expressions of a shared cultural and political identity. This phenomenon has both a positive side (as the embodiment of a sense of membership and political community) and a dark side (insofar as the membership of some in the political community comes at the expense of others). Thus constitutions may express both community and exclusion, solidarity and domination. But constitutions are not only passive vehicles for the expression of already-existing identities and relations of power; they can also function as engines for a shared identity, particularly through their protection of a body of civil and political rights for all citizens. Constitutional rights may lie dormant, but the possibility remains that in the hands of activists they will come to life in unexpected ways.

The national identity that is inscribed in a constitutional document is neither fixed nor stable. Writing a constitution is merely the beginning of an unending dialectic between text and people (Norton, 1988, p. 468) The notion of identity contained within a constitution is always open to disruption by contrary notions of national selfhood. As Spivak would have it: 'The text has no stable identity, no stable origin, no stable end' (Spivak, 1976, p. xii). Constitution-makers attempt to write a national identity. In other words, they attempt to pass from the imagined idea of the nation to the realised state. In attempting to write the definitive narrative of the nation, constitution-makers cannot erase the other narratives of national selfhood against which it was composed. Constitutions therefore contain the seeds of their revision. As Brannigan has pointed out: 'At the heart of the writing of national identity, is also its contradiction, its frustration, its impossibility, and waiting within these aporetic spaces, the other' (Brannigan, 1996, p. 69).

In culturally plural or divided societies, the expressive and the creative potential of constitutions exist side by side. The success of the constitutional project in such societies depends on political actors' ability both to express existing cultural identities and to forge shared political identities that can bridge the distance between different groups. Whether the creation of a shared political identity requires institutional recognition for diverse cultural identities is a subject of some controversy among the contributors to this volume. Some argue that constitutionalism in divided societies requires both that states recognise identities through their policies and that the cultural distinctiveness of each segment of society has some presence within the constitutional document itself. Others worry that the constitutional entrenchment of group differences can sometimes be a double-edged sword, aimed at eradicating unjust hierarchies among groups but inadvertently reinforcing differences that impede a sense of shared political community. These discussions deepen and illuminate, without resolving, what Martha Minow has called the 'dilemma of difference': that we often cannot overcome unjust inequalities without reasserting differences we might ultimately wish to erase (Minow, 1990, chapter 1).

Constitutions, as Alan Cairns instructs us in the opening essay, may be Janus-faced. On one side, they benevolently and impartially secure the rule of law and an order of equal rights and liberties for their citizens. But the goods that constitutions provide for citizens can often be understood by way of contrast with their stance toward non-citizens. The logic of constitutional inclusion and protection has had its counterpart in the logic of constitutional exclusion and subjugation. In some constitutional regimes, it almost appears that the value of constitutional protection can only be thoroughly enjoyed by some if it is simultaneously denied to others. Historically, constitutions have sometimes embodied this contrast by combining their exclusion of some persons from full membership or citizenship with an attribution of the moral, cultural or racial inferiority of those persons. This combination of negative cultural meanings with legal exclusions from civil and political rights is what Cairns labels 'constitutional stigmatisation'.

Cairns' comparative study of five historical cases of constitutional stigmatisation offers a fascinating and troubling portrait of the family resemblance among them. The cases begin with what Cairns calls, generically, the 'imperial constitution', a classification which points toward the broad similarity between colonial orders' exclusion of subject peoples from self-governance and their reliance upon claims of the cultural 'backwardness' of those peoples to justify strong hierarchies of rule. These regimes are interesting not only because their rationalisations of hierarchical rule echo throughout the other cases, but also because the struggles for liberation of colonised peoples have informed the political claims of subjugated groups in constitutional orders that are not usually regarded as structures of colonial rule. As Cairns points out, the claims for Aboriginal self-government in North America would not have the same resonance in a world where European powers still held sway in Africa and elsewhere. Thus 'the message of imperialism, ... as well as the message of its ending, was not restricted to the imperial rulers and the ruled. Both messages had larger consequences for the domestic politics of societies outside the imperial orbit that were divided by race/culture' (p. 16). Cairns moves from this general discussion to an exploration of Canada's treatment of Indians during most of the nineteenth and twentieth centuries as an example of 'internal colonialism'. His three remaining cases are apartheid in South Africa, segregation in the American South, and Jews in Nazi Germany.

The similarities among these cases are striking, sometimes chilling. In each case, constitutional regimes aimed to protect or enhance the racial or cultural integrity of ruling groups, whether through laws against miscegenation (as in Nazi Germany, apartheid South Africa, and the American South) or through attempts to educate 'backward' peoples into civilised world views (as in imperialist regimes and Canadian policy toward indigenous peoples). As Cairns puts it, 'much of the rhetoric and ideology that justifies stigmatisation appears to be a universal toolkit' (p. 31). But of course there are important dissimilarities among these cases as well. Their policies toward subordinate groups ranged from paternalism to extermination, according to whether their characterisations of 'otherness' were cultural (and potentially changeable) or biological (and permanent).

Cairns is reluctant to draw unambiguous conclusions from the study of constitutional stigmatisation. There is a strong tendency among contemporary political and constitutional theorists - reflected in some of the contributions to this volume - to conclude that the best remedy for constitutional stigmatisation is positive constitutional recognition for formerly excluded groups. But such positive recognition, Cairns argues, suffers from an important similarity with constitutional stigmatisation: it singles out an ethnic, national, or indigenous minority for distinctive treatment under the law. Cairns does not disagree with other contributors who argue that such devices are sometimes necessary and constructive, but he cautions that they should be used carefully, with an open mind as to whether the gains they secure outweigh their sometimes hefty costs.

Vivien Hart's contribution, 'The Contagion of Rights: Constitutions as Carriers', traces a flow of the influence of constitutional rights and principles from established constitutional regimes to African countries and -

incipiently - back again. Focusing especially on the relationship between Britain and its African colonies during the process of decolonisation in the 1950s and 1960s, Hart shows that while Britain was unwilling to entrench the European Convention on Human Rights (ECHR) into its own legal system (notwithstanding its leading role in developing the Convention), it did encourage the entrenchment of Convention rights in the 'independence constitutions' of the newly self-governing states. Concerns about ethnic and racial identity directly undergirded the entrenchment of such rights, which were seen by both African elites and by British negotiators as important pragmatic protections for minorities. For the former, the minorities in question were principally the African ethnic groups bound together by the (often arbitrary) territorial borders of colonial rule. Although interethnic harmony was undoubtedly a concern for the British as well, there is no doubt that they were also motivated to protect the civil rights - especially the property rights - of white settlers and foreign investors. In other words, both African elites and British decision makers were motivated by a distrust in the propensity of new political authorities to wield governmental power even-handedly, and they favoured the entrenchment of rights as a device for protecting their principal constituencies from political abuses. Hart's analysis suggests that the failure of independence constitutions to entrench women's rights as reliably as they entrenched the rights of religious and ethnic minorities highlights the extent to which these constitutions were seen as pragmatic devices for the security of the core interests of established elites. To the extent that rights were taken seriously in these constitutions, they were embraced less on the ground of moral principle than as practical political tools for achieving some commonality of interest among rival ethnic communities.

As Hart makes clear, even this more pragmatic understanding of constitutional rights had little political effect. The independence constitutions did not last for long; in most cases they gave way to traditional (and patriarchal) local authority structures. Nor did they actually secure minority rights while they lasted. But the historic impotence of constitutionalised rights in African states does not negate the legacy of those rights altogether. The promise of constitutional solutions to the problems of ethnic conflict, and of rights as guarantors of basic minority interests, continues to inform proposals for political reform. Moreover, the residue of paper rights in existing constitutions - including, in some cases, rights against sex discrimination - provides a toehold for activists, and there is some evidence that the litigation of such rights may be on the rise. As Hart puts it, 'Once installed, rights provisions may take on unexpected life - may be contagious' (p. 53).

Further, a rise in constitutional activism in non-Western settings may yield a new blend of universalistic and regional conceptions of human rights, including a blend of individualistic and collective rights. Hart offers the provocative suggestion that as the thought and practise of rights protection spreads, it may both give new content to Western understandings of rights and inspire new processes for the identification and specification of rights. Drawing on the South African case, Hart argues that the combination of international human rights discourses, of the mobilisation of international women's rights organisations, and of local women's activist involvement in constitutional negotiations yielded an unprecedented dissolution of strong hierarchies between civil and political rights, social and economic rights, and women's rights in the South African Constitution of 1996. As Britain, under Tony Blair's Labour government, entrenches the ECHR into its own law, it will be very interesting indeed to see whether the legacy of British constitutionalism in Africa will come home to roost in unexpected ways.

As Cairns' and Hart's contributions disclose, rights-based constitutionalism may be a double-edged sword for minorities or marginalised groups. The rights enshrined in a constitution may be defined in ways that exclude some citizens from their shelter, or may secure rights (for example, an equal right to vote in a majoritarian political system) which benefit the politically strong without protecting the politically weak. The protection of group-specific rights in constitutions or in legislation may, as Cairns points out, sometimes function to reinforce the social distance between social or cultural groups. At the same time, the very presence of rights instruments in a constitutional order often gives at least symbolic expression to the ideal of equal citizenship, and may be taken up as a political resource by marginalised groups in different ways and at different times.

Whereas Cairns and Hart explored the relationship between social identity and constitutional rights from a legal and historical perspective, Melissa Williams' essay explores this relationship from the standpoint of political theory. The constitutional protection of rights is a key element of liberal understandings of justice. Yet it is not difficult to perceive that these rights often function to preserve the advantage of some social groups over others. As feminist critics of liberal conceptions of justice and impartiality have argued, there are circumstances in which treating disadvantaged groups justly may require treating them differently. Universal or difference-blind rights of citizenship may be a tool for justice toward these groups, but they may also serve to preserve existing hierarchical structures of power and stratifications of privilege and wealth. If this is the case, Williams asks, how can we design processes for defining the content of basic legal and constitutional rights and institutions that will overcome the tendency to bias?

Recent democratic theorists have tended to converge on a general answer to this question: that justice toward marginalised groups requires that rights and legislative policies be defined within processes that are inclusive and deliberative. Williams pursues this claim by exploring how conceptions of deliberative democracy aspire to impartial political decisions, where impartiality entails both inclusiveness and absence of bias. She then considers the ways in which deliberation is likely to be complicated by differences of group identity, particularly when those differences coincide with inequalities of wealth and power. These difficulties become most apparent when one moves from the level of the theory of democratic deliberation to the level of institutions and practices. In particular, the move from theory to practice raises the difficult question of how to motivate parties to deliberate in a spirit of impartiality. Drawing on some examples from other contributions to the volume, Williams concludes that it often takes a combination of powerful moral arguments and a high level of political mobilisation among marginalised citizens for such transformative discussions to take place.

The role of constitutions in both creating and expressing cultural identities is particularly clear in Patrick Hanafin's exploration of the Irish constitution and its relation to the conflict in Northern Ireland. Articles 2 and 3 of the Irish Constitution of 1937 express an irredentist view of the Irish nation as including the counties of Northern Ireland. Whether these articles express a symbolic view of the nation or an actual legal claim to a right of sovereignty over those counties is a matter of some dispute in the legal interpretations of Irish courts. What is clear, however, is that the irredentist nationalism expressed in the constitution is a barrier to the resolution of the conflict in Northern Ireland, as it gives credence to unionist scepticism about the Irish government's willingness to accept their right to play a significant role in the governance of the region. But Hanafin argues that there is good reason to believe in the Irish government's recently expressed willingness to amend those two articles of the constitution as part of a new political settlement in Northern Ireland. The strong identification of Irishness with both Catholicism and nationalism shows signs of weakening in the Republic of Ireland, where popular sentiment may well support the new agreement.

Meanwhile, public opinion in Britain is not generally supportive of the hard line unionist position. Thus while both sections in Northern Ireland have historically relied upon a felt bond with their respective 'homelands', the sentiment may no longer be mutual: popular opinion in both 'homelands' is increasingly supportive of a political settlement, including power sharing arrangements, in Northern Ireland. The political future of Northern Ireland, then, depends importantly on the changing national identity of the Irish Republic both at the level of popular political culture and in the text of the constitution.

The key obstacle to such arrangements is the hard-line position of both unionist and nationalist leaders in Northern Ireland. As Hanafin points out, the depth of the hostility of the two sections makes it difficult for any institutional solution of the conflict to take hold: there is a limit to the extent to which formal institutions can resolve deep ethno-cultural conflicts. This problem provides the central theme for Damian O'Leary's comparison of three different approaches to the constitutional project in Northern Ireland.

Damian O'Leary's contribution focuses on the political conflict in Northern Ireland as an instance of cultural conflict, and is highly critical of past efforts to resolve the conflict because of their neglect of its cultural dimensions. O'Leary traces two paths of constitutional order in Northern Ireland: the path of liberal majoritarianism and that of consociational democracy. The former, he argues, characterised the history of the province from 1921 to 1972, and led predictably to the dominance of the Protestant majority and a Catholic sense of grievance at being excluded from significant political influence. As Patrick Hanafin's essay details, Articles 2 and 3 of the Irish Republic's constitution inscribe a Catholic and nationalist identity as the core content of Irishness, with the implicit identification of northern Protestants as the hostile 'other'. The liberal majoritarian institutions of Northern Ireland until 1972 presented the obverse constitutional image, subordinating nationalist and Catholic identity for the sake of Unionist, Protestant identity. The 1972 crisis known as 'Bloody Sunday', in which British paratroopers opened fire on civil rights protesters, made clear the unsustainability of a majoritarian approach to governance. The alternatives proposed since then have all involved some form of 'power-sharing' or consociational democracy, in which institutions balance the political clout of the Protestant majority with guarantees for the political influence of the Catholic minority. While O'Leary accepts some of the institutional features of consociationalism, he argues that these are insufficient to secure a constitutional settlement. The conflict in Northern

Ireland is not only a conflict over religion and ethnicity, but has become imbued with a strong sense of a tradition of 'Irishness' on each side. Each section has come to attach strong positive cultural meanings to its own identity and strong negative meanings to the identity of the other. Consociational solutions alone are too formalistic to overcome the cultural meanings that have grown up around the conflict, O'Leary argues, and he offers a third approach, 'substantive constitutionalism', as an alternative.

'Substantive constitutionalism' makes space for cultural identity in three ways: through the principle of *just recognition*; through procedural innovations aimed at bringing *complex voices* into dialogue with each other; and through efforts to build extra-state political interaction between cultural groups in the form of *complex publics*. O'Leary concludes his contribution by sketching out a number of political proposals which go beyond consociational arrangements and aim to build intercultural recognition in these three modes.

Richard Iton's essay continues to explore the challenge of cultural divisions to existing constitutional settlements, but extends the inquiry to the cases of the United States and Canada. Drawing on Pierre Vallière's infamous characterisation of francophone Quebeckers as 'white niggers of America', Iton advances the controversial and thought-provoking thesis that cultural divisions pose a greater threat to the political health of the United States than to that of Canada. If we understand political health in terms of the capacity of political institutions to channel social and political conflict toward peaceful settlement, he argues, American racial divisions are a graver political illness than is Quebec separatism.

Iton examines the interaction of two principal axes of political conflict in both countries: the struggle between the political right and the political left over the future of the welfare state, and conflicts surrounding the recognition and accommodation of racial and linguistic differences. Iton suggests that the effective resolution of struggles over the welfare state requires the presence of a healthy political left to counterbalance the robust political right that has emerged in both countries. Although ethno-cultural conflict has frustrated the emergence of a national left in both countries, he argues, the geographic concentration of francophone Canadians, combined with a weak federal system, has permitted the separation of cultural from economic issues and rendered the latter more tractable at both provincial and federal levels. In the United States, in contrast, the geographic dispersion of African Americans has contributed to the inseparability of issues of race and class. Whereas welfare policy is not suffused with issues of cultural difference in Canada, it is thoroughly 'racialized' in the United States - and consequently impedes the political effectiveness both of the poor and of African Americans. Iton offers a fascinating account of the ways in which the parties of the right in both countries - the Reform Party in Canada, the Republican Party in the United States - have been able to turn minorities' aspirations for political recognition to their own political advantage.

While many constitutional regimes are under pressure internally as a product of the politics of identity and recognition, they are simultaneously being challenged by rapidly changing economic, cultural and political dynamics on a world scale. These transformations, taken together, fall under the heading of 'globalisation', and they have far-reaching implications for the future of the constitutional state. In his essay 'Globalisation and Governance', Jan Aart Scholte offers a broad and helpful overview of the factors that contribute to globalisation and of the changing face of political organisation and governance. Scholte defines globalisation as the rise of *supraterritorial* relations between social, economic and political actors. Thus the networks of relationships in which such actors participate are decreasingly bound to a specific territory or the borders of a particular state. He traces the consequences of the rise of supraterritorial relations for the structure of the state: they include a decline in sovereign authority, increasing multilateralism in policy making and a retreat from welfare provision. As the role of central state governments in policy making declines, other loci of decision making are becoming more important. Substate actors (such as city, state or provincial governments), regional actors, and multinational actors are gaining a higher profile. Moreover, these changes involve not only different political bodies, but private organisations such as multinational corporations and non-governmental organisations as well. These changes, however, seldom create new mechanisms of democratic accountability to accompany the relocation of decision making power. As Scholte suggests at the end of his essay, the processes of globalisation may have grave implications for constitutional democracy.

Robert O'Brien's essay picks up these themes where Scholte leaves off by examining closely the ways in which newly emerging regional regimes endanger democratic self-rule. O'Brien separates out the constitutional (rights-protecting and government-limiting) from the democratic (popular sovereignty) elements of constitutional democracy: the former are aimed at protecting rights and limiting government for the sake of those rights, whereas the latter aspire to popular sovereignty. O'Brien argues that regional integration in Europe and North America - specifically, the

European Union and the North America Free Trade Agreement - tend to have strong features of restrictive constitutionalism and are low in the scale of democratic responsiveness and accountability. The processes of regional integration have been elite-driven, often overriding popular opposition in member states. The influence of capitalist interests has been visible both in formulating the terms of integration and in promoting the agreements during political campaigns. Meanwhile, O'Brien argues, a popular and effective political community has not yet emerged on the regional scale. National labour organisations have not, until quite recently, developed alliances with parallel organisations in other countries. But this may be changing: women's organisations, labour unions and environmental organisations are beginning to form more transnational coalitions. The growth of such grassroots coalitions, O'Brien argues, is the most important source of hope for the revitalisation of democratic accountability and responsiveness in the integration process.

Robert Vipond concludes the volume, as he did the conference, with an instructive overview of the lessons about constitutionalism that we might draw from the various chapters' inquiries. His essay, 'Constitutionalism as a Form of Conflict Resolution', considers the constitutional project as a tool for mediating and managing intergroup conflict within societies. Every society contains political cleavages of one sort or another, and these cleavages must be addressed within the constitution if political institutions are to provide a source of stable political order. Vipond reads the essays in the volume as commentaries on three different ways in which constitutions have been used to manage political conflict. The strategy of constitutional stigmatisation, described in Alan Cairns' essay, attempts to resolve conflict by establishing one group as the permanent victor and another as the permanent loser. History, however, has taught us that few constitutional losers are content to remain in that position permanently, and that this strategy eventually produces further conflict. The second strategy, which Vipond describes as characteristically American, attempts to resolve intergroup conflict by creating institutions that are neutral as between the various groups. In practice, however, such neutrality rarely seems possible, and the United States Constitution has not mediated racial conflict in a manner that recommends it as a model for other societies. The third strategy, toward which constitutional practice seems to be moving and which many of the essays in this volume recommend, is the strategy of the 'culturalised' constitution. This approach secures some basic rights for all citizens but also makes space for the expression and recognition of distinct group identities in giving practical content to those rights.

2 Constitutional Stigmatisation[1]

ALAN C. CAIRNS

Constitutional Stigmatisation

This is not the paper I planned or was asked to write. The topic suggested by Peter Russell was 'Rights, Identities, and the New Constitutionalism'. The focus, as I understood it, was to see constitutions as instruments to respond to needs for recognition in complex, heterogeneous societies. Charles Taylor has written sensitively on this subject (Taylor, 1992), one which perhaps comes naturally to Canadian scholars as they survey the multiple competing identities whose constitutional reconciliation has thus far eluded the best efforts of constitutional reformers over several decades.

However, for better or worse, I have resisted the temptation to focus on Canada, and also the suggestion that I address the 'New Constitutionalism'. To link the issue of identity with constitutional statements about who is a valued member of the civic community, and who is either not positively valued, or is explicitly devalued, is to realise that constitutions can be Janus-faced. They may declare who is among the elect, or they may identify categories of people who are beyond the civic pale. In extreme cases, exclusion is clearly stigmatising, in that it makes public, official statements about who is and who is not a worthy member of the community. Such constitutional statements simultaneously denigrate or demean those who are kept outside the community and exalt those who are included. The positive recognition accorded to the latter receives an additional bonus with the reminder that others who share the same territorial space are not their equals. This discriminatory constitutional policy deserves a name - I call it constitutional stigmatisation.

This chapter explores five cases where the constitution and/or constitutional policy specifically denigrates or stigmatises a people by defining them as 'other', as non-citizens, as unworthy of possessing or incapable of handling civic rights. Initially, the paper examines two colonial situations: (1) an omnibus category, colonised peoples, under the generic rubric 'the constitution of imperialism', which treats the latter as the master instrument of alien rule in recent history, and (2) 'Indians in Canada', as an example of internal colonialism. The following two brief case studies, (3)

'Apartheid', and (4) 'Blacks in the American South' have been jointly examined by several authors as classic examples of segregation (Cell, 1982; Fredrickson, 1981). According to Fredrickson, segregation results from 'systematic and self-conscious efforts to make race or color a qualification for membership in the civil community'. South Africa and the American South tended to 'a kind of *Herrenvolk* society in which people of color however, numerous or acculturated they may be, are treated as permanent aliens or outsiders' (Fredrickson, 1981, pp. xi-xii). The final example of constitutional stigmatisation, (5) 'The Third Reich and the Jews', examines the background to the darkest episode in twentieth century western history, the Holocaust.

Given the limited space at my disposal, and my even more limited competence, this is a topic for the macroscope, not the microscope. Further, each of the case studies is, unavoidably and appropriately, morally and politically sensitive. They deal with intercultural/interracial encounters that, especially in the case of Jews and the Third Reich, make us ashamed of the atrocities we can inflict on each other. Students of the Holocaust refer to the difficulty of finding appropriate language that combines analysis and moral sensitivity to an evil that almost defies comprehension (Marrus, 1987, pp. 201-202). Accordingly, the analysis that follows is designed to underline the brutal price we pay when constitutional policy defines some of us as 'other', when citizenship is treated as a scarce resource, unavailable to many who receive daily reminders of the coercive powers of the state. 'Once the concept of "otherness" takes root', writes Slavenka Drakulic in *The Balkan Express*, 'the unimaginable becomes possible. Not in some mythological country but to ordinary ... citizens.' (Drakulic, 1994, p. 3).

The Constitution of Imperialism

> The conquest of the earth, which mostly means the taking it away from those who have a different complexion or slightly flatter noses than ourselves, is not a pretty thing when you look into it too much. What redeems it is the idea only. An idea at the back of it; not a sentimental pretense but an idea; and an unselfish belief in the idea - something you can set up, and bow down before, and offer a sacrifice to. (Joseph Conrad, *Heart of Darkness*, cited in Said, 1993, p. vii).

The domestic examples, discussed below, of civic exclusion and internal hierarchies of power, reward, and recognition based on the categorisation of distinct peoples as superior or inferior drew some of their legitimacy from the international arena dominated by European powers, particularly from the theory and practice of imperialism.

European imperialism was the classic example of non-recognition applied on a global scale. It assumed the cultural (and possibly racial) superiority of the imperial overlord, and the cultural (and possibly racial) inferiority of the subject peoples. The treatment of the latter varied, depending *inter alia* on the presence or absence of a sizeable settler population, the nationality of the imperial power, and the latter's view of where the subject people could be ranked on the global cultural and racial hierarchy from whose heights the carriers of European civilisation looked down on the rest of humanity. In the most elementary model that was natural to the imperial mentality, European civilisation was at the top, the cultures of Asia and the Middle East were in the middle, and tribal peoples - often thought of as surviving examples of the childhood of the human race - were at the base, and hence had the longest distance to travel before they could catch up.

In the hierarchical world view of imperialism, superiority and inferiority neatly divided those in charge from those that were their charges. The imperialist mentality was summed up in the evocative title of a book that sought to explore it - *The Lords of Human Kind* (Kiernan, 1972). The early British Victorian travellers in pre-imperial Africa, for example, proudly defined themselves as British, Christian and White - each category of which contrasted them favourably with the African peoples they encountered.

The imperialist mission, or more accurately, the moral obligation of the British people - according to the missionary explorer David Livingstone - was to bring Christianity, Civilisation, and Commerce to the peoples of Africa, and thus raise them in the scale of humanity. In the different terminology of Gerrit Gong, Europe applied a 'standard of civilisation' to the peoples its merchants, proconsuls, etc., encountered as Europe extended its influence around the globe. Peoples who did not meet the standard were either taken over or accorded less than full rights in the international community. Once imperial law and order was formally instituted, often following quick and decisive application of superior force, the colonised peoples adapted to the new world, and exploited the opportunities it held out. Ultimately, however, those who were judged and found wanting by standards that were not their own came to experience their subject status as a humiliation (Gong, 1984, p. 246). The indignity and resentment were compounded for those who acquired western education, adopted the lifestyles of their imperial masters, and still found themselves rejected.[2]

Although differences in the various settings of empire were profoundly important for individual colonies - Algeria was not the Gold Coast - determining, for example, how long the state of tutelage was expected to last, they paled in significance before the ubiquitous reality - the universal assumption of the unfitness of subject peoples to rule themselves. They were variously described as children or wards. More positively, they were sometimes thought of as pupils being schooled in the virtues of advanced civilisations - the latter defined as vanguard civilisations in touch with the future (See Thornton, 1965, esp. chapter 4, 'Doctrines of Civilization'). While to be a pupil held out the possibility of graduation, it was, nevertheless, a demeaning status for it rested on an explicit premise of cultural (and sometimes racial) inferiority. The humiliation inherent in imperialism induced Nehru to speak of freedom 'from contempt' as crucial to the dignity of those who had been colonised (Perham, 1970, p. 184).[3]

In addition, therefore, to the constitutions of individual colonies, there existed what can properly be called a generic imperial constitution. The governing class and the administrative arm were largely recruited from the metropole and were responsible to the political capital in the Mother country across the water. The imperialist elites saw their governing, leadership role as natural. They brought a complacent arrogance to their task - one which they seldom saw as ending in any future that would concern them (See Hobsbawm, 1987, chapter 3; Thornton, 1978, pp. 10, 39, 49, 56, 59, 95). Accordingly, the identity message transmitted to the subjects of empire was unambiguous - in a world of competing cultures/races their way of life, cultural achievements, governing capacities, etc., were seriously deficient. Therefore, they must be taken care of, and administered by superior others. In many cases, cherished customs and practices were prohibited by the imperial administration.

Imperialism was the enemy of empathy between the rulers and the ruled. A common citizenship was unthinkable. Equality was, by definition, a violation of the imperial relationship. Missionaries and settlers, Thornton noted, in spite of their many differences, shared the belief 'that the native ... was not of the same moral order as themselves ... he was ... an outsider.' The understanding that fellowship makes possible was absent. 'No imperialism in practice ever broke free of its own insistence in the social superiority of its agents' (Thornton, 1965, pp. 196-98).

It is only a slight exaggeration to say that imperialism defined the world for our grandparents, no matter which side of the ruling divide they were on. For many, of course, the experience of imperialism was vicarious, rather than personally encountered. Canadians, for example, especially of British background, belonged to the British Empire, but they were not involved in the running of its affairs. Nevertheless, they received reassuring messages of their importance from the ubiquity of the colour red on the world's maps. The constitution of imperialism, in other words, distributed potent messages that bolstered the identities of some and eroded the sense of self-worth of others. The message of imperialism, therefore, as well as the message of its ending, was not restricted to the imperial rulers and the ruled.[4] Both messages had larger consequences for the domestic politics of societies outside the imperial orbit that were divided by race/culture. To make the same point slightly differently, the contemporary strength of Aboriginal nationalism in Canada and the support - both Aboriginal and non-Aboriginal - for the inherent right to self-government, would either not exist or would be much weaker if European empires still held sway over much of the world beyond Europe. The fact that, by the second half of the twentieth century, colonialism, formerly seen 'as an agency of civilization ... had become not only morally repugnant but also a crime against humanity' (Jackson, 1990, p. 107), transferred moral capital from settler majorities in Canada and elsewhere to minority indigenous peoples.

Indians in Canada, Confederation to the 1969 White Paper

> It would be incorrect to convey the impression that Euro-Canadians invariably look down upon Indians, but it would be equally misleading to pretend that Indians are not a stigmatised people within Canadian society (Dyck, 1991, p. 4).

The British North America (BNA) Act elevated Canadians of British background above their fellow citizens with its preambular declaration that Canada was to have a constitution 'similar in principle' to that of the United Kingdom. This constitutional support for Britishness was reinforced by the particulars of the constitutional monarchy at federal and provincial levels, by the British doctrine of parliamentary supremacy, by the continuing institutional link of the Judicial Committee of the Privy Council (until 1949) and the Westminster role in the formal amending procedure (until 1982).

Recognition of the French-Canadian nationality in the 1867 settlement was expressed in the provincial autonomy and provincial jurisdictions given to a Quebec no longer bound with Upper Canada (the future Ontario) in the United Province of Canada (Silver, 1982, chapter 2).

The strong constitutional affirmation of Britishness was reinforced by the assimilating doctrine of anglo-conformity outside Quebec that assumed the absorption of immigrants into the English-speaking majority in terms of both language and cultural norms. The global map with its ubiquitous splotches of imperial red confirmed for the doubtful that to be British was to be somebody. Searchers for a positive example of the (constitutional and everyday) politics of recognition need look no further than the British in Canada in their heyday.

Searchers for the counter-case in Canada of demeaning, or stigmatic, or negative recognition find their example in the status Indian population. The Indian people did not participate in the discussions that led to the BNA Act. They were jurisdictionally allotted to the federal government under section 91-24 ('Indians, and lands reserved for the Indians'). Under this authority and building on pre-Confederation practice, a special branch of the federal government administered their affairs, applying an act - the Indian Act - that pertained exclusively to them. They were a specific, legally defined population, with clear rules for gaining or losing Indian status.

On the basis of a special act, and a special branch of government responsible for its administration, a pattern of differential treatment evolved that set the Indian people apart from other Canadians. They were physically separated from the rest of the Canadian population by the reserve system. With some exceptions, they were deprived of the federal franchise until 1960. This not only deprived them of the basic political resource of democracies, but it symbolised their civic exclusion from full membership in the Canadian community. The Hawthorn-Tremblay Report of 1967 spoke simple truth when it defined their past status and treatment as 'citizens minus' (Hawthorn, 1967, vol. 1, p. 6)[5] - a label also specifically applied to Indian women in a later publication (Jamieson, 1978). As the role of the state expanded and provincial governments came to play an enhanced role in providing services in the 1960s, the special Indian link with Ottawa left them progressively behind other Canadians in the quality of government services.

Status Indians were defined as wards, often compared to children, and their cultures were officially denigrated. A cultural assault was mounted against the potlatch, the sundance, and the traditional methods of selecting their leaders. The residential school system separated Indian children from their parents. Residential schools were employed as instruments of religious conversion, of cultural assimilation, and for the displacement of Aboriginal languages by English and French. As total institutions, it now appears that they were also sites for sexual and other abuses of the young by powerful adult authority figures from another culture. A pass system introduced in 1882 attempted to control Indian movement off the reserves in western Canada. Although its enforcement was sporadic - applied by some Indian agents until the 1930s - it nevertheless justifies its description by the historian F. Laurie Barron 'as a form of selectively applied administrative tyranny' (Dickason, 1992, pp. 314-15).

The Indian future was seen either as disappearance as disease born of contact took its toll, or as absorption into the general population as state-led social engineering achieved its objective of their assimilation into the majority society. The government goal, as enunciated in 1920 by Duncan Campbell Scott, deputy superintendent general of Indian Affairs, was 'to continue until there is not a single Indian in Canada that has not been absorbed into the body politic and there is no Indian question, and no Indian department' (Dickason, 1992, p. 327). Given this goal, reserves were viewed as schools for civilisation. The territorial separation of the reserve system was therefore temporary until old customs and practices were eroded. In a sense, the overall thesis was a version of Durham's policy of assimilating the 'backward' French-Canadian population by weakening the role of tradition and the appeal of nationality, and by encouraging liberal freedoms, individual ambitions and a politics that brought French and English together in collaborative endeavours in a single political unit. He had no doubt that the victor would be the mid-19th century version of the culture of modernity practised by the rapidly growing English-speaking population culturally linked to the aggressive, expansive American culture to the south (Ajzenstat, 1988). Durham's dream was short-lived. The goal of assimilation for Indians - based on the non-Durham strategy that separation was an instrument of assimilation - was official policy until the 1970s, receiving its most powerful expression in the 1969 federal government White Paper, which proposed abolishing the Indian Act and winding down the Indian Affairs Branch in order to expedite the assimilation of the Indian peoples into the majority society (Canada, 1969).

In sum, status Indians - a legally defined people - were singled out for special treatment that assumed their cultural inferiority. Defined and treated as wards, they were a subject people with little official input into the policy and administration that was designed to transform them into replicas of the change agents in charge. Their identity was rejected and then attacked by the majority society. 'From birth to death most Indians have been caught in a situation where they have had to listen to one unvarying and unceasing message - that they are unacceptable as they are and that to become worthwhile as individuals they must change in the particular manner advocated by their current tutelage agents.' Few Indians accepted the invitation, as 'to have done [so] would have been to accept the principle of their own worthlessness' (Dyck, 1991, p. 27). Their relation to the constitution, as it applied to them, is appropriately described as stigmatising (See Royal Commission on Aboriginal Peoples, 1996, esp. vol. 1).

Not surprisingly, the separate treatment originally seen as transitional has confirmed and reinforced the separate identity it was intended to overcome. The negative differential treatment of the past has solidified a sense of Indianness that is now the basis for a constitutional philosophy of parallelism. In many cases, the sense of Canadian citizenship among Indians is weak (Boldt, 1993, pp. 50, 73-74, 83, 108).

The immediately following two case studies - apartheid in South Africa and segregation in the southern United States - highlight the efforts of dominant white groups to implement and maintain the policy of social separation and economic unification which was their response to pressures to modernise in racially divided societies (Cell, 1982, pp. 81-82, 104, 169-70, 233). As Cell convincingly argues, the massive machinery of segregation was not required when economies were largely rural and racial hierarchy and paternalism governed race relations (Cell, 1982, pp. 11-13). Segregation, which reached its fullest expression in apartheid, is more than the white supremacy which preceded it. Nor does physical separation exhaust its meaning.

> Segregation ... is an interlocking system of economic institutions, social practices and customs, political power, law, and ideology, all of which function both as means and as ends in one group's efforts to keep another (or others) in their place within a society that is actually becoming unified. Both the structure and the dynamics of segregation are thus profoundly paradoxical. Social patterns and economic trends appear to run in opposite directions. To its members such a society may appear to be normal, logically and permanently divided. But if the groups that compose it were truly separate, if they really lived their lives apart, if economy and society were indeed plural or dual, there would be no need for segregation ... the essence of the system ... the crux of segregation

> is the monopoly by the dominant group over the political institutions of the state (Cell, 1982, p. 14).

Although segregation/apartheid presupposes beliefs in the racial/cultural inferiority of the groups whose interactions with the dominant it seeks to control in the latter's interest, those beliefs are only necessary supports, not sufficient conditions for the emergence of a segregationist regime. Although urbanisation and industrialisation confronted the American South and South Africa with new realities of economic interdependence and an intensified cheek-by-jowl existence, they did not dictate the response. The segregation response, subsequently fine-tuned into apartheid in South Africa, was a political response that prevailed over alternatives that were considered but rejected (Cell, 1982, p. 231). Following which, the system of segregation acquired its own momentum. The power relationship which sustained segregation was in turn sustained by an intellectual system, a legitimating ideology. For a time, this provided a justification for the power-holding white community to enjoy a disproportionate share of the benefits of interdependence, benefits, which were psychological as well as material.

Apartheid

> Political, economic, social, cultural and sexual segregation were cast [in apartheid doctrine] as divinely ordained, historically vindicated and the foundation of a just and harmonious society. 'Being white' meant being socially and culturally distinct, politically and economically privileged and physically segregated from all those who were not (Posel, 1987, p. 439).

Apartheid has been defeated, weakened by its contradictions and by international opinion that turned South Africa into a pariah state. By the 1960s, it had become one of those words that symbolised a philosophy and a policy subject to universal opprobrium. It emerged as official state policy following the 1948 election victory of D. F. Malan. In one sense, it was a continuation of an array of past policies of segregation and unequal treatment of the non-white people of South Africa - Indian, coloured and African.[6] In spite of these continuities, the policy was a departure from the past in two important ways. (1) It was based on an explicitly articulated philosophy or doctrine. (2) It was rigorously implemented in its heyday - as a battery of legislation comprehensively covering the interactions of white and non-whites, especially Africans who numerically dominated the non-white category.

The guiding philosophy was 'separate development'. A *volk* - often defined as a god-given entity/category - should develop according to the dictates of its inner evolving logic. The members of a *volk* should not become a pale and necessarily imperfect imitation of another contiguous *volk*, for to do so would be a sacrifice of cultural integrity.

Apartheid justified the overall rightness of European political rule. This gave Europeans legal control of the major settings in which interracial/intercultural contact occurred, especially in the economy, where the presence of low-paid - usually migratory - African workers serviced the burgeoning economic expansion that sustained white prosperity.

The policies that gave substance to the apartheid regime involved massive interference in the life of society.[7] (1) *Labour and Work*: A comprehensive system of labour regulation controlled the mobility of Africans - where they could work, and the jobs to which they could aspire (also limited by Bantu education policy). (2) *'Communal apartheid'*, in Giliomee and Schlemmer's phrase: This included the statutory classification of every individual as native, a coloured person, or a white person (The Population Registration Act of 1950). Territorially distinct group areas within the Union were later supplemented by the homelands policy, destined to give the appearance of parallel development, while simultaneously justifying the exclusion of Africans from South African citizenship (their citizenship was to be in impoverished homelands). The 1949 Prohibition of Mixed Marriages Act forbade white-black intermarriage, followed by the 1950 Immorality Act, which prohibited extra-marital intercourse between whites and blacks. This symbolically significant prohibition of the most intimate forms of contact was reinforced by legislation requiring separate amenities for black and white, including park benches, entertainment facilities, sporting activities, eating areas, etc. (3) *Politics*: Apartheid was designed to preserve white control. There were no Africans in the Union Parliament, and the representation of Africans by whites ended in 1959. Disenfranchisement not only symbolised their outsider status, but deprived them of the political influence that might have challenged the disproportionate share of the benefits of an interdependent society enjoyed by the white minority.

Apartheid was a system designed to manage interdependence, especially economic, based on a plentiful supply of cheap labour, while preserving white rule and white privilege. This difficult juggling act required a low evaluation of black, especially African, capacity. The Bantu Education Act (1953) was the servant of separate development by providing an education for a subordinate status, which simultaneously undermined African self-worth. School textbooks taught the superiority of whites. A 1983 study reported that 79 percent of English-speaking whites and 69 percent of an Afrikaner elite group believed that the 'Bantu was a child who was some centuries behind the white man in development' (Giliomee and Schlemmer, 1989, p. 95).

The apartheid system, especially the pass laws, annually made petty criminals of hundreds of thousands of Africans, who queued up for a 'two minute trial in Commissioner's court on the way to a short-term jail sentence' (Davenport, 1991, p. 544). Rigorous enforcement of the pass laws contrasted with the relative indifference of the police to the widespread 'violence and lawlessness' of township life (Marks and Trapido, 1987, p. 50). Those on the receiving end of apartheid were constantly humiliated by a system that subjected them to innumerable large and small restrictions, failed to provide security, and routinely denied their self-worth while giving lip service to separate development.

The absolutely central assumption of apartheid was the impossibility of a common society, and thus of common citizenship. The Tomlinson Commission that reported in 1955, as full-blown apartheid was implanted in the statute books, began with the basic premise '"that there is little hope of evolutionary development" towards a common society, and "not the slightest ground for believing that the European population, either now or in the future, would be willing to sacrifice its character as a national entity and as a European racial group."' It considered that this should be accepted as '"the dominant fact in the South African situation"'(Davenport, 1991, p. 340).

The correlation of whiteness and blackness with superiority and inferiority respectively, the absence of a common citizenship, the exclusion of Africans from political power, and the reality of economic interdependence managed by Europeans justified, to its beneficiaries, the disproportionate share of goods (and status) that flowed to the power-wielding European minority. Systematic stigmatisation of the black majority, reinforced by a comprehensive battery of supportive legislation that structured the meeting points of white and black to the advantage of the former, closely paralleled the situation in the American South, discussed in the following section.

Blacks in the American South: Reconstruction to *Brown v. Board of Education*[8]

> To most whites, blacks simply did not count, indeed were invisible (Nieman, 1991, p. 120).

> We have seen the mere distinction of color made in the most enlightened period of time a ground of the most oppressive dominion ever exercised by man over man (James Madison, cited in Eastland and Bennett, 1979, p. 2).

In his classic study, *An American Dilemma*,[9] the Swedish social scientist Gunnar Myrdal described the contemporary condition of blacks (then Negroes) in the United States. Myrdal's analysis is now a half a century old. His belief that the American creed of the moral equality of individuals would vanquish the ideology of white racism that contradicted it may have given excessive influence to values and ideas, and probably exaggerated the hegemony of the American creed among the latter. Nevertheless, his massive research still communicates a remarkable 'feel' for the psychological reality of southern racism toward the end of the period I propose to examine. Consequently, I have employed Myrdal as a primary reference. He wrote at a time in the early forties when the caste-like system of black-white relations in the American South was in apparent full vigour, albeit challenged by changes in the intellectual and moral climate partly triggered by World War II. Myrdal's more than 1000 pages come as close as is humanly possible to providing a comprehensive analysis of American society and the position of blacks within it. His concentrated focus was on the South, which contained three-fourths of the Negro population when he wrote, and where segregation and discrimination were most pronounced (Myrdal, 1944, vol. 2, p. 574). He described two ways of life sanctioned by an ideology of race inequality, enforced by state power, embodied in hundreds of regulations and reinforced by customs that extended to the minutiae of social interactions.

Myrdal quickly realised that understanding the position of blacks dictated that his main focus would be the beliefs and behaviour of the ruling white majority. The latter subscribed to 'whole systems of firmly entrenched popular beliefs' about blacks and race relations 'which are bluntly false ... [but serve] opportunistic *ad hoc* purposes' for the majority (Myrdal, vol. 1, p. lxxiii; see also vol. 1, pp. 54-55). The white majority, holding virtually 'all ... economic, social, and political power ... naturally determines the Negro's "place".' The life of the latter, in matters big and small, including the Negro's 'opinions on the Negro problem' are reactions to the constraints and humiliations imposed by the majority (Myrdal, 1944, vol. 1, p. lxxv).

The backdrop to Myrdal's study was the still-living memory of slavery and the justifying belief in black inferiority that rationalised it. The long reach of the past was underlined by his comment that 'what we are studying is in reality the survivals in modern American society of the slavery institution' (Myrdal, 1944, vol. 2, p. 577). The racial doctrine that supported slavery defined slaves as property that could be owned, exploited, and bought and sold. The racial hierarchy of slavery was legitimated by a philosophy of social inequality that pervaded the social system of the American South up to the Civil War of the 1860s. The Reconstruction constitutional amendments of the 1860s, which were designed to give full citizenship rights to blacks, and a constitutional guarantee of equality were, in effect, overturned by the southern states in subsequent decades.

From 1830 to 1914, the basic white supremacist views common 'to almost all shades of white opinion' – including 'Negrophobe and "paternalist"'- embraced an integrated set of propositions. Whites and blacks differ 'physically, intellectually, and temperamentally'. In some of the preceding, including intelligence, blacks are inferior. Where such differences are not permanent, they can be overcome only over very long time periods. These differences explain and justify strong opposition to miscegenation that would generate either a 'short-lived and unprolific breed' or an inferior 'type'. White racial prejudice, given the preceding, is understandable when blacks seek equal status. According to George M. Fredrickson, 'it follows ... that a biracial equalitarian (or integrated) society is either completely impossible, now and forever, or can be achieved only in some remote and almost inconceivable future. For all practical purposes the destiny of blacks in America is either continued subordination - slavery or some form of caste discrimination - or their elimination as an element of the population' (Fredrickson, 1971, p. 321).

When Myrdal wrote, eighty years after the freeing of the slaves, he found a systematic policy of racial inequality embedded in a justifying theory, legislation that implemented the theory, and elaborate social practices of everyday life that gave the support of routine to inequalities that white beneficiaries viewed as the natural order. In contrast to other non-coloured groups destined to be Americanised, Negroes were considered unassimilable, and indeed were 'excluded from assimilation' (Myrdal, 1944, vol. 1, pp. 53-54, 57). Further, as he noted, the boundary between blacks and whites was intended to be fixed and permanent, and it 'is directed against the whole group' (Myrdal, 1944, vol. 1, p. 58).

Various statutory restrictions, supplemented by intimidation, effectively denied the franchise to blacks, 'against the intention and spirit of the amended Constitution' (Myrdal, 1944, vol. 1, p. 430).[10] Myrdal claimed that every category of deprivations and injustice was linked to Negro disenfranchisement (Myrdal, 1944, vol. 1, p. 512). It was the master exclusion from which all others flowed. By contrast, in the North, where Negroes voted in proportion to their numbers, they had equitable access to community services (Myrdal, 1944, vol. 1, pp. 500-501).

The customary separation of the races that followed the Civil War was strengthened by three waves of legislation from the late 1880s into the twentieth century. State legislatures and municipal councils introduced 'a mountain of laws and ordinances to formalize and to put the force of law behind what had been largely customary arrangements' (Nieman, 1991, p. 108). Southern blacks encountered a maze of regulations - from ubiquitous signs distinguishing 'white' and 'colored' facilities (where the latter were invariably inferior), and extending to separate Bibles in courtrooms - all to remind blacks that they were viewed and treated as a 'degraded caste' (Nieman, 1991, pp. 108-109).

A panoply of Jim Crow laws separated blacks and whites in restaurants, libraries, theatres, parks, playgrounds, schools, buses, public meeting places, sports, stores, railroad cars, etc. Interracial marriage was prohibited. Rules of etiquette governed social interactions when blacks and whites met. Blacks did not take the lead in conversation; they were deferential in the presence of whites; they were rarely addressed formally - as Mr. or Mrs. The social function of the etiquette of conversation was to serve as a reminder of the superiority of whites. The broader rules governing all social relations sought to keep whites and Negroes separated, and to reinforce Negro inferiority (Myrdal, 1944, vol. 2, pp. 611-15). In Myrdal's summary, '*what white people really want is to keep the Negroes in a lower status*' (Myrdal, 1944, vol. 2, p. 591, italics in original). These rules of social intercourse were constant reminders of the caste system of southern society. The overall purpose of segregation was public and explicit - to minimise social contacts, and where they were unavoidable to ensure that the guiding norm was inequality. According to Myrdal, the anti-amalgamation doctrine that the preceding social controls were designed to support was built on the concern for 'race purity', a concern based on the imputed biological inferiority of the Negro. The white majority's 'rank order of discrimination', accordingly, put the bar against intermarriage and sexual intercourse between black men and white women at the top of necessary prohibitions, with discrimination in jobs, access to credit, and public welfare at the bottom (Myrdal, 1944, vol. 1, pp. 58-61, 102).

Blacks were poorer, less educated, had shorter life expectancies, received inferior health care, held the menial jobs, had much less access to government social services, and could not count on equal application of the laws. Physical violence by whites against blacks was almost a caste privilege, undertaken with minimum concern for or fear of the law. Law enforcement in the South in 1940 was described as 'absent when Negroes were the victims (whether whites or other Negroes were the criminals), and over-enforced when whites were victims and Negroes the violators' (Rose, 1944, p. xl). Nieman commented that 'blacks were members of a despised caste and stood outside the protection of the law ... police brutality and disregard for the rights of blacks suspected of crime were pervasive... Lynching ... [to support white supremacy] made a mockery of the rule of law' (Nieman, 1991, pp. 118-19). In sum, blacks were in but not of the society. They were not fellow citizens.

In *Slavery and Social Death*, Orlando Patterson defined slavery as the 'permanent, violent domination of natally alienated and generally dishonoured persons' (Patterson, 1982, p. 13). Glenn Loury, commenting on Patterson, stresses his focus on the 'systematic dishonoring of enslaved persons,' based on the 'hierarchical symbolic relations of respect and standing between masters and slaves', from which masters extract honour and slaves experience 'extreme social marginality' (Loury, 1995, p. 69).

The formal ending of slavery doubtless diluted the degree of continuing dishonouring of blacks in the American South. It remains true, however, that for the next century the de facto constitution of southern society systematically applied not only a policy of non-recognition to its black population but, in Patterson's terms, a policy of dishonouring blacks, or in the terms of this essay a policy of stigmatisation. It logically followed that the degradation of blacks by 'the legal system assured that even whites of the lowest social and economic position were superior to blacks' (Nieman, p. 120). The ceiling above which blacks could not rise was at the same time a floor below which whites could not fall.

Given the plain words of the Reconstruction amendments following the Civil War, the rules and practices that defeated their purpose can best be described as a counter-constitution. Southern whites, to put it differently, after the official demise of slavery, learned to work the US constitution in order to frustrate its intent by nullifying the Reconstruction amendments. According to Myrdal, southern whites came to see their violations, sanctioned by time, as being constitutional (Myrdal, 1944, vol. 1, pp. 446-48).

The Third Reich and the Jews: Background to the Holocaust[11]

> The attempted annihilation of the Jews of Europe was a state-sponsored project with the aim of killing every man, woman and child of the Jewish people in pursuit of an ideological fantasy (Pulzer, 1997, p. 20).

The policy of the Third Reich systematically isolated the Jewish people, deprived them of full citizenship rights, limited their access to various professions and occupations, defined and registered them, and stigmatised them by the requirement that they wear a yellow badge. They were publicly excoriated by Hitler and other leading Nazis as the cause of Germany's problems. The attack on the Jews flowed from the racial definition of the German nation - a *Volk* . As early as 1920, the programme of the Nazi party stated: 'Only members of the nation may be citizens of the State. Only those of German blood, whatever their creed, may be members of the nation. Accordingly, no Jew may be a member of the nation' (quoted in Kershaw, 1995, p. 233).[12]

Prior to the establishment of the Third Reich in February 1933, with Hitler as Chancellor, German Jews had an ambiguous identity. On the one hand, the Weimar constitution, framed by a committee chaired by a Jewish minister of the interior, appeared to give them the freedom and equality they had long sought. They were devoted to the 'German language as vehicle of their spirit and ethos' (Yahil, 1990, p. 20), proud of German culture, and integrated into the growing German economy. Yet they retained their Jewish identity as a distinct group, partly because in spite of their possession of equal citizen rights, they were not fully accepted by most Germans (Yahil, 1990, p. 20). Pulzer states that there was no 'consensus that the Jew was a citizen like any other' in the half-century preceding Hitler's seizure of power (Pulzer, 1992, p. 23). Anti-Semitism, introduced into German politics in the 1870s, soon became an enduring feature, accepted by the German people 'as a familiar element of their political discourse' (Dawidowicz, 1986, p. xx). Hence the Weimar Republic was unable to deliver on its promise of equality for Jews. The gap between promise and performance underlined 'the difference between the *pays légal* and the *pays réel*' (Dawidowicz, 1985, p. 46).

In 1933, legislation removed rights and democratic legal protection from all Germans (The Emergency Regulation in Defense of the People and the State, February 28, 1933) (Yahil, 1990, p. 54).[13] This was quickly followed by an 'Enabling Act' (Law for Removing the Distress of People and Reich, March 23, 1933) giving legislative authority to Chancellor Hitler (Yahil, 1990, p. 56). This gave the Nazi government authority for four years to pass legislation that violated the constitution - authority renewed by Hitler in later years (Dawidowicz, 1986, p. 51). Concurrently, Germany became a one-party state under the control of the National Socialist Party.

The regime was consolidated by laws allowing the Nazi government to 'coordinate' unions, independent organisations and societies, including political parties, which led to their suppression or regrouping and management by the state. Regime consolidation based on racist ideology steadily isolated and ostracised the Jews. Jewish judges, prosecutors, lawyers and notaries had their activities restricted; Jews were removed from senior positions in the state bureaucracy; Jewish doctors and pharmacists were removed from the National Health Service. Jewish ritual slaughter of animals for food was prohibited (Yahil, 1990, p. 65). By the end of 1933, an objective with nineteenth century roots, 'the exclusion of Jews from public life, government, culture, and the professions' had been achieved (Dawidowicz, 1986, p. 59). The absence of German resistance to the repudiation of the legal equality that had been guaranteed to Jews in 1869 suggests the weakness of that concept in German political culture, and the survival of negative stereotypes. 'There is ample evidence', according to Peter Pulzer, 'of a relatively easy acceptance [by the German people] of pariah status for a significant section of German citizens' (Pulzer, 1992, p. 347).

The 1935 Nuremburg Laws furthered the divorce between the Jews and the majority population. The Reich Citizenship Law differentiated state subjects from Reich citizens. The former was 'a person who enjoys the protection of the German Reich and who in consequence has specific obligations towards it.' The latter, a citizen of the Reich, by contrast, was 'a subject of the State who is of German or related blood, who proves by his conduct that he is willing and fit faithfully to serve the German people and the Reich.' Further, 'the Reich citizen is the sole bearer of full political rights in accordance with the Law' (Yahil, 1990, p. 71).

The 1935 Law for the Protection of German Blood and German Honour was based on the premise that 'the purity of German blood' was the precondition for the future 'existence of the German people'. This law was described by the courts 'consistently and repeatedly' as a 'fundamental law' or 'one of the most important laws of the National Socialist state' (Müller, 1991, p. 105). It prohibited marriage between Jews and 'subjects of the state of German or related blood', and forbade sexual relations outside marriage between them (Yahil, 1990, pp. 71-72).[14] In the same year, 1935, an effort was made to register every Jew. Jewish organisations were prohibited from using the phrase 'German Jews' in their titles, to be replaced by 'Jews in Germany' (Yahil, 1990, pp. 80-81).

The overall purpose of this battery of discriminatory legislation and policy was to isolate the Jewish population, exclude them from the official category of citizens, and stigmatise them by the requirement to wear a yellow badge (applied in 1941 to all Jews of the Greater Reich) (Yahil, 1990, p. 293). The laws forbidding intermarriage and sexual relations were part of an unrelenting effort to segregate the Jews, the better to prevent the defiling of Aryan purity. These developments, precursors to the 'Final Solution', were accompanied by an ideological onslaught that denigrated Jewish life and culture, defined Jews as subhuman, and gave a cloak of legitimacy to random and organised acts of violence against the Jewish 'other' by both the state and private citizens. Separated 'legally, politically, and socially' from the Germans, they were 'outside the protection of the state ... completely at the mercy of the secret police, without access to law or courts' (Dawidowicz, 1986, p. 68). For the Aryan majority, belonging 'to the national community [which] explicitly excluded the Jews ... implied acceptance of the exclusions it imposed' (Friedländer, 1997, p. 116; see also p. 164). This reduced solidarity with and empathy for Jews, who were placed outside the citizenship bonds of mutual responsibility.

While not all the regulations and policy described above were explicitly constitutional in the narrow technical sense, they were - from a larger perspective - clearly constitutional.[15] Technically, their constitutionality derived from the 1933 Enabling Act. Technicalities aside, their fundamental purpose - the redefinition of the relations of the German population to the German state in terms of the most basic category of membership, citizenship, and the inferior category of subject - classifies them as constitutional in terms of their subject matter.

State constitutional policy was based on the premise that rights and duties should be correlated with racial differences. National Socialist theory defined the state as the chosen political expression of the *Volk*. Accordingly, citizenship was not based on individual rights, 'but derived from membership in the *Volk*' (Dawidowicz, 1986, p. 67). State policy sensitive to the latter, was simultaneously, deliberately and precisely designed to humiliate the Jewish population, to undermine their feelings of self-worth, to deny them the German identity they had assumed, and to reduce their interaction with the non-Jewish population. The pervasive contrast between the 'inferior' Jew and the 'superior' German of pure blood had the intended effect of stimulating and exaggerating race pride among the latter. National Socialist policy in this period was an extreme and comprehensive example of stigmatising a people. If the anti-Semitism of many Germans remained mild, it was constantly reinforced by the regime's relentless anti-Jewish propaganda, which sustained at least a 'tacit acquiescence' in the state's anti-Jewish policy (Friedländer, 1997, pp. 4, 324, 331-32). The policy 'of depersonalization and dehumanization of Jews, [their reduction to the status] of "non-persons"' (Kershaw, 1993, p. 106) or a functional equivalent, was a necessary if not sufficient condition for the Holocaust that followed.

Conclusion

> ... there is an interdependence between the individual and collective processes of identity formation. Thus, individuals expect to recognize themselves in public institutions. They expect some consistency between their private identities and the symbolic contents upheld by public authorities, embedded in the societal institutions, and celebrated in public events. Otherwise, individuals feel like social strangers; they feel that the society is not *their* society (Breton, 1984, p. 125, italics in original).

Constitutions can be Janus-faced. They may impartially and benignly distribute equal rights to all. Or, more ambitiously, as Canadians have tried to do in recent constitutional exercises, they may seek to identify and positively embrace many of the diversities of a heterogeneous society - although that effort, which is always under-inclusive, leaves some groups bewailing their exclusion, or their inferior recognition. Finally, a constitution may be an instrument of exclusion, massively favouring some members of society, while excluding or denigrating others. In divided societies, therefore, one purpose of a constitution (or of high state policy if 'constitution' is narrowly defined) may be to degrade, demean, and remove from the category of fellow citizens an identifiable subgroup of the population. Their removal from the category of fellow-citizens is one of the most symbolically aggressive actions a state can take against a portion (perhaps the majority) of its population. This role or purpose may appropriately be labelled as stigmatising.

Although stigmatising policies, or their absence, are applied by individual governments, including colonial governments, we misinform ourselves if we overlook the international climate of values and ideas that wash across borders and inform both rulers and ruled. Policies towards Canadian Indians before World War II were a spillover from the ideological assumptions that sustained the massive reality of European empires. The end of the empire and the United Nations leadership role on behalf of racial equality redefined South Africa from being a 'white dominion' to a pariah state. Much of the impetus for the post-World War II retreat of Jim Crow laws in the United States came from the Cold War necessity of making American democracy credible in the ideological conflict with the Soviet Union. While individual states are not prisoners of this international *zeitgeist* - which does not always speak with a single voice - they cannot entirely escape its influence on how they interpret and respond to domestic realities.

Surveying these five cases, one is initially struck by the similarities of the beliefs in racial/cultural superiority that serve as a connecting thread. The protection or enhancement of the racial or cultural integrity of the ruling groups is a constant - hence the almost paranoid fear of miscegenation in Nazi Germany, apartheid South Africa, and in the American South, and the imposition of standards of 'civilisation' by imperialists, who, in effect, set exams that had to be passed before their wards could be treated as self-governing adults.

Much of the rhetoric and ideology that justifies stigmatisation appears to be a universal toolkit. One is, however, simultaneously struck by the dissimilar purposes the generic rationale can be adapted to. These range from Nazi policy towards the Jews - obviously devoid of any suggestion that Jews might be beneficiaries of their exclusion from the German people - to much imperial policy in Africa and Asia which justified the installation of alien rule as the vehicle for subsequent emancipation of the colonised from wardship to self-rule. This suggests that the ideology of racial/cultural superiority is not itself the determinant of the package of policies it comes to justify. The latter depend on numbers, whether difference is viewed as biological or cultural, and the purposes of those who take charge of the lives of others. Nazi policy towards Jews, for example, was economically irrational. It removed productive labour from the economy, and subsequently devoted extensive resources to mass murder at the very time that Germany was losing the war. It can only be explained by a ritual obsession with racial purity. The range of policies and treatment to which beliefs in superiority could lead explains John Cell's repeated suggestion that there were much worse policies than segregation, including complete exclusion (Cell, 1982, pp. 175-76, 227-28), and even elimination as was the fate of the Beothuks in Newfoundland, the aborigines in Tasmania, and was the objective of Hitler's policy towards the Jews.[16]

One crucial difference in the nature of hierarchical rule over non-citizens defined as 'others', is whether the difference in ways of life, mastery of nature, or in whatever is seen as confirmation of inferiority is considered to be biological or cultural in origin. If the latter, and the culture of those in charge is open to members of the subject community, alien rule can be thought of as transitional. If the former, as in the American South and South Africa, it will be thought of as permanent. Clearly, an imputation of racial inferiority is much more wounding than an attribution of cultural inferiority that can, at least in theory, be overcome, although both designations are humiliating.

Stigmatisation that is based on law, rather than simply embedded in customary behaviour, is both more offensive to the recipient and more effective in controlling behaviour.[17] The offence is compounded when, as in apartheid South Africa, the American South, Nazi Germany, and to a somewhat lesser extent for status Indians in Canada, law and regulation aspire to comprehensiveness - to reach into the minutiae of behaviour. Comprehensive stigmatisation law is the voice of the state ostracising the unworthy.

The elaboration of law to regulate the minutiae of interdependence reaches its apogee in urban settings when the frequency and intensity of economic and potentially of social interaction threaten to overcome the separateness deemed essential to the ruling group. Spatial coexistence in common urban settings can only be prevented from blurring cleavages by a massive intrusion by the state in sites of potential interaction varying from swimming pools and restaurants to intermarriage. A ruling group that seeks to maintain a unified economy and social separation requires the instrument of law to achieve its objectives. An unregulated proximity will generate intimate encounters that will erode barriers between groups sustained only by custom.

Although the constraints on the ruling group, whether elite colonial officials, Indian agents in Canada, or the ruling white minority in South Africa, were not uniform, they too were controlled by the hierarchical system from which they benefited. They were not to let the side down, and were obligated to observe restrictions on forms of contact with their 'inferiors' that sustained the mystique of their right to be in charge. In sum, they had an obligation to conduct themselves as members of the governing class (Cell, 1982, pp. 15, 234).

Stigmatising state policy underlines the central significance of citizenship as a constitutional category. When a people is divided into citizens and others, and the latter are also systematically denigrated, the fellow-feeling that binds a people into a common society is deliberately fractured. To be put outside the community of full citizens is an official public badge of inferiority - an official statement that one is unworthy. The stigmatised group is variously defined as childlike, or incompetent, or subhuman, or as animals, or all of the preceding. For the stigmatised, the negative consequences may vary from the receipt of casual insensitivities to lynching and genocide. The privileged majority - or minority, as in apartheid South Africa - has a remarkable capacity to accept its privileges as natural and deserved. The complacent and satisfying acceptance of their caste superiority by the majority is embedded, in the examples noted above, in a justifying set of racial/cultural beliefs that acquires the status of an official ideology. Nazi Germany excepted, this ideology typically includes some belief that segregation, imperial rule, or wardship, will ultimately benefit the subject peoples by fostering their separate development, preparing them for self-government, or elevating their position on the ladder of civilisation, or if nothing else, providing paternal rule for those incapable of self-rule. Even slave owners deeply believed in their own necessity, which added a sweetness to their power over others. These reassuring beliefs are bolstered by the coincidence of the racial/cultural divide with the citizen/non-citizen divide which gives an aura of naturalness (and possibly permanence) to the latter. The superior/inferior distinction pervades the entire society, reinforced by the conforming daily behaviour of beneficiaries and victims - with the latter often developing self-hatred as they come to accept the official justifications for their subordination.

I would like to be able to conclude this comparative analysis of massive constitutional stigmatisation with lessons for our era in which positive constitutional recognition, often to be supplemented by positive policies of affirmative action, is widely urged. Support for such catch-up measures for those who carry the legacy of past discrimination appears entirely reasonable. Further, although appropriate constitutional policy instruments may not always be available or discoverable, a constitution that positively embraces the diversities of a heterogeneous society is preferable to a constitution that distinguishes between the elected and the unworthy.

Beyond the preceding, I have only a minimal and yet possibly important conclusion tentatively to offer. Positive constitutional recognition that singles out an ethnic, national, or indigenous minority for preferential treatment may weaken or even sunder the civic ties which support a common citizenship. The singling out of a people for special constitutional treatment, even if the latter is intended to be positive, may come with a price tag. Special treatment underlines difference, and difference invites judgement that begins with the premise that the recipients of preferential recognition or treatment are not standard members of the 'we' community. The extent and nature of the institutionalisation or recognition of difference inform the reaction of the rest of society. Recognition that is primarily symbolic, such as multiculturalism policy, has lesser consequences for perceptions of community - who is 'one of us'? - than recognition in the form of jurisdictional powers.

Special asymmetrical status for Quebec, with enhanced jurisdiction and powers beyond those of other provinces, will necessarily weaken the ties of a common citizenship between Quebecois and other Canadians. For such a large and powerful political community, the diminished feelings of responsibility for each other that follows may be an acceptable price. For the much smaller, more dependent Aboriginal nations of several thousand people, a constitutional politics of apparently positive jurisdictional recognition that weakens ties with the majority society needs to be carefully considered to ensure that the gains out-balance the losses, and that the latter are not discovered after the fact. What has the goal and appearance of positive recognition may, in the alchemy of politics, turn out to be its reverse. The constitutional enshrinement of difference, even of positive difference, should never be undertaken lightly. Not all forms of asymmetrical citizenship are oxymorons, but some unquestionably are.

Notes

1. I wish to thank Russell Isinger and Andrew Staples for excellent research assistance, Jean Laponce for providing written comments on an earlier draft, and the discussants and questioners at various academic sessions who have helped me clarify my thoughts.
2. See Jackson, 1990 (esp. pp. 17, 71-74, 76, 85, 102-108, 143) for an incisive analysis of the rise and fall of justifications for European imperialism.
3. Thornton observes that 'men do not allocate a secondary and subordinate place to other men without developing a contempt for them. They can justify their dominance only on the assumption that these others are not worthy to share it. The subsequent anti-colonialist campaigns have accordingly had as their principal objective the release of whole peoples from this contempt, which is the most searing of all forms of bondage' (Thornton, 1965, p. 158).
4. When imperial powers also had stigmatised minorities at home, imperial and domestic policies tended to move in tandem. C. Vann Woodward noted the parallel between the surge of American imperialism in the Philippines, Hawaii and Cuba at the turn of the century and the enhanced popularity of racism at home. Subsequent international events - the Holocaust, the Cold War and the United Nations' spotlight on racism - encouraged the decline of Jim Crow and moves toward integration (Woodward, 1974, pp. 74, 130-133).
5. The report argued for a 'Citizens Plus' status for Indians (Hawthorn, 1967, vol.1, pp. 396-97).
6. Indeed, G.M. Fredrickson minimizes the discontinuity between the 1910-1948 segregation era and the post-1948 apartheid era, viewing the latter as 'essentially an outgrowth of the former' (Fredrickson, 1981, pp. 240-41). Simultaneously, however, he indicates major changes introduced to the segregation regime by the nationalists, which seem far from trivial.
7. See Giliomee and Schlemmer, 1989, chapter 3, for this and the following paragraph.
8. See Nieman, 1991, for an excellent survey.
9. Rogers M. Smith has recently criticized Myrdal's thesis that the 'American dilemma' is the clash between the normatively hegemonic, democratic American creed, with its values of the moral equality of individuals, and the discriminatory treatment of blacks, expressive of prejudice, expediency, and self-interest. Smith's thesis, buttressed by massive research, is that the American creed is only one among several traditions, constantly jostling with other deeply embedded rival traditions that would restrict citizenship to the latest version of the 'chosen' (Smith, 1997, pp. 8-9, 22-24).
10. See Myrdal, 1944, vol. 1, pp. 479-86, for Southern techniques for disenfranchising the Negroes.

11. Major sources for this section are Dawidowicz, 1986, chapter 3; Yahil, 1990, chapter 3. *Documents on Nazism, 1919-1945;* Noakes and Pridham, 1974, provides a helpful 'insider' perspective on the movement of policy and opinion, especially chapter 15, 'Antisemitism, 1933-1945.' Saul Friedländer's *Nazi Germany and the Jews: Volume 1, The Years of Persecution, 1933-1939* (Friedländer, 1997), eschews clinical language and its distancing effect in a brilliant analysis which involves the reader in intensely human portrayals of individual Jews caught in the ever-tightening grip of the Nazi state.
12. Jews, of course, were not the only internal enemies of the German state. Indeed, the initial attacks of the Nazi government were on the left - the Social Democrats and the Communists. Subsequently, homosexuals, the genetically 'unfit', gypsies, Jehovah's Witnesses, and many others enlarged the category of outsiders who could be purged in the interest of the purity of the *Volk.*
13. As Kershaw observes: 'With one blow, all the personal liberties protected in a liberal democracy had been eliminated by an emergency decree that, though specifically aimed at Communists, could be effortlessly extended to all other presumed "enemies of the state" and was to last for the duration of the Third Reich' (Kershaw, 1995, p. 218).
14. The concern for racial purity fitted in with a pervasive eugenics strain in Nazi ideology, which led to extensive sterilisation and euthanasia, along with the elimination of inferior peoples (Kershaw, 1995, pp. 235, 237-238).
15. In reality, 'constitutional' meant little more than the expression of the Führer's will. The constitutional reality was described in 1938 by the head of the Nazi Association of Lawyers as follows: 'The real characteristic of constitutional law in the Third Reich is that it does not represent a system of competencies but the relation of the whole German people to a personality who is engaged in shaping history. We are in a juridical period founded on the Führer's name, and shaped by him. The Führer is not backed by constitutional clauses, but by outstanding achievements which are based on the combination of a calling and of his devotion to the people... Whether the Führer governs according to a formal written Constitution is not a legal question of the first importance' (Noakes and Pridham, 1974, p. 254). In 1935, Hitler stated in a major speech 'All of us, my comrades, and especially you who hold positions of leadership in the State and the movement, will not be judged by your observance of forms but by your successful realization of our programme , i.e., by the measure in which you defend our *völkisch* life' (Noakes and Pridham, 1974, p. 257). See also (Müller, 1991, chapter 9, 'Nazi Jurisprudence') for a chilling description.
16. Hence Heribert Adam's critique of efforts to equate apartheid with the Holocaust (Adam, 1996).
17. Woodward concludes a discussion of the decisive impact of restrictive law compared to custom with the statement that 'the Jim Crow laws put the authority of

the state or city in the voice of the street-car conductor, the railway brakeman, the bus driver, the theater usher, and also into the voice of the hoodlum of the public parks and playgrounds. They gave free rein and the majesty of the law to mass aggressions that might otherwise have been curbed, blunted, or deflected' (Woodward, 1974, pp. 107-108).

3 The Contagion of Rights: Constitutions as Carriers

VIVIEN HART

Introduction

The late twentieth century has been an era of constitution-making, as constitutions have become badges of legitimacy for regimes seeking acceptance from their own citizens and in the eyes of the world. Among the formal rules and relationships of governance embodied in modern constitutions, rights are ubiquitous. Even Britain, famous for its anomalous uncodified accretion of constitutional conventions, practices and laws, and its 'Anglo-Saxon' antipathy to formal rights, elected a government in 1997 pledged to incorporate the European Convention on Human Rights into British law as part of a new constitutional settlement. In this essay, I examine one early contribution to the diffusion of rights after World War II, the creation of 'independence constitutions' as British colonies in Africa became nations. The rationale for the contested inclusion of rights drawn from the new European Convention on Human Rights was different in Britain from Africa. Regardless, in the short term this innovation had little effect in either place. In the long term, however, this episode can be seen as laying one part of the foundations of international rights politics. Transferring western rights to Africa was always a problematic exercise. Its unexpected consequences may now include the possibility that influence is a two way street, in which Europe can learn from Africa.

Amongst rights instruments, the 1996 South African Constitution is widely regarded as 'state of the art' (Kentridge, 1996). A comprehensive list of civil, political and social rights stands at the head of this Constitution (Act 108 of 1996, Chapter 2). This bill of rights was compiled under the unprecedented constraint of Principle 2 of thirty four Constitutional Principles laid down in the Interim Constitution of 1993:

> Everyone shall enjoy all universally accepted fundamental rights, freedoms and civil liberties, which shall be provided for and protected by entrenched and justiciable provisions in the constitution (Act 200 of 1993, Schedule 6).

Principle 2 was expansively interpreted by advisors (de Vos, 1997). As a result, an African nation has become exemplary of a maturing international politics of human rights. From origins in the aftermath of World War II, the human rights cause has been institutionalised in governmental and nongovernmental organisations, acquired expert practitioners and repositories, and penetrated both national and international political cultures. In this political arena, movements formed in the name of rights and claimants aware of the power inherent in their language and symbolism now frame and legitimate their demands in rights terms, and are effective in many different political circumstances. Rights politics may be driven by idealism or cynicism, implemented or evaded, but no longer ignored.

Ironically, the evolution of an international rights politics owed much of a negative kind to South Africa. The massive violations of human rights there prior to 1990 exemplified the problems for which rights were to be the solution, 'succeeded in generating many new norms', and instigated rights-based movements with the apartheid regime as a target: 'South Africa has taken no positive part in the development of international human rights jurisprudence on account of its policy of apartheid. From a negative perspective, however, South Africa's contribution has been considerable' (Dugard, 1995, p. 171). The translation of South Africa from rights pariah to rights exemplar is at least in part due to the formative interaction, as a mode of resistance, of the anti-apartheid movement with the international rights movement. Well before State President de Klerk's momentous commitment to a negotiated settlement and a bill of fundamental rights, the ground was being prepared and international experience absorbed within South Africa. During the 1980s, an oppositional legal community was 'gearing itself for the introduction of a different Constitution with a Bill of Rights', and, in meetings with representatives of the banned organisation, winning the support of the African National Congress for a strategy of constitutionalism and rights (van Wyk, 1995, pp. 135-6; Kentridge, 1996, pp. 241).

The African continent has in the past been presented by students of constitutionalism as 'a vast graveyard' for the practice, as opposed to the rhetoric, of liberal democratic constitutionalism. The metaphor couples the prominence of the language of western constitutionalism and rights in post-colonial African political discourse with the evidence that, as 'scholars predicted: "few African governments have valued them other than as rhetoric."' (Okoth-Ogendo, 1993, p. 66; Nyerere, 1993) In examining an apparent paradox of 'commitment to the idea of the constitution and rejection of the classical notation of constitutionalism', H.W.O. Okoth-Ogendo speculates that the exigencies of power and poverty block the advance of what might otherwise be a desired development of liberal constitutionalism in Africa: 'Constitutionalism is the end product of social, economic, cultural, and political progress; it can become a tradition only if it forms part of the shared history of a people' (Okoth-Ogendo, 1993, p. 80; Ghai, 1993).

If timing is all, then the South African commitment to rights in the 1990s can be both explained and rescued from the African 'graveyard' prediction by its emergence within and because of an international rights culture. South Africa's particular history to a degree sets it apart from the African states created by 'independence constitutions' in the 1950s and 1960s (Mamdani, 1996). But the constitutional histories of African peoples have not been immune to reciprocal influences, including structural and cultural traditions. Thus the relationship of indigenous discourses to the artificial implant of a western rights discourse in Africa is an issue for the development of constitutionalism in South Africa as much as for its continental cohorts. South Africa may have drawn heavily upon international experience in the 1990s, but its recognition of communal and customary rights and traditional authorities has been attributed to an African rights consciousness with distinctive characteristics, distinguishable from both European and American formulae (Steiner and Alston, 1996, pp. 689-706). Then too, Christof Heyns reminds us that, while the potential of the international compendium of rights to provide diverse African nations with a 'common common law for human rights' must not be ignored, nor must the flawed origins of these rights in deeply oppressive colonial powers (Heyns, 1995). 'Human' rights thus have a complex and contested history which challenges simple explanations of their pervasive appearance in late twentieth century constitutional texts. The passage of western rights to Africa as a legacy of colonialism, their place in African political development, their return to the west as a model by the South African example, is a history more of the pragmatic and political uses of rights more than of idealism. What stands out in this episode is the uncertain and non-linear course of the transnational diffusion and establishment of rights politics.

'The doctrine of fundamental rights was contagious', Anthony Lester has written of this history, 'spreading not only with Napoleon to the civil law countries of Europe but also with the independence movement to the overseas British Empire' (Lester, 1984, p. 48). Codified fundamental rights were part of the shared history of neither the British people nor their African colonial subjects in the post-war years. How has the diffusion of western liberal constitutional theory and practice, so influential in recent constitutional change, occurred? A premature gift by Okoth-Ogendo's analysis, a final act of cultural imperialism to Africanists, western fundamental rights were also included in African independence constitutions in the former British colonies at a time when their introduction in Britain itself was resisted by the state. The sheer unexpectedness of the British Parliament granting strong rights instruments in the 1950s renders the making of these independence constitutions of interest in the British as well as the African context. This historical moment is an object lesson in the complexity of the transfer and adoption of political discourse and practice, the different cultural meanings, motivations, and above all the contradictions. The original constitutions stood only briefly, and it was tensions between their introduction and their context which were most evident at the time. Yet this episode was one of the early building blocks in the half-century work of the creation of modern international rights politics, with consequences for later constitutional change in both Britain and Africa.

In the remainder of this essay, I consider some published evidence of the views of British and African elites in the process of making independence constitutions in British Africa. Both these elite groups entered a dialogue new to them about the uses and content of rights. The constitutions they wrote carried the rights created in the European Convention on Human Rights to Africa. At the time, this transfer appeared neither to create an active rights politics in the recipient nations nor to impact on the embryonic rights politics at home. Both British and African politics were affected, but in both the impact came more in the long than the short term (Heyns, 1995).

From the start, rights were a means of the recognition and protection of African identities, racial, tribal, ethnic, religious, customary, and–although often constructed through their silence on the matter–gendered. This essay is in danger of reproducing the silencing of women's voices by its focus on the elites, mostly men, who negotiated the new constitutional settlements and left copious official records of their thinking. Their preoccupation was usually the imminent threat of conflict or secession on lines of race, ethnicity or religion. The words of women are much harder to retrieve and such a research project is beyond the scope of a short and derivative account. But it must be remembered not only that women participated and spoke, but also that the recognition of women's rights and gendered difference may be the hardest test for the sincerity of rights talk. Rights for women have been potentially powerful and subversive propositions for all colonial, post-colonial, and traditional or customary authorities, cross-cutting every other identity, be it of race and ethnicity, religion or class. Women were active in African independence movements in the 1950s and I have noted some of their claims and the disappointing outcomes below. By the 1990s, women were powerful in the South African constitutional process of the 1990s and empowered by the outcome. In the decades between, one route by which some women tried to re-enter the public debate was via occasional attempts to activate dormant constitutional rights (Cook, 1994). The recent intersection of these efforts with an emerging international women's movement for human rights and with women's prominent role in the South African constitutional negotiations has happened both within and despite of the history outlined here.

Britain and the Diffusion of Rights

From 1957, when the Gold Coast achieved independence as Ghana, through the 1970s, a succession of British colonies in Africa, the Caribbean and the Pacific achieved independence. As part of the process of legal separation and state formation, Britain bequeathed each a written constitution, devised in negotiations and conferences between colonial, African and other resident groups, lawyers, civil servants and assorted advisors (de Smith, 1964). The diffusion of the Westminster model of parliamentary government by this means has often been noted. In addition, almost all these independence constitutions contained a clause entrenching fundamental civil rights and freedoms. Rights were guaranteed without discrimination on racial, ethnic and religious grounds; in rare cases sex discrimination was also outlawed. Few independence constitutions survived long and, even where rights clauses were continued in later constitutions, they were rarely enforced in the early post-colonial years. But, as Okoth-Ogendo argues, the fact that constitutions were both demanded and replaced by African state elites and ephemeral and honoured mostly in their breach, should not be a reason for ignoring these texts but for examining their place in the development of constitutionalism in and of Africa (Okoth-Ogendo, 1993).

Imperial rule had long accustomed Britain to writing 'constitutions' for its dominions and colonies. The charters granted to American colonies were early examples, the British North America Act of 1867, mapping Canadian government and only patriated to Canada in 1982, one of the most lasting (Zines, 1991). Constitutional guarantees of human rights were demanded for India as early as 1895 (Lester, 1984, 48). The Irish constitutions of 1922 and 1937 included enforceable rights. The Simon Commission on the Indian Constitution in 1930, however, had typically rejected for the British sphere of influence those models of rights developed in 'European states formed after the War' because 'experience has not shown them to be of any great practical value' (Cowen, 1961, p. 114; de Smith, 1964, p. 164). Declaratory Bills of Rights eventually appeared in the post-war constitutions of India (1950) and Pakistan (1956), but no constitution in Britain's dependent territories in the mid 1950s contained entrenched rights and nor did the 1957 constitution of independent Ghana. Nigeria's independence constitution of 1959 did, and thereby marked the beginning of a new era for British and post-colonial rights practice. Previously, if there was an official British view of rights at all, it was one of contemptuous dismissal. At the Nigerian Constitutional Conference of 1953, Colonial Secretary Oliver Lyttelton 'contrived to put himself and most of the other delegates in the room in good humour by laughing out of the conference room' the idea that the UN Declaration might be incorporated (de Smith, 1964, p. 167). But in 1959, the Nigerian Constitution drafters entrenched rights clauses borrowed from the European Convention on Human Rights (ECHR). What, if anything, had changed on the British side of this relationship, and with what impact on Britain's own rights politics?

As a leading member of the Council of Europe, Britain had been closely involved in drafting the European Convention of Human Rights and was indeed the first nation to ratify it. The post-war Labour government, however, was a reluctant constitutional reformer. In fully traditional vein, it resisted encroachment on the doctrine and practice of parliamentary sovereignty, to which the proposed European Convention represented a major threat. Lord Chancellor Jowitt in particular was adamantly against the ECHR, spitting resentment at a proposal which he was reported to believe 'would be a disaster which would undermine the whole of English law and the system of administering it and that we ought to have nothing to do with the Convention' (Marston, 1993, p. 815). But the Cabinet could see the difficulty of rejecting such a Convention as much as the difficulties arising from ratification: 'for political reasons we must - in some form or another - accept this draft Convention' (Marston, 1993, p. 817). However complacent about the protection of rights under British common law and parliamentary government, Britain was becoming a public sponsor of a European system which must not become, as the Foreign Office put it, 'like the similar professions of the Communist Governments, a hollow mockery' (Marston, 1993, p. 809). In the end, Jowitt and his colleagues had to be content with a middle course, endorsing the new rights regime while ensuring that the European Court of Human Rights would have no direct jurisdiction and individual Britons no direct right of petition (Lester, 1984; Marston, 1993).

British subjects were emphatically not to gain enforceable or fundamental rights. It was 1965 before a later Labour government granted the right of individual petition, 1997 before yet another Labour government was prepared to incorporate the ECHR into British law, albeit still with no judicial power to overthrow legislation (Lester, 1984; Human Rights Bill, 1997). What it would not give at home, however, Britain granted to Nigeria at what, in this context, seems the early date of 1959. One problem seen by Britain during the drafting of the ECHR was whether the Convention would be automatically applicable to its empire. As the Colonial Secretary noted in 1950: 'The Convention, if applied to the colonies, cannot be other than an embarrassment to Colonial Governments'. While rejection of this possibility would make the Colonial Office 'very glad', he could understand the political criticism which would arise from international circles (Marston, 1993, p. 193, p. 816). For indeed, as Heyns observes, 'the countries involved in this lofty enterprise' of writing an international rights convention, 'were also the main perpetrators in what was increasingly being recognised as the gross and systematic human rights abuses which colonialism constituted in large parts of the world' (Heyns, 1995, p. 254). Even more than in the grant of rights at home, the colonial issue exposed the hypocrisy of Britain's role in drafting the ECHR.

A solution for the colonies was found. The UK first ensured that applicability to colonies would be voluntary and 'with due regard ... to local requirements'. Then, in 1953, Britain brought most of its territories under the Convention (Vasak, 1963, p. 1209). There was no dramatic effect (as there was none yet in Britain), but perhaps a degree of restraint upon British and colonial government actions, including the possible embarrassment of making a public derogation from time to time (Vasak, 1963, pp. 1212-14). However, this extension of the ECHR to the colonies provided a fig leaf to those who sought to downplay the grants of enforceable rights in subsequent independence constitutions by a Britain opposed in principle to such instruments. Lord Wilberforce stated the conventional British wisdom, in an appeal brought to the Privy Council from Bermuda: 'constitutional instruments drafted in the post-colonial period' were 'greatly influenced by the European Convention for the Protection of Human Rights and Fundamental Freedoms... That Convention was signed and ratified by the United Kingdom and applied to dependent territories'(*Min. Of Home Affairs v. Fisher* (P. C.) [1980]). In this view, the UK was merely transferring an existing guarantee which it had previously held in trust for its possessions, a technical rather than a principled inclusion. Innovation lay only in the entrenchment abroad of what would not be entrenched at home, that is in the mechanisms for enforcement not in the possession of rights.

Comments at the time, however, suggest that new rationales for rights were emerging in British circles. In the Nigerian negotiations during 1959, British officials advanced from outright rejection to the discovery of some practical advantage in rights clauses. Pragmatism rather than any new appreciation of the principle seems to have changed minds. In 1952, internal Colonial Office papers had repeated the traditional distaste, regardless of Britain's public commitment to both the United Nations and Council of Europe rights regimes. In addition to a general guarantee of equality, the 1953 Self Government Statute codified traditional common law rights to freedom of religion, opinion, association, the rule of law and fair judicial procedures. This statute, it was noted, contained 'a feature ... which is alien to practise in the Colonial territories ... the inclusion of a chapter laying down a code of fundamental rights', no doubt 'there under the influence of the United Nations Declaration of Human Rights' (Goldsworthy, 1994, pp. 169-70, letter from Sir T. Lloyd to Sir W. Strang, 9 May 1952). Notes on an inter-departmental meeting the following month elaborated:

> On Chapter II concerning Fundamental Rights it was agreed that although none of those present saw any advantage in including this chapter, it would be more harmful to try to get it excluded now than to leave it in. The Colonial Office position was safeguarded in so far as it could be said that the Statute was produced by the Sudanese themselves, and was not a British draft. In this way the Colonial Office could argue against using it as a precedent for draft colonial

> constitutions (5 June 1952, FO 371/96855, in Goldsworthy, 1994, p. 170).

Within a year, anticipating the independence of two major West African colonies, the Gold Coast and Nigeria, a more positive attitude began to emerge. In 1953, Colonial Office staff noted that a revised colonial constitution for the Gold Coast must combine internal self-government with British retention of several 'essential powers', including the power 'to protect any section of the population from discriminatory or oppressive treatment'(Minutes by Sir C Jeffries and Mr Lyttelton, 9 February 1953, CO 554/254, in Goldsworthy, 1994, p. 189). The imperatives of protection were strong for nations with boundaries created by Europeans, where regional, ethnic and religious groups were maybe (as the Governor of Nigeria asserted loftily in a paper on constitutional issues) 'held together solely by the influence of British officials'(Governor Sir J. Macpherson, 16 March 1953, CO 554/254, in Goldsworthy, 1994, p. 191). The 1957 Ghana Constitution laid down a guideline of racial equity both to win consent from and provide reassurance to a divided population.

S. A. de Smith sums up that when 'there emerged political situations in which a transfer of power could not be effected without guarantees against the prospective abuse of authority by a new set of rulers, precedents already set in the international sphere could be drawn on by the constitution-makers'(de Smith, 1964, p. 174). Certainly the belief that the British only granted rights out of a profound distrust of the new nations was prevalent; a suspicion that 'the advocates of a Bill of Rights are really concerned to palm off a second class democracy by circumscribing the people ... because they do not trust non-whites, and feel that if the non-whites were an enfranchised majority they would prejudice the whites' (Cowen, 1961, p. 115). It became apparent that among protected minorities would be both the white population and potential overseas investors. The Monckton Commission on the Constitution of Rhodesia and Nyasaland in 1960 attached the 'utmost importance to the Bill of Rights ... [which] will help to reassure Europeans and Asians who find themselves outnumbered by Africans in all three Territories'(Report, 1960, p. 151). In the same year, the report of the Kenya Constitutional Conference concluded that it was 'the firm view of Her Majesty's Government that justiciable fundamental rights be provided', and that it was 'important to include protection for property rights' (Kenya Constitutional Conference, 1960, p. 9). The Attlee government in Britain had been particularly concerned that the introduction of the ECHR, by protecting the rights of property owners, might interfere with the development of a planned economy (Marston, 1993, p. 813; Zines, 1991, p. 36, p. 53). Governments during the fifties appear to have turned this around, using rights on behalf of the 'Europeans [whose] main concern was to secure their land and property rights' (Ghai, 1967, p. 180). The British, Julius Nyerere commented, 'without saying so ... devised constitutions which pre-supposed a basically capitalist society' (Nyerere, 1993, p. 14).

By the time of the Nigerian constitution-making process in the late 1950s, Colonial Office civil servants had developed a rationale for grants of rights in independence constitutions. Vasak believed that 'the success of the Nigerian experiment' finally secured this new attitude: 'it is no secret that the "draftsmen" of the Colonial Office in London have ... in mind the spirit of the Convention, whenever, anywhere in the world, the peaceful evolution of the British Commonwealth runs up against the problem of national, racial or tribal minorities' (Vasak, 1963, p. 1223). Yet the irony noted by observers, of the application abroad of what was unacceptable at home, seems not to have ruffled the serenity of the British government. John Kendle noted the same blind spot in the closely associated development of federal structures for independence constitutions. The considerable expertise on federalism accumulated within the civil service remained insulated from British political discourse. By the 1950s, Colonial Office 'civil servants were at ease with the federal idea', as they were becoming with the idea of rights: 'This shift in attitude in Whitehall and Westminster could easily have led an observer to conclude that the British might yet find the federal idea attractive in other forums than the colonial. This of course would have proved to be a mistake... As long as the British were playing with other people's sovereignty and not their own, the federal idea had little fear for them' (Kendle, 1997, p. 149).

In 1962, Dwight Holland commented that views on how best to protect rights in British Africa had recently 'changed radically', away from traditional parliamentarism towards a new enthusiasm for bills of rights (Holland, 1962, p. 145). The inherent contradictions, so plain in the British role in drafting the ECHR and diffusing its principles in independence constitutions, took several more decades to explode at home. Anthony Lester, for one, predicted that these contradictions, placidly taken on board at the time, could not for ever be swept under the carpet: 'What passes for wisdom in the United Kingdom', he wrote in 1984, 'is an ever more isolated view among the modern democracies of the nature of human rights and of their protection against the misuse of public powers; and it has become a barely tenable position for the United Kingdom to maintain ...' (Lester, 1984, 47). The contagion of rights, however, spread only outwards at the time.

African Perspectives

In 1963, Karel Vasak could not 'help being struck with the fact that it is principally the United Kingdom which has been behind the veritable "dissemination" of the European Convention throughout the world and especially in Africa' (Vasak, 1963, p. 1223). The British, however, were pushed more than pulled by their own emergent rationale: 'In general', Holland wrote, 'it may be said that the pressure has come from the emerging independent territories themselves, rather than from the United Kingdom, which has adopted the role of passive agreement rather than that of positive encouragement in this matter' (Holland, 1962, p. 145). A change of heart of the British government was essential, but the leadership coming from indigenous elites has sometimes been ignored or underestimated. On this point, for example, de Smith was dismissive: 'The traumatic experiences of the Second World War, the Atlantic Charter, the United Nations Charter, even the Universal Declaration of Human Rights, failed to stimulate local demands for constitutional bills of rights ... though they speeded the movement to self-rule'(de Smith, 1964, 174). Each side in the negotiations sought to establish 'what they conceived to be democratic constitutions', Julius Nyerere later recalled. But whereas the British government had been primarily concerned to 'safeguard special interest groups', African leaders 'were demanding the kind of freedom for themselves' that they believed existed in the metropolitan country: 'The systems we knew were those of Europe–and occasionally the USA' (Nyerere, 1993, p. 14; Von Eschen, 1997). Evidence can be gathered from diverse sources of such autonomous demands, that the question was on the agenda way ahead of British sympathy and usually at the urging of racial and religious minorities.

Authorship of the Sudan Self Government Statute of 1953, with its declaration that 'All persons in the Sudan are free and equal before the law. No disability shall attach to any Sudanese by reason of birth, religion, race or sex'(Chap. 2, Article 5), had been disavowed by the Colonial Office. The statute was, according to an explanatory Sudanese memorandum, 'essentially Sudanese in origin ... drafted on the basis of recommendations by the

Sudanese themselves, and of discussions with Sudanese of widely differing opinions' (Egyptian Society, 1953, p. 55). The inclusion of sex as a prohibited ground of discrimination set off events which illustrate the difficulties for any social group of attaining anything more than formal declarations of rights. The establishment in 1956 of a committee to draft a permanent constitution 'sparked off a lot of activity by feminist societies and unions for the realisation of political rights for women'. But this in turn created a backlash of substantial and effective opposition to giving any effect to equal rights (Fawzi, 1959, pp. 247-49).

In the Gold Coast independence negotiations, the official opposition was able effectively to veto any settlement. Opposition leader, Dr K.A. Busia, summarised their objective in a letter to the Times: 'an agreed Constitution that safeguards the minority rights of the Northern territories, respects the identity of the Ashanti nation, provides for an independent judiciary, and secures the legal freedom of every citizen' (22 Sept 1956). Ghana did not entrench ECHR rights. The Ghana Constitution Order in Council did, however, guarantee that 'No law shall make persons of any racial community liable to disabilities to which persons of other such communities are not made liable' (Article 31). Meantime, pressure within Nigeria for independence with comprehensive rights was building.

The Nigerian Bill of Rights, following the text of the ECHR, was a response to Nigerian demands. So much confidence was placed in the protection of rights guarantees that Nigerian leaders insisted that 'the Chapter of the Constitution containing the Bill of Rights was promulgated even before the independence elections' (Heyns, 1995, p. 257). This text became the model for 'neo-Nigerian' constitutions in the majority of later African independence constitutions. It was 'the conduit for the importation of the Western articulation of the concept of human rights into modern African human rights law' (Heyns, 1995, p. 258). Acceptance by both Britain and Nigeria, however, represented no idealistic recognition of the human rights of the individual. The point was the potential of rights instruments to offer some safeguard against the fear (of the departing colonial rulers) of the abuse of power and the fear (among Nigerians) of the exploitation of internal divisions and majority power over minorities. The various independence negotiations, in which both federal and rights solution figured large, are a classic example of the use of constitutional devices to pre-empt or transform conflict. At the risk of over simplifying, in Nigeria the fear that federalism would be a shortcut to regional secessions and the break up of the nation led to a greater reliance on national government and unified citizenship rights, to control the tensions created by ethnic diversity. Shortly afterwards, in Kenya, the fragmentation of the coalition against Britain into competing ethnic groups before the constitution was finalised, led to a complex federal system 'that validated ethnic citizenship in autonomous regional governments' (Ndegwa, 1997, p. 606).

At the 1953 Nigerian constitutional conference, Nigerian representatives had asked for: the inclusion of 'certain basic human rights' especially for citizens of the Muslim Northern region. In accounts by African lawyers, there is no mention of Lyttelton's ridicule. By 1958, drafting a bill of rights was the priority, at the behest of 'the small ethnic groups who feared oppression by dominant groups after the British government had withdrawn from the country' (Odumoso, 1963, p. 94, p. 122). A year earlier, a Minorities Commission had been established as a result of the difficult constitutional negotiations. Because of the British government's fear that regionalism would lead to disintegration, the Commission was instructed that a structural solution was to be recommended only 'if all else failed'. Sir Henry Willink's report 'pronounced against the creation of new regions and proposed, as one means of allaying the fears of the minorities, the inclusion in the Nigerian Constitution of provisions guaranteeing certain fundamental rights' (Vasak, 1963, p. 1216). The Commission's logic, leading to a recommendation to apply the ECHR, is further evidence of the developing rights rationale:

> Provisions of this kind in the Constitution are difficult to enforce and sometimes difficult to interpret. Nevertheless, we think they should be inserted. Their presence defines beliefs widespread among democratic countries and provides a standard to which appeal may be made by those whose rights are infringed. A government determined to abandon democratic courses will find ways of violating them but they are of great value in preventing a steady deterioration in standards of freedom and the unobtrusive encroachment of a government on individual rights (quoted in Vasak, 1963, p. 1217).

Chief Awolowo, who participated in both 1953 and 1958 meetings, remained critical of the independence constitution clauses, as 'inadequate in that they do not contain any of the fundamental social rights contained in the Universal Declaration of Human Rights' (Awolowo, 1966, p. 120). This omission, according to Karel Vasak, placed the Nigerian Constitution 'among those which emerged from the Revolution of 1789' rather than those of the post-war European settlement which included social rights. It was in line also with the influence, though relatively minor compared with that of the ECHR, of American rights ideas. Thurgood Marshall, then at the height of his achievements with the NAACP, attended the Kenya Constitutional Conference as a Group Special Adviser to the African Constituency Elected Members. They must surely have sought his unparalleled expertise on civil rights. As Colonial Secretary Iain Macleod noted, he brought with him a 'very helpful paper', taken into account in the final draft (Kenya Constitutional Conference, 1960, p. 9). The fact that these, and not for example the German formula, were the crucial influences upon independence constitutions was a consequential choice of direction for African rights. It left open, as Heyns observes, 'the central preoccupation of Africa over many years ... the conflict between communalism and individualism' (Heyns, 1995, p. 263).

Awolowo noted also that the ECHR ban on sex discrimination in the exercise of its rights and freedoms disappeared in the Nigerian text and even that 'several clauses allow discrimination ... against the female sex' (Awolowo, 1966, p. 121; Vasak, 1963, p. 1218). The omission seems not to have been discussed in the formal negotiations, but conveniently enabled the exclusion of Muslim women in the Northern region from suffrage rights (Vasak, 1963, p. 1218 n. 43). The general omission was a setback for all women who had been active in Nigerian politics before this date, from the Igbo 'women's war' of 1929 to the elitist Lady Oyinkan Abayomi, educated in Britain and wife of a Yoruba chief, who was active in women's organisations in Lagos from the 1920s. In 1944 Abayomi was a founder of the Nigerian Women's Party, established 'to seek by constitutional means' citizenship for the entire Nigerian population, and to improve women's conditions 'by recognition of their equal status with men' (Johnson, 1986, p. 246). The fate of women who provided vital support for the National Council for Nigeria and the Cameroons may have been typical. Despite an NCNC female leadership training course begun in 1959 with the motto 'What the men can do the women can', women slipped into support roles. In the constitutional negotiations with other nationalists and British officials, the NCNC abandoned its full female suffrage claim and accepted the exclusion of northern women from voting rights (Van Allen, 1976, p. 82).

Within independence movements, it has been suggested, 'women were fighting not just for the political independence of their country nor for generic "civil rights" but for clearly defined objectives based on their specific needs'(Cutrufelli, 1983, p. 170). Thus, in parts of Nigeria where the base for women's involvement in anti-colonial struggles was market women's organisations, marginalisation from the national settlement may have resulted, as women made limited 'demands related to market activities' and to retaining their autonomy in existing social roles (Hay and Stichter, 1990, p. 148). In a pattern resembling that of nineteenth century British women, in Nigeria and other African states women's first demands were often for voting rights and representation, not for equal rights. Imperial powers were also more likely to grant this right. In 1959, it was reported that female suffrage was a recent but spreading development in Africa. Yet Sudan denied the vote to women (despite their strong non-discrimination clause), apparently encouraging 'an incipient feminist movement' to form. Variable suffrage rights were maintained in independence constitutions in west (Nigeria), east (Uganda) and central Africa (Rhodesia and Nyasaland). Despite such variations, it was claimed at the time that 'the mere recognition of women's rights is important, regardless of the meaning of the vote' (El Hamamsy, 1959, p. 482, p. 473). And in at least one case, inequities in voting rights did themselves generate a broader critique of discrimination. In 1958, Kenya's coastal Muslim women 'successfully petitioned the colonial government to protest discriminatory legislation that denied them the vote but gave it to women of other ethnic communities'. But in the end it appeared that this campaign 'resulted as much from ethnic pride as from a desire for equal rights' (Strobel, 1976, p. 183, p. 210).

Rights on paper were, then, neither necessarily replicated in law nor observed in practice. In matters of sex equality, as of other rights, formal recognition was often or usually as far as the effect of independence constitutions went. As Yash Ghai has pointed out, indigenous legitimations of power, including patrimonialism and religion, and 'more fundamentally, ... the character of the state and the nature of the process of accumulation in most Third World countries ... undermine constitutionalism'(Ghai, 1993, p. 192). And yet, he suggests, the legacy of independence constitutions has not altogether vanished:

> Only a handful of countries still have the constitution they adopted on independence; yet, despite political vicissitudes in which military or other authoritarian regimes replaced democracy, aspirations for the return to the constitutional values of the

independence period for the resolution of their problems animates the peoples of these countries (Ghai, 1993, p. 190).

A Two Way Bridge?

During the 1950s, the drafting of independence constitutions became a mechanism for spreading the discourse of constitutional rights. The British government was no leader in this diffusion of international human rights ideas, but was reluctantly pushed by a mixture of informed demand from their colonies, fearfulness about the future and a dawning recognition of the interests of British settlers and businessmen. The demand for constitutions to include rights came from the elites of the new nations. The common ground on both sides of these negotiations was that rights were a defensive mechanism. Only in the 1960s, and in Caribbean independence constitutions drawing upon the new Canadian Bill of Rights, such as those of Trinidad (1961) and Jamaica (1962), were rights included for their own merits rather than as a defence against fundamental social divisions. Jamaica, representing a convergence and synthesis of previous developments in both Africa and Canada, also set a textual pattern followed in most independence constitutions of the 1960s and including the firm establishment of sex in the list of prohibited discriminations.

Anti-discrimination guarantees on grounds such as race, tribal membership or religion could be construed as conflict resolution devices, mediating currently problematic social divisions and active sources of hostilities. Adding sex interjected a pervasive and potentially much more subversive classification, which cut across other identities, contravened the bulk of colonial and customary law and challenged social practice in familial relations, the division of labour and the ownership and transmission of property, the distribution of political power through representation, authority structures and the formal definition of citizenship. If constitution-makers had simply lifted their texts from international instruments, then we might have expected sex discrimination to be outlawed in every independence bill of rights. The pivotal Ghanaian and Nigerian texts clearly selected only attributes serving their immediate needs, and these did not include sex. Even in texts where sex discrimination was proscribed it was also institutionalised, most prominently in political representation and the definition of citizenship and its transmission to children.

The development of women's rights, whether originally excluded or included and ignored, offers one example of how the gap was bridged between the early and defensive introduction of rights and the proactive and central debate in 1990s South Africa. When the full story of the intervening years is told, it may provide part of the answer to Ghai's conundrum of the survival from the independence texts of the aspirations of the constitutional rhetoric, despite the pragmatism or even cynicism of their introduction and implementation. Once installed, rights provisions may take on unexpected life - may be contagious, as Lester proposed. The infection may lie dormant for years; the slow take-up of the possibilities offered by the ECHR and European Union rights in Britain, the eventual toe in the water of women using the national and regional rights existing on paper in Africa to take their cases to court, demonstrate this potential (Collins and Meehan, 1994; Cook, 1994; Quansah, 1992; Stamp, 1995).

When such experiments with women's rights began to occur in Africa, they did so in parallel with the blossoming of an international rights movement. So long as women's lives and politics remained distinct and separate from men's, national developments probably followed the same international pattern described by Elissavet Stamatopoulou. She has criticised the international community for the separation of women's human rights from the discourse and practice of international human rights theory and law. Institutional separation of the two accentuated the problem, when, almost as soon as the UN pronounced the principle of sex equality, it created at the operational level both a Commission on Human Rights and a separate Commission on the Status of Women to which women's rights issues were sent (Stamatopoulou, 1995, p. 36, pp. 40-42). A - maybe the - prime factor in the emergence of women's rights consciousness in Africa has been the work of international organisations, from the first UN Decade of Women and promulgation of the UN Convention on the Elimination of All Forms of Discrimination Against Women (1979) to the 1993 Vienna World Conference on Human Rights in which women's rights were re-integrated into general rights discourse (Stamatopoulou, 1995, p. 36). The effect of the Vienna recognition can be seen in the full guarantees of women's rights and social and economic rights alongside traditional political and civil rights in the new South African Constitution. Advisors to the Constitutional Assembly 'rejected the distinction between first-, second- and third generation rights' which 'flies in the face of the Vienna Declaration of 1993 that all human rights are universal, indivisible and interdependent and interrelated' (de Vos, 1997, p. 3).

Henry Steiner and Philip Alston couple, as I have done above, two processes: 'a horizontal trend among states', the result of decolonisation or external pressure; and a 'vertical' trend of 'links between the spread of such types of constitutions and the achievements of the human rights movement in constructing an international system of norms, institutions, and processes' (Steiner and Alston, 1996, p. 710). The South African Constitution of 1996 prioritised the international for domestic use (de Vos, 1997, pp. 1-2). Advisers on the implementation of Constitutional Principle 2 warned that 'National Bills of Rights are not "universally accepted fundamental rights" in the sense that they lacked general acceptance and were generally the product of particular historical and political circumstances' (de Vos, 1997, p. 2). In the case of the independence constitutions, the horizontal and vertical went together. While the ECHR could be said to have a degree of international acceptance, it was itself the product of local historical circumstances.

This paper about the ECHR and the development of rights in post-colonial Africa has only touched upon the most distinctive African contribution to the conceptualisation of rights, that input of indigenous ideas of communalism which attempts to redress the imbalance of the ECHR in favour of individualism. 'It is perhaps worth noting', Heyns wrote, 'that the European system is bound to undergo far-reaching changes in the next few years, when a large number of countries where a less individualistic orientation prevails will become participants in the system' (Heyns, 1995, p. 263). Heyns is thinking primarily of the absorption by western Europe of countries in the former Soviet sphere of influence, with legal roots in German rather than Anglo-American practice; their entry into the European human rights regime will add to the pressure already felt in Britain from its membership of the European Union, to come to grips with the role of social and economic as well as civil and political rights. In South Africa, van Wyk noted, a 'special feature ... was the way in which the position of women was addressed from the outset' (van Wyk, 1995, p. 141). Western societies, like African societies, are structured by gender, and traditional female gender roles are often particularly affected by the formulation of social and economic rights. Land and property rights, rights in development programmes, family, health and education rights, have been as crucial as suffrage and citizenship rights for African women (Cook, 1994; Howard, 1986, chapter 8). The pre-emptive mobilisation of South African women in the constitutional process of the 1990s, demonstrated how women had realised the extent to which their future was implicated in the formulation of a new framework of rights (Bazilli, 1991; Kaganas, 1994; Kadalie, 1995).

The recognition of the indivisibility of rights, framed in Vienna, may spur the contagion of rights to become a two-way process. One far-reaching change specific to the United Kingdom, implemented by the Human Rights Bill going through Parliament in the Spring of 1998, is the incorporation of the ECHR into British law. It will go against the British tradition of dispensing outwards rather than drawing sustenance from innovations elsewhere. But as Britain prepares to incorporate the individualistic ECHR (thus locking in a conceptualisation of rights dating from the 1940s and unchanged from that disseminated in the 1950s) the South African experience is timely. South African women's constitutional politics offers a model and a moral, not only for women but for the engagement of all citizens in the process of the formulation and legitimation of new constitutional frameworks. When it comes to the content of such frameworks, Heyns for one wonders: 'Would it be hoping for too much that, based on our many years of experience, Africa - and in particular South Africa - may provide some of the components of a workable solution' to a new rights regime in which individual and collective rights are both recognised (Heyns, 1995, p. 263). Sydney Kentridge similarly has proposed that 'the experience of the formulation of the fundamental rights in the South African Constitution ... may be worth considering by those who are pressing for a bill of rights for the United Kingdom' - chickens coming home to roost indeed, almost fifty years after the expatriation of rights from Britain to Africa (Kentridge, 1996, p. 254).

4 Impartial Justice and Partial Perspectives[1]

MELISSA S. WILLIAMS

Introduction

The legal protection of fundamental rights, whether through constitutional or legislative devices, is a key element of liberal understandings of justice. A just political order secures these rights for its citizens without bias or favour; ideally, it treats all citizens impartially, without regard to social position or personal attributes. As liberal justice has been understood until recently, this aspiration requires a scheme of constitutionally entrenched rights that are blind to differences that, as John Rawls famously expressed it, are 'arbitrary from a moral perspective' (Rawls, 1971, p. 511).

This understanding of justice has undergone serious challenge in the last decade, as feminists and others have tackled the problem of reconciling the aspiration to democratic equality with the persistent fact of social and cultural difference. These theorists offer a profound critique of the ideal of universal citizenship, arguing that we can no longer understand democratic equality to be adequately served by a programme of uniform rights for all. Membership in certain kinds of groups coincides with significant social, political and economic differences among citizens. Treating these citizens as full and equal members of the political community may sometimes require that we redefine our just obligations in a manner that acknowledges and accommodates social difference. At times, this may require that we recognise difference explicitly in the form of different rights or different treatment (See esp. Young, 1990).

I use the term 'social difference' to denote differences that follow the lines of membership in what I call 'marginalised ascriptive groups'. These groups have four characteristic features: (1) patterns of social and political inequality are structured along the lines of group membership; (2) generally, membership in them is not experienced as voluntary; (3) generally, membership in them is not experienced as mutable; and (4) generally, there are negative meanings assigned to group identity by the broader society or the dominant culture. Each of these characteristics distinguishes marginalised groups from voluntary associations, as well as from cultural groups that do not suffer economic, social or political disadvantage.[2] Often, these groups have historically been excluded from the full enjoyment of civil and political rights. In other words, marginalised groups have often suffered what Alan Cairns calls 'constitutional stigmatisation' in his contribution to this volume. Paradigmatic examples of marginalised ascriptive groups include women, African Americans, and Aboriginal peoples in North America, Australia and New Zealand.

The difference-based challenge to liberal understandings of justice proceeds not only at the level of formal, institutionalised rights, but also at the level of theory-formation itself. That is, the conception of fairness as difference-blindness enters the scene not only in the application of principles of justice, but also in the theoretical formulation of those principles. Thus critics note that one of liberal theorists' favourite methods of theory-generation, the hypothetical decision making situation - of which the best known contemporary example is Rawls' original position - is designed so as to exclude considerations of social difference from influencing the formulation of basic principles of justice, including the scheme of basic rights and liberties that should be enshrined in the constitution.

Yet this difference-blind approach, critics argue, results in standards of justice that fail to treat members of marginalised and disadvantaged groups as full and equal citizens. (Okin, 1989; Young, 1990; see also Minow, 1990) Quite inadvertently, liberals have built bias into their principles of justice by defining those principles through a process that totally abstracts from social particularity. In short, what appears just from within liberals' hypothetical decision making situations often functions in ways that reinforce and reproduce certain social groups' marginalisation.

We can see how a difference-blind scheme of rights may reinforce patterns of social privilege and disadvantage by borrowing some examples from other contributions to this volume. Alan Cairns' study of constitutional stigmatisation outlines some of many ways in which constitutions may entrench different sets of rights for different sets of people, creating distinct classes of citizenship. As I have noted above, many contemporary marginalised groups were historically stigmatised in the ways Cairns describes. At the least, most contemporary marginalised groups were once excluded from full political rights, particularly the franchise. In the wake of this history, a scheme of difference-blind civil and political rights would appear to be the surest route to justice. But note the ways in which the introduction of putatively universal and impartial rights have functioned in other settings to reinforce existing patterns of privilege. Vivien Hart notes that the entrenchment of basic civil rights in the 'independence constitutions' was often driven by colonial desires to protect the property interests of white settlers and foreign investors. Thus the entrenchment of universal rights to property had the consequence of frustrating independence governments which sought to pursue development through the devices of a planned economy, including, presumably, land reform (Hart, this volume, pp. 46-47). As Damian O'Leary points out in his essay, the institutions of majoritarian democracy in Northern Ireland secure a universal right to the franchise for both Protestant and Catholic voters. Yet the difference-blind instrument of single-member district plurality elections guaranteed the permanent underrepresentation of the Catholic minority in Stormont. As O'Leary notes, these facially neutral electoral processes were accompanied - not coincidentally, from the Catholic perspective - with patterns of Catholic underrepresentation across the most important institutions of Northern Ireland: in the judiciary, police force, the civil service, and so on (O'Leary, this volume, pp. 94-98).

The critical observation that difference-blind rights may function to conceal a built-in bias in constitutional principles does not, however, automatically yield an alternative. If difference-blindness is not, by itself, sufficient to secure justice toward marginalised groups, what principles and procedures should we adopt in their stead?

Recent theoretical attempts to address this question have produced two distinct approaches to defining justice so that it is responsive to social difference. The first I call the 'juridical' model of justice toward groups, and it basically accepts the ideal of liberal impartiality. On the basis of that ideal, the juridical model begins with the premise that justice should be defined through a process of reasoning that is shielded from the tug and pull of particularist political interests. In other words, justice should be defined *prior to politics*, and in fact should serve to define the boundaries within which a diversity of political goals may be sought. As the 'right is prior to the ... good', (Rawls, 1971, p. 31), the just is prior to the political. It is a 'juridical' model of justice insofar as it contains the implicit assumption that justice, once defined in the abstract, should be interpreted and enforced by judges and other agents of a neutral and impartial state. On this view, the difference-based critique of liberal justice leads us to incorporate the distinctive concerns of marginalised groups into the process of philosophical reasoning that culminates in a conception of justice. Once we have corrected the bias of liberal justice in this way, the resulting principles will function *truly* impartially, and will no longer systematically reproduce existing patterns of inequality.

In contrast, the 'political' solution to the problem of difference rejects the notion that justice can be defined prior to politics. Instead, its advocates maintain that standards of justice can only avoid reproducing inequality if they are defined *within* a political process that provides the opportunity for marginalised groups' perspectives to be expressed and heeded. In this model, our duties of justice are not defined prior to a process of political discourse, but within it. Justice does not merely define the boundaries within which politics can take place, but is itself reshaped as a result of a public deliberation. Justice is not defined analytically, but discursively. It is important to emphasise that it is not just a matter of applying justice politically once we have defined it analytically; the definition itself must be politicised, because viewing justice from the standpoint of these groups can mean radically reconceiving some of the fundamental principles of justice.

I have argued elsewhere that the political approach to defining justice toward groups not only has important advantages over but is actually implicit (although undeveloped) in the juridical approach (Williams, 1995). Nonetheless, the political approach itself leaves us with unanswered questions that are so fundamental that it renders the aspiration to justice itself suspect. When the command to attend to the particularity of perspectives on issues of justice enters the public sphere, we seem to be in danger of losing any firm ground from which we can evaluate the competing justice claims of different social groups. Consequently, the political approach would seem to lead us to a precipice at which we must choose whether to abandon the ideal of justice as impartiality altogether, as some difference theorists have already done (Young, 1990).

The clash between these two approaches to reconciling equality and difference brings to light a profound need to reconceive the aspiration to impartial justice and, in the process, to reconsider the relationship between the political and judicial spheres within constitutional democracies. Despite the strength of difference-based critiques of liberal bias, the conclusion that impartiality is impossible is premature. What is clear is that a great deal of work remains to be done in reconceiving impartiality in the wake of the critique from difference. But this theoretical task must not begin from the supposition that our thinking about justice can or should remain insulated from the numerous and conflicting claims about equality and fairness that are at play in the realm of politics. The competition of both ideas and interests that lies at the heart of political life inevitably - and, I would argue, quite properly - informs judges, political philosophers, and citizens in their judgements about justice. The challenge we face is not to eliminate the links between politics and the impartial rule of law, as both models of justice toward groups have hitherto done, but to develop further our understanding of the relationship between the political and the juridical that best fulfils our aspirations for justice.

As we embark upon the project of addressing this challenge, it is sensible to begin with an inquiry into discursive approaches to defining the terms of political co-operation, and into the place social difference has in political discourse. As noted above, the difference-based critique of liberal justice makes clear that justice towards marginalised groups requires that legally protected rights be defined through a process that directly includes the voices of those groups. This essay, then, attempts a first step toward the formulation of a political conception of justice toward groups by examining the relationship between three theoretical constructs: the ideal of impartiality, the theory of deliberative democracy, and the notion of group-based differences. In what ways do the now-burgeoning theoretical models of deliberative democracy rely upon an ideal of impartiality as the criterion of legitimate democratic discourses? What happens to the model of deliberative democracy and its embedded ideals impartiality when we add social difference into the mix? In what ways does difference enhance deliberation, and in what ways does it impede impartial political judgement? Finally, what empirical and institutional lessons might we take from a study of the place of difference in deliberative democracy?

Impartiality as Constitutive of the Deliberative Model

Theories of deliberative democracy are concerned with the problem of political justification in the face of moral disagreement; they aim to provide a solution to that problem. As a theory of political legitimacy, deliberative democracy aims at a politics in which collective decisions are grounded in reasons acceptable to all who are affected by them. Deliberative democrats assume that such decisions can only emerge from a process of shared and inclusive public reasoning among equal citizens. The standard of discursive legitimacy requires, then, that both the content and the context of political decision making is consonant with the ideal of free public reasoning among equals (Cohen, 1996; Cohen, 1989; Manin, 1987).

Recent discussions of deliberative democracy (see, e.g., Cohen, 1989; Manin, 1987) offer an ideal of deliberation of which the following is a very rough sketch: We make arguments to one another about the requirements of the common good, and try to persuade one another of our understanding of that good. There are at least two important requirements which participants must meet: they must offer *reasoned* argumentation; and arguments must be aimed at what is *common* rather than what is particular to individual or group. Claims regarding particular individuals or groups must be framed not in terms of their narrow interests, but in terms of shared commitments to public ends, including the public end of justice. In speaking, participants take up their identity as citizens concerned with the common good, not that of bearers of particular interests. The reasons we appeal to must not be reasons which we can expect others to recognise as reasons; we must not appeal, e.g., to conceptions of divine authority which other participants in the discussion do not share. We must enter the conversation with sufficient open-mindedness that we can be persuaded by the arguments of others.

How does such persuasion come about? We hear ways of characterising issues of joint concern that are novel to us, that cause us to see those issues in a different light, and that do a better job of making sense of the facts of the case than do the accounts we had hitherto affirmed. We narrow the range of disagreement through this process, and our collective decisions reflect a greater degree of a common sense of the matter than we had possessed in advance of the discussion. To the extent that no voices were silenced in the deliberative process, and everyone's arguments were listened to sensitively and open-mindedly, the decision we arrive at has a greater legitimacy than it could have had through any other method of decision making.

The principle of impartiality permeates characterisations of the ideal of deliberative democracy in at least four ways: (1) The structure of the deliberative situation is itself impartial, insofar as participants are characterised as standing in relations of perfect equality to each other. None has any structural advantage in getting her views heard sympathetically by others; everything turns on the persuasiveness of the arguments themselves. Consequently, the outcome will not reflect any systemic bias in favour of some perspectives and against others. In short, relations of power have no place within the deliberative process, and so it avoids being 'partial' in the sense of 'biased'. (2) Second, the deliberative process is impartial in the sense that it is *inclusive* (and so not 'partial' in the sense of 'incomplete').

The ideal of deliberation rests on the assumption that no relevant social perspective was excluded or ignored in the formulation of the common interest in whose name a policy is enacted. (3) Third, the reasons participants offer in defence of their interpretations of shared ends are themselves 'impartial' reasons, in the sense that they appeal to the interests that all participants share rather than to the partial interests of some subset of participants. In a deliberative process, the argument that what is good for General Motors is good for the country, without a more specific account of how other affected social actors will benefit from the flourishing of General Motors, simply carry no persuasive force. (4) Finally, impartiality is a feature not only of the spirit in which participants should *speak*, but also of the spirit in which they should *listen* and *judge* each other's speeches. The judgements that participants reach are based not on their interests but on their honest evaluations of the persuasiveness of the reasons offered.

I find this ideal of democratic decision making very appealing, and I am among those who have argued that some such model of deliberative democracy is a necessary presupposition of any coherent defence of marginalised group representation (Williams, 1998). Yet for a number of reasons I remain very unsettled about the adequacy of the ideal of deliberative democracy as a model of justice toward marginalised groups. The remainder of this essay continues to explore some of the reservations and worries I have about the capacity of deliberative democracy to serve the end of justice toward marginalised groups, and to see what resources we might have for answering them. It proceeds by asking the general question, What is the relationship between deliberative democracy and a 'politics of difference'? How can a politics of difference enhance the capacity of deliberative democracy to produce just political decisions?

Pluralism, Difference, and Justice in Deliberative Democracy

A plurality of perspectives is a necessary presupposition for deliberative democracy; otherwise, there would be nothing to be gained from discussion. Pluralism enhances deliberation because it expands the number of alternative understandings of a problem we can entertain in attempting to resolve it. In particular, the presence of a plurality of points of view or of opinions within political discourse presumably strengthens our judgements and our decisions by allowing us to anticipate some of the weaknesses and pitfalls that attend any particular perspective. It allows decisions to be more complete, to comprehend a greater array of social and political possibilities and to foresee a greater number of social and political consequences of our decisions.

So far, it is clear that many different forms of social diversity will enhance the deliberative process, and that marginalised group perspectives constitutes a dimension of pluralism which will contribute at least as much to the comprehensiveness of political decisions as any other. Indeed, there may be good reasons to suppose that they will contribute more, since their perspectives have historically tended to get ignored in the political process. They may see things about social forces that are not readily apparent to others, and what they see may turn out to be extremely valuable for the formulation of good public policy. This notion lay behind some of the strongest arguments for the extension of the franchise to women in the US woman suffrage movement at the beginning of this century. Activists, notably Jane Addams, argued that changes in industrial production and the dynamics of increasing urbanisation meant that social functions (hygiene, waste disposal, health) which formerly had been performed within the household now needed to be addressed as matters of *public* policy. Because women were the agents within the household who had performed these social roles, Addams argued, they had a knowledge about such needs that men generally did not possess. Women should have an equal place in politics, therefore, because the formulation of good public policy depended crucially upon their input into the decision making process.

While the foregoing account makes a great deal of sense of the ways in which a more inclusive deliberative politics serves our interest in the *soundness* of political judgements, however, it does not tell us much about the ways in which a deliberative politics of difference can serve the end of *justice*. That is, while it presents reasons why the perspectives of marginalised groups might improve social policy, it does not give an account of how including those perspectives within the deliberative process will help to ameliorate groups' marginalisation in the society at large, i.e., to increase the justice of social and political arrangements. The dynamics of deliberation through which marginalised group perspectives could reshape public understandings of justice in ways that help to dismantle the social structures of inequality, I believe, must be somewhat different from the dynamics of deliberation that existing models of deliberative democracy presuppose (and which I have roughly sketched above). It is here that my concerns about the limitations of the deliberative model arise.

To explain, let me begin by sketching a description of the dynamics of a deliberative politics which includes the voices of marginalised groups and serves the end of ameliorating the structures of inequality that sustain their identity as such. In such a process, members of marginalised groups explain how an existing practice functions to reproduce their marginalisation and prevents them from being able to participate as full and equal members of society. For example, women might undertake to explain to men how the practices of sexual harassment impede their ability to perform their work or to rise through the ranks in their careers. People with disabilities might try to explain how much time it takes them to navigate their way through a city which was not built with them in mind, and how participating in some spheres of social life and employment is simply impossible for them, not because of the nature of their disabilities but because they are physically prevented from entering the relevant spaces. Other participants in the discussion - men, or persons without disabilities (the 'temporarily able-bodied', as some describe us) - listen to their accounts, and learn to see their own practices from a new angle. But there is more to it than this: for in order for the arguments to have any impact on the social structure of inequality, the listeners must also learn to see their own practices as oppressive to others, as unjust. Finally, they must be willing to change those practices, even though doing so will almost certainly be damaging to their own interests as they have understood them until now. As Iris Young expresses this dynamic in a defence of group representation,

> Group representation unravels the false consensus that cultural imperialism may have produced, and reveals group bias in norms, standards, styles and perspectives that have been assumed as universal or of highest value. By giving voice to formerly silenced or devalued needs and experiences, group representation forces participants in discussion to take a reflective distance on their assumptions and think beyond their own interests. When confronted with interests, needs and opinions that derived from very different social positions and experience, persons sometimes come to understand the limitations of their own experience and perspective for coming to a conclusion about the best policy for everyone (Young, 1994, p. 136).

Now, there are at least four ways in which this account of a deliberative process that contributes to the end of justice differs from the account of deliberative decision making I sketched above:

(1) First, although the participants in the discussion may be equally situated with respect to one another (though it is not yet clear how this can come about), power relations are a necessary feature of the deliberative agenda. It is only by making the unjust consequences of their power visible to privileged groups that marginalised group perspectives can have any chance of transforming prevailing understandings of the requirements of justice. Yet models of deliberative democracy generally are silent on the relationship between inequalities of social power and the process of deliberation. This omission is traceable in large part to the influence of Habermasian theory upon views of deliberative democracy: Habermas' theory of communicative action explicitly abstracts from relations of power to construct an 'ideal speech situation' which is free from the relations of power which inhibit 'systematically undistorted communication' (Habermas, 1990).

(2) Second, participants in a difference-sensitive deliberative process are present as bearers of distinct and identifiable interests, and not simply in their (generalised or universalised) role as citizens. The diversity of perspectives that are brought to bear on discussions of public policy is not simply the diversity that comes from participants' mastery of different bodies of knowledge and experience, but is a diversity that specifically reflects social structures of inequality, the lines of group difference along which positions, wealth, opportunity, political influence, etc. are unevenly distributed.

(3) Third, because of the more immediate relationship participants bear to identifiable interests, the aspiration to impartiality is much more demanding within the second model of deliberation than within the first (although that, too, is quite demanding). Let's place ourselves in the role of a participant in deliberation whose presuppositions are being challenged by another participant. The first model asks us to listen to the other's account of the common good and to evaluate it in a spirit of impartiality, without attending to the question whether or not our interests would be served by such a conception. The second model asks us to go beyond that, to listen sympathetically to another's claim that our practices treat them unjustly. Indeed, it asks us to listen sympathetically to the claim that

the fulfilment of our interests comes at the cost of a just regard for their interests. Where the other's arguments are strong, it asks us to revise our evaluation of our own practices, to judge them unjust, and to forgo the interests they serve in the interest of justice. Whereas in the first model of deliberation we can 'bracket off' the question of how our interests might be affected by a change in policy, in the second model we cannot avoid attending to that question, since the point of the other's claim is that current arrangements unjustly prefer our interests to theirs.

(4) Finally, the outcome of the deliberative process that is specifically responsive to group difference is impartial in a different sense from the impartiality of outcomes in extant models of deliberative democracy. It is still impartial in the sense that it does not favour some groups over others, but it goes beyond this in that it must also be *transformative*; it must *correct* the past biases of social arrangements in ways that other models of deliberative democracy seldom contemplate.

Thus, the view of deliberation that emerges if we focus on the contributions of a discourse involving marginalised groups to collective understandings of justice appears more radical than the more common views of deliberative democracy would seem to admit. A deliberative politics of difference makes sense only as a transformative politics, one which contemplates not only 'a fairer distribution of resources and power between groups we expect to remain hostile' but also the emergence of 'a more comprehensive understanding that validates the worth of each group' (Phillips, 1993, p. 160). But at the same time as it presents a more radical view of democracy than most other deliberative models, it also seems to run the risk of being even more naively utopian than those models, which have themselves often been criticised for their lack of realism concerning human psychology and motivation, for making 'heroic assumptions about participants' (Johnson, 1998). If participants in deliberative democracy as normally described are 'heroic', then participants in a deliberative politics of difference would seem to have to be divine.[3]

Furthermore, a deliberative politics of difference might seem to be self-contradictory, for some of the reasons I have alluded to above: Participants are equal participants in the deliberative process, but the fact of their social inequality permeates political discourse. Participants are meant to judge each other's speeches impartially, but their identifiable interests lie just beneath the surface of arguments concerning justice.

In fact, I do not believe that the ideal of a deliberative politics of difference *is* naively utopian under all circumstances; the trick is to be more specific about the circumstances in which it is conceivable that privileged groups will relinquish some of their privilege in response to marginalised groups' justice claims. What could possibly motivate a disposition in privileged groups to listen impartially to claims of marginalised groups in the manner I've described?

It seems to me that there are there are two principal sources of the motivation of the powerful to heed the voices of those who are less powerful: (1) the desire to be just, or at least to be able to justify one's position (both in the sense of one's beliefs and in the sense of one's social standing) to others (see Scanlon, 1982); and (2) the need to stem conflict in order to avoid its costs. Both of these can serve as motives to listen and to try to understand a situation from the standpoint of another, even a less powerful other. In fact, if we look to the most profound historical moments of the inclusion of oppressed groups into democratic politics - the Civil Rights amendments, the woman suffrage amendment, the Civil Rights Act, South African democracy, the inclusion of First Nations in Canadian constitutional negotiations - all have in common the fact that a new responsiveness to oppressed groups arises with *both* a failure to be able to justify current practice *and* a social mobilisation of the oppressed which threatens potentially high costs to the dominant group/class should it fail to resolve the conflicts. We may soon be able to add Northern Ireland to this list if the Belfast Agreement of 10 April 1998 (discussed in Patrick Hanafin's and Damian O'Leary's contributions to this volume) succeeds. There, again, a massive political reform involving a partial transfer of political power from a relatively strong to a relatively weak group will have emerged as a response both to a persistent sense of the injustice of political arrangements and to the tragic costs of violent conflict.

What this suggests, however, is that the motive of a common good of justice and the motive of interest are in fact much more closely intertwined than prevailing models of deliberative democracy admit. It is a threat to the interests of privileged groups that inclines them to be open to a redefinition of the requirements of justice. The same connection between interest and justice is of course present for marginalised groups as well, though it appears in a different form: as many opponents of group recognition have noted, acknowledging group-based claims of injustice creates a motive for groups to assert disingenuous claims, and to wield a 'victim' status as a tool of political power. This is not a dynamic I wish to deny, although of course I do not draw the same conclusion from it as do opponents of the 'politics of difference'.

Thus, by examining the tensions between the politics of difference and the ideal of deliberative democracy we can bring to the surface some important defects in the latter. In particular, models of deliberative democracy are imperfect tools for deepening our understanding or advancing the end of democratic egalitarianism so long as they remain solely within the realm of ideal theory, and so long as they continue to assume a sharp disjuncture between a politics of interest and a politics of deliberation. Instead, this exploration suggests that we should conceive of politics as consisting of a continuum between perfect solidarity and the unbridled battle of interests.

If we choose to think of politics and of the possibilities for egalitarian deliberation in this way, I believe that we will find that a concern for the capacity of political processes to approximate the ideal of impartiality depends crucially upon (a) social circumstances, in particular the degree to which marginalised groups are politically mobilised; and (b) the structure of political institutions. Both of these factors can create pressures upon privileged groups to cooperate in a deliberative mode with less privileged groups. The political mobilisation of marginalised groups creates pressures in the manner I have described above. Political institutions can themselves create incentives for deliberation through decision rules that move in the direction of consensus or unanimity as a requirement of legitimate or binding political decisions (as in John C. Calhoun's system of concurrent majorities, or as with supermajority rules), as well as through norms of public discourse themselves. As Jon Elster has recently argued, the publicity of political argument can, by itself, have the effect of moderating the play of interests in political decision making even where interest is what motivates participants, a dynamic he describes as 'the civilizing effects of hypocrisy' (Elster, 1995).

I began this essay with an acknowledgement that the legal protection of rights, whether through statutory or constitutional devices, is a key element of our understandings of justice. How does a conception of deliberative democracy which attends to social difference - what we might call a deliberative politics of difference - affect our conception of rights? This question is too deep to probe in a brief essay, but the foregoing suggests some preliminary answers.

Although there are key civil and political rights which we should expect any legitimate constitutional regime to protect - rights to freedom of mobility, of speech and press, of religion; rights to vote and hold political office - these basic rights have a different particular content in different constitutional regimes. The freedom of speech may or may not include a right to use hate speech, for example; the right to vote may exist within a single-member plurality system of elections or a scheme of proportional representation. A deliberative politics of difference entails the conviction that the process of giving specific content to civil and political rights - and, I should add, to social rights as well - should include the voices of marginalised groups, and that the content of those rights should not function to reinforce unjust patterns of social, cultural, economic, or political inequality. A scheme of rights which avoids unjust inequalities may be articulable in difference-blind terms, but in some circumstances it may require some group-specific rights. I do not think there is a universally valid answer to the worry that Alan Cairns rightly raises in his essay in this volume (p. 34), that group-specific rights reinforce the social distance between groups, reproduce intergroup hostility, and jeopardise marginalised groups' prospects for equality.

The participation of formerly excluded groups in the process of rights-definition will probably produce unexpected outcomes and novel ways of thinking about rights. Vivien Hart's account of the participation of women's organisations in the South African constitutional negotiations provides a clear and fascinating example of these possibilities: it led to a dissolution of a clear hierarchy among civil, political and social rights, a hierarchy that has been integral to liberal understandings of rights (Hart, this volume). Thus, while I see no reason to worry that a more deliberative process of defining legally protected rights will jeopardise the *security* of those rights, it is undoubtedly true that it will transform their *content*.

The main thrust of this essay has been, however, that we face a deep puzzle when we raise the question whether a genuinely deliberative politics of difference is possible. The short answer is that it is *not impossible*, but that we need to know a great deal more about the institutional forms that can realise it and the social and historical circumstances which can motivate the powerful to engage in it.

Notes

1. This essay is part of a larger research project, *Reconstructing Impartiality*, for which I have received funding from the Social Sciences and Humanities Research

Council of Canada. I am grateful for that support. I also wish to acknowledge that there is some overlap between the arguments I present here and the lengthier discussion in (Williams, forthcoming).
2. For further discussion of marginalised ascriptive groups, see (Williams, 1998).
3. Cf. Rousseau's description of democracy: 'If there were a people of gods, it would govern itself democratically. So perfect a government is not suited to men' (Rousseau, 1978, p. 126).

5 Issues of Territoriality and Identity in the Irish Constitution

PATRICK HANAFIN

Introduction

> I think it's time to admit that both parts of Ireland are failed conceptual entities. That is, the ideas which created them and the ideologies which sustained them have withered at the root. If 'Northern Ireland' has visibly broken down, the 'Republic' as once conceived has visibly broken down. And since 1969 each has helped to expose the inner contradictions of the other (Longley, 1994).

Alternating periods of peace and terrorist hostility since 1994 have been the backdrop against which the latest efforts to resolve the Northern Ireland question by constitutional means have taken place. The Framework Documents of February 1995 (Northern Ireland Office, 1995a; Northern Ireland Office, 1995b) reflected a new willingness on the part of the British and Irish governments to solve the problem on the basis of a model of shared authority whereby internal institutions would be created which respected both traditions in Northern Ireland. This aspiration towards solving the Northern Ireland conflict has been given further impetus by the conclusion of the Belfast Agreement of 10 April 1998.

On a symbolic level, the acceptance in principle on the part of the Irish Government to amend Articles 2 and 3 of the Irish Constitution of 1937 represented a shift from the irredentist view held by the framers of the Constitution to an officially recognised post-nationalist paradigm. This made explicit a fundamental change in the attitude of the Republic of Ireland towards Northern Ireland. In legal terms given the acceptance by the Irish Supreme Court in a number of cases of the constitutional validity of Articles 2 and 3, this proposal represents a profound change. This softening of the Irish Government's position on the constitutional claim has not occurred suddenly, but is the culmination of a gradual shift towards consensus on the part of mainstream nationalist opinion. At a more profound, yet intangible level, it was the apogee of a reinvented *zeitgeist*.

The Constitution and the Idea of the Nation

The Irish constitutional text can be viewed as an evolving narrative that is transformed in tandem with shifts in the construction of Irish identity. Thus, it is constitutive of a shared history but also purports to constitute this history. The original idea of the nation reflected in the Irish Constitution of 1937 is very much that of its framer Eamon de Valera. A former revolutionary turned statesman, his idea of nationhood was firmly rooted in an idealist peasant landscape of the memory. However it may have been the case that Mr. de Valera was suffering from an early case of false memory syndrome as such a peasant ideal never existed in reality. The dominant political and social discourse of 1930's Ireland was Roman Catholic, socially conservative and irredentist. All these elements were reflected in the Constitution and indeed, it may be argued, were co-extensive. The need to combine the notion of the imagined or invented Irish nation with the reality of partition was demonstrated in Articles 2 and 3 of the Constitution of 1937. These articles taken together include the so-called national claim to the six partitioned counties of Northern Ireland while simultaneously recognising the reality of partition.[1] The inclusion of these articles was a move on de Valera's part to appease both extreme nationalist opinion at home and also an attempt not to upset relations with the Commonwealth.

The absence of a declaration of a republic in what is otherwise a typically republican constitution can be explained in terms of maintaining a degree of civility in Ireland's relationship with its former colonial dominator. It is also interesting to note that Articles 2 and 3 appear with Article 1 in a discrete section entitled 'The Nation'. The articles dealing with the workings of the new state, Articles 4-11, are included in a separate section entitled 'The State'. This would appear to signify that the imagined ideal of the Nation is a distinct entity from the legal reality of the twenty-six county state, as indeed the territorial unit of the state is not co-terminus with the idea of the Irish nation. This reflects in a symbolic manner the unfinished business of the nationalist project. As Smith has put it, this incompleteness 'is not merely an insult, it is a negation of the nation' (Smith, 1971, p. 223). Thus the idea of the Irish nation is simply that, an idea based on an assumed cultural homogeneity, whereas the state is a territorial reality, a political unit. It also suggests that the aspiration for a united Ireland was to take a back seat to the immediate need of developing the twenty-six county state. In the words of Richard Kearney, the new state: 'allowed a purely rhetorical aspiration for a United Ireland to replace any policy for achieving it in reality' (Kearney, 1988, p. 239).

The desire to enshrine the values of the ruling elite in the Constitution revealed it to be not so much a neutral legal document for a post-colonial pluralist democracy, but an expression of the values of a deeply conservative ruling class. In effect, the fiction of the claim to Northern Ireland was integral to the rhetorical nationalism of the ruling party, Fianna Fail. That it was little more than rhetoric can be seen in Article 3's negation of Article 2's claim, 'pending reintegration of the national territory'. However, it remained of powerful symbolic importance, forming one of the two pillars of the Constitution - Nationalism and Catholicism. Whilst Articles 2 and 3 *per se* did not form an intractable barrier to a resolution of the Northern Irish question, they provided yet another rationale, if rationale be needed, for Unionist opposition to any co-operation over Northern Ireland (Cruise O'Brien, 1994, pp. 155-56). Thus, the postcolonial conception of Irishness was not an inclusive one. Rather it pandered to a certain elitist ideal of essential (namely, Catholic and nationalist) Irish identity. The northern Protestant population as a result was not seen by the new elite in southern Ireland as part of the postcolonial Irish national family. In this sense the northern Protestant became, to paraphrase Norton, the 'territorial liminar [who was] identified with the adjacent, usually hostile, nation' (Norton, 1988, p. 55).

Legal Interpretation of Articles 2 and 3

The Irish courts have, on a number of occasions, been given the opportunity to interpret Articles 2 and 3. In the case of *Boland v An Taoiseach* ([1974] I.R. 338) the Sunningdale Agreement of 1973 was challenged on the basis that it infringed Articles 2 and 3 of the Constitution of 1937. This challenge was ultimately unsuccessful with the Supreme Court ruling that the Sunningdale Agreement was not a true treaty, but a communiqué containing declarations and assertions of policy. Article 5 of the Sunningdale

Agreement stated that:

> The Irish Government fully accepted and solemnly declared that there should be no change in the status of Northern Ireland until the majority of Northern Ireland desired a change in that status.

The Supreme Court distinguished an inter-governmental communiqué from a treaty. Thus, because a communiqué lacked an internationally binding quality, a court was not required to interfere with the executive process, even if such process infringed any articles of the Constitution.

In subsequent cases, two models emerged as to the interpretation of Articles 2 and 3. Firstly, there is the aspirational model. In the case of *Re Article 26 and The Criminal Law (Jurisdiction) Bill 1975* ([1977] I.R. 129) O'Higgins CJ stated obiter that the national claim to unity existed not in the legal but the political order and that it was one of the rights which was envisaged in Article 2. Thus, he claimed that the Constitution in this regard expressed aspirations and aims rather than legal rules. It was the political entity of the nation as opposed to the legal entity of the state that possessed rights even if such rights were not recognised by law.[2] Secondly, there is the legal claim model exemplified by the dictum of Hederman J in the case of *Russell v Fanning* ([1988] I.R. 505). In this case Hederman J stated that:

> ...the reunification of the national territory is by the provisions of the Preamble of the Constitution and Article 3... a constitutional imperative and not one the pursuit or non-pursuit of which is within the discretion of the government or any other organ of state ([1988] I.R. 505, p. 537).

In the case of *McGimpsey v Ireland* ([1990] 1 I.R. 110) the Anglo-Irish Agreement of 1985 was challenged as being contrary to Articles 2 and 3 of the Constitution. Barrington J in the High Court, in analysing the competing models of interpretation of Articles 2 and 3 was of the view that even though he preferred the aspirational model he could not find anything in the Constitution, even under the legal claim model which was offended by the Anglo-Irish Agreement. On appeal to the Supreme Court, it was agreed that the Anglo-Irish Agreement was not in any way inconsistent with the provisions of Articles 2 and 3. Finlay CJ stated that:

> ...the only reasonable interpretation of Article 1 taken in conjunction with the denial of derogation from sovereignty contained in Article 2(b) of the Anglo-Irish Agreement is that it constitutes a recognition of the de facto situation in Northern Ireland but does so expressly without abandoning the claim to the reintegration of the national territory. These are essential ingredients of the constitutional provisions in Articles 2 and 3 ([1990] 1 I.R. 110, pp. 120-21).

The Supreme Court concluded that Articles 2 and 3 constituted a claim of legal right. The Supreme Court's decision in *McGimpsey v Ireland* is important in that it resolved the ambiguity over which model of interpretation was the correct one, coming down in favour of the legal claim model. Thus, Article 2 was seen as being a declaration of the extent of the national territory as a claim of legal right. The reintegration of the national territory was accordingly to be viewed as a constitutional imperative. Article 3 was interpreted as prohibiting the enactment of laws with any greater area or extent of application or extra-territorial effect than the laws of the Irish Free State pending the reintegration of the national territory. Moreover, the restriction imposed by Article 3 pending the reintegration of the national territory in no way derogates from the claim as a legal right to the entire national territory.

From Hibernia Irredenta to Post-Nationalist Ireland?

Notwithstanding constitutional interpretation of Articles 2 and 3, it would seem that the irredentist ethos of the Constitution of 1937 does not fit comfortably the current model of Irish society, which in recent years has begun to confront the sacred cows of nationalism and Catholicism. Thus, in asking whether the Irish nation is still irredentist, it is necessary to examine recent shifts in the Irish societal paradigm. It is now at least arguable as to whether the national claim to Northern Ireland still reflects the attitude of the Irish people to Northern Ireland. The clause in the Joint Framework Document of February 1995 that speaks of the willingness on the part of the Irish Government to amend Articles 2 and 3 of the Constitution reflects this new ethos in Irish political culture. The inclusion by the Irish government in the Belfast Agreement of 1998 of a clause which would put to the people of the Republic of Ireland in referendum the question of amending the constitutional claim to Northern Ireland marks a decisive shift in the thinking of the political elite in southern Ireland. The strategy of the Irish Republic is to seek conciliation with the United Kingdom over Northern Ireland rather than adopt a conflictual approach. Since the Anglo-Irish Agreement of 1985 this has increasingly been the approach of southern governments. The Agreement allowed the Irish government for the first time since the creation of the six-county unit to engage in some form of governance of Northern Ireland, even if only of an indirect or peripheral nature. Thus the United Kingdom has come to be seen as a partner rather than a barrier to the resolution of the conflict.

Moreover, Irish identity has undergone a profound change since the monolithic Catholic nation of De Valera's imagining. Today Irish society is as fragmented and diverse as any other modern state and the idea of an all-inclusive nationhood sits uneasily with this reality. Changes in the law in the areas of contraception, divorce, sexual orientation and passive euthanasia have loosened the grip of the Catholic hierarchy on collective morality and demonstrated the fractured nature of societal opinions on issues of personal autonomy (Hanafin, 1996; Hanafin 1997b). The old certainties of Mother Ireland and mother church are no longer acceptable in a widely differentiated society, coming to terms with a belated adolescence and cultural maturity (Hanafin, 1997a). Thus, the period since the introduction of the Constitution has seen Ireland's imagined community becoming less cohesive and less willing to adhere to the old certainties of Nationalism and Catholicism. As Longley has noted: 'cultural change and changing awareness of culture, in the Republic and even in the North, have already exposed political Irishness ('the ethos on which the independence movement was built') as now more a prison than a liberation'(Longley, 1994, p. 180).

However this perceived shift in the societal paradigm is not accepted by all shades of opinion in Ireland. There are groups who view almost as a crusade the reinsertion of the old certainties in public and legal policy. However, these forces in society proved to be less politically powerful than their rhetoric would lead one to believe. The recent referendum on the amendments to Articles 2 and 3 was carried with 94.39 per cent of those who voted supporting the changes. Thus the post-irredentist thesis has passed its first test.

The form that the amended Articles 2 and 3 will take was outlined in the Belfast Agreement of 10 April 1998. The revised wording that will now appear in the Constitution reads as follows:

Article 2

It is the entitlement and birthright of every person born in the island of Ireland, which includes its islands and seas, to be part of the Irish nation. That is also the entitlement of all persons otherwise qualified in accordance with law to be citizens of Ireland. Furthermore, the Irish nation cherishes its special affinity with people of Irish ancestry living abroad who share its cultural identity and heritage.

Article 3

1. It is the firm will of the Irish nation, in harmony and friendship, to unite all the people who share the territory of the island of Ireland, in all the diversity of their identities and traditions, recognising that a united Ireland shall be brought about only by peaceful means with the consent of a majority of the people, democratically expressed, in both jurisdictions in the island. Until then, the laws enacted by the Parliament established by this Constitution shall have the like area and extent of application as the laws enacted by the Parliament that existed immediately before the coming into operation of this Constitution.

2. Institutions with executive powers and functions that are shared between those jurisdictions may be established by their respective responsible authorities for stated purposes and may exercise powers and functions in respect of all or part of the island.

3. The State may exercise extra-territorial jurisdiction in accordance with the generally recognised principles of international law.

4. If a declaration under this section is made, this subsection and subsection 3, other than the amendment of this Constitution effected thereby, and subsection 5 of this section shall be omitted from every official text of this Constitution published thereafter, but notwithstanding such omission this section shall continue to have the force of law.

5. If such a declaration is not made within twelve months of this section being added to this Constitution or such longer period as may be provided for by law, this section shall cease to have effect and shall be omitted from every official text of this Constitution published thereafter.

The overwhelming vote in favour of the amendment reflects the reality of a fragmented Irish nation. The rhetorical overlay of the Constitution with regard to territorial matters has been exposed as just that, mere rhetoric. The bounded national subject of Irish constitutional discourse has been revealed as an elite construction.

'You can't personify Unionism' - Northern Ireland's Identity Crisis

> I learnt of a great many things on my first day at school... I discovered that I lived in Belfast and that Belfast lived in Ireland and that this combination meant that I was Irish. The grim young bint we were loaded with was very fervent on this point... [she] told us that the occasional Misguided Soul would try to call us British but that of all things to call us this was the wrongest. No matter how the Misguided Souls cajoled, insisted or pleaded, our names would remain Irish to the core, whatever that meant... in the spirit of compromise (ever with me even then), I dubbed myself 'Ripley Irish British Bogle' (Mc Liam Wilson, 1989, pp. 13-14).

While official opinion in the south is moving towards a less hard-line stand on national unity, political opinion within the North of Ireland is ambivalent on the issue. Northern nationalists and in particular the breakaway extremist elements that have emerged in the wake of the Belfast Agreement do not support the latest proposals for peace in Northern Ireland. Unionist opinion is fractured in the aftermath of the Belfast Agreement. The Official Unionist Party has suffered from internal dissent as a result of the leadership's support for the proposals. More extremist Unionist opinion remains steadfast in its opposition to any form of conciliatory dialogue with nationalism (Browne, 1995, p. 10; Ellis, 1995, p. 5). This appears at first glance to be the result of the Ulster unionist's subjective sense of cultural homogeneity and definition of the cultural Catholic community in Northern Ireland as Other. Thus, unionist Ulster sees itself as a community apart within the wider framework of the United Kingdom. It is not a question of unionists desiring an independent Orange Free State but rather remaining part of the United Kingdom. Thus, unionists define themselves not as a self-contained ethnic state or nation but rather as part of the imagined community of the United Kingdom. In so doing they define themselves negatively *vis-à-vis* the cultural

Catholic community of Ulster whom they see as part of the imagined community of Ireland. However it is ironic that public and official opinion in the United Kingdom does not relish the idea of embracing Ulster unionists as part of the British imagined community of today. Thus, as Gallagher has written:

> ...opinion polls in Britain since the mid-1970s have shown a consistent majority in favour of a united Ireland and a withdrawal of British troops from Northern Ireland... The very concept of 'British withdrawal' would, of course, make no sense if Northern Ireland was seen as part of Britain...
>
> ...it is questionable whether the 'British nation' can be said to include the Ulster Protestants if the mainland British do not consider them to be part of 'us' (Gallagher, 1995, 722).

To complicate matters further, it may be argued that Ulster unionists do not form an undifferentiated mass. Within the Unionist community there are differing views. Jennifer Todd has argued that there exists an appreciable difference between what she terms 'Ulster Loyalists' and 'Ulster British'. The Ulster Loyalists define themselves as members of the Ulster Protestant community first and foremost and any identification with Britain is only secondary. For Todd the '...Protestant people of Northern Ireland are emphasised in Ulster loyalist writings and speeches over and above the British connection' (Todd, 1987, p. 6). On the other hand, the Ulster British see 'Greater Britain' as the community with which they have most empathy with only 'a secondary regional identification with Northern Ireland' (Todd, 1987, p. 11). In the recent referendum on the implementation of the Belfast Agreement required as part of the majority consent approach of the British and Irish governments demonstrated that Unionist opinion is divided on the issue. 71.12 per cent of those who voted supported the constitutional changes proposed by the Belfast Agreement. This demonstrates a questioning of the homogeneous Unionist nation and that the hard-line voices of Unionism have lost their appeal for a people jaded by a bitter conflict.

Models for Constitutional Reform

In an attempt to resolve the conflict at a constitutional level a number of attempts have been made to create structures that would allow both traditions to receive equality of treatment and equal recognition. The attempts that have been made to date have been far from successful, due in the main to either flaws in their conception or due to the extreme difficulty of applying institutional reform measures to a deep-rooted ethno-national conflict.

Since the suspension of the Northern Ireland Parliament in 1972, a number of initiatives have been attempted in order to arrive at a satisfactory constitutional settlement of the Northern Ireland conflict. In 1973 the concept of consociationalism (Lijphart, 1982; O'Leary, 1989) underpinned the establishment of a power-sharing executive and assembly. The *Northern Ireland Constitution Act 1973* provided that the Secretary of State for Northern Ireland was henceforth to be the formal link between the United Kingdom and Northern Ireland. It was the Secretary of State who was to appoint the members of the Executive from among the members of a seventy-eight member unicameral Assembly. The Sunningdale Agreement of 9 December 1973 where the Irish Government, the Government of the United Kingdom and representatives of unionist and nationalist parties in Northern Ireland agreed to set up two all-Ireland institutions, led to the eventual demise of this consociational project. Firstly, a Council of Ireland was to be established, comprising six members from the Irish Government and the Northern Irish Executive. Secondly, a Consultative Assembly was to be established which was to comprise thirty members each from the Northern Ireland Assembly and the Parliament of the Republic of Ireland. However, this decision was not greeted with enthusiasm by unionists. It was the wrath of Ulster Unionists towards the Sunningdale Agreement that eventually led to the demise of this attempt at power sharing.

The Anglo-Irish Agreement of 1985 created an Intergovernmental Conference that gave the Irish government a formal consultative role in the affairs of Northern Ireland. The Agreement stated that no change could be made to the constitutional framework of Northern Ireland without the consent of a majority of the people of Northern Ireland. Direct rule continued but the Intergovernmental Conference was to act as a framework within which both sovereign states would strive to accommodate the rights and identities of the two traditions which exist in Northern Ireland. However this model is not free from difficulty. As Todd has noted:

> It highlighted the problems of institutionalising equal status. If the role of the Irish government was simply a pragmatic device to even the power balance and gain greater benefits for nationalists in the short

> term, its very existence - a nationalist representative in the policy arena while unionists lacked any such representative - marked a new form of inequality for unionists. If, on the other hand, the Irish government's position was *de jure* - an expression of the equality of the traditions - this required that it abandon its role as partisan protector of the nationalist minority and become a co-partner in administering the region. But even-handed administration, by either the British or Irish government, required a clearer view of the rights of each community (Todd, 1995, p. 823).

The beginnings of the latest initiative were contained in the Framework Documents of 1995. This initiative is made up of two documents. The first *A Framework for Accountable Government in Northern Ireland* contains proposals for the internal government of Northern Ireland and was published by the British Government alone. This is the so-called Strand One of the proposed resolution to the conflict. The second document *A New Framework for Agreement: A Shared Understanding between the British and Irish Governments to assist Discussion and Negotiation involving the Northern Ireland Parties* was a joint publication of the British and Irish governments and is concerned with relations between both parts of Ireland (Strand Two of the proposed solution) and also with relations between the United Kingdom and Ireland (Strand Three). *A Framework for Accountable Government in Northern Ireland* proposed new political institutions in an effort to create an atmosphere of equality between all parties to the Northern Ireland stalemate. To this end, the Document proposed the establishment of a new form of Executive and Assembly for the province. At an executive level a collective presidency was suggested. This was to be elected by proportional representation. The collective presidency's powers included nominating chairs of the proposed new assembly, referring legislative proposals to the courts and the vetoing of proposals made by the Assembly. Moreover the Presidency was to operate unanimously which in effect would have given the power of veto to each of its members.

The proposed Assembly was initially to consist of ninety members. This proposed Assembly differed from the Stormont model of 1921-1972 and from the Sunningdale model of 1974, in that simple majority rule would not have been the model adopted. It was proposed that weighted majorities would be used when legislation of a controversial nature was being voted on, in an attempt to prevent majority dominance. The power of the collective presidency to veto legislation would, it was hoped, also prevent such an eventuality. The British Government stated that it would adhere to a policy of rigorous impartiality in relation to the internal governance of Northern Ireland and that there would be what it termed 'parity of esteem' between the two traditions. Moreover, the British Government acknowledged the fact that there can be no purely internal resolution of the Northern Ireland problem. Thus the basis for any settlement must be a three strand approach; North-North, North-South and East-West relations. To this end the second Framework Document deals with North-South and East-West relations.

A New Framework for Agreement recognised that no settlement can come about without the consent of the majority of the people of Northern Ireland. Moreover, both governments agreed to amend their constitutional provisions in relation to Northern Ireland. Thus Ireland stated its willingness to amend Articles 2 and 3 of the Constitution of 1937 and Britain was prepared to amend the *Government of Ireland Act 1920* as part of a wider settlement.

After the publication of the Framework Documents, the peace process was marked more by inertia than progress. In November 1995 the Irish and British governments introduced the Twin Track initiative. The purpose of this initiative was to prepare the ground for all-party negotiations. It established a phase of preliminary talks designed to examine the basis, format and agenda for all-party negotiations. It also established an International Body to examine the decommissioning of illegal arms, to be chaired by former United States Senator George Mitchell. The International Body on the Decommissioning of Arms published a report on 24 January 1996. This document proposed six principles of democracy and non-violence and an elective process to take negotiations forward. This initial period of 'peace' was punctuated by the ending of the IRA cease-fire on 9 February 1996, with the Canary Wharf bomb in London. However, the British and Irish governments decided to go ahead with the election of an all party negotiating body. Following elections in May, the all-party negotiations began on 10 June 1996. Sinn Fein was excluded from taking part in the negotiations until such time as the IRA reinstated its cease-fire. It was not until 19 July 1997 that the IRA announced the reinstatement of its cease-fire. Sinn Fein entered the negotiation process in September 1997.

The publication in January 1998 of a revised blueprint towards a settlement of the Northern Ireland conflict by the British and Irish governments was intended to speed the peace process along. Instead it provoked rancour on all sides and was seen as a fudge (Mullin, 1998, p. 4). The document provided that the Irish Government would remove Articles 2 and 3 from the Constitution. In exchange for this, the British Government pledged to delete from the *Government of Ireland Act 1920* references to the sovereign territory of Northern Ireland. The blueprint also outlined details of a Northern Ireland Assembly. Strand Two of the Framework Documents was to be amended to provide for a new agreement between the British and Irish governments to replace the Anglo-Irish Agreement of 1985. As far as Strand Three of the negotiations was concerned the blueprint proposed a Council of the British Isles. This intergovernmental council will include representatives of the British and Irish governments, the Northern Irish administration and the devolved institutions of Scotland and Wales. The introduction of an intergovernmental Council of the Isles was initially looked upon with disdain by Sinn Fein, as downplaying the importance of Strand Two institutions and making even more remote any possibility of a united Ireland.

The initial proposals contained in the Framework Documents and the later revised blueprint were subjected to substantial negotiation and alteration during the currency of the multi-party talks process. The outcome of these talks was the conclusion of the Belfast Agreement of 10 April 1998, which forms the basis for the democratic resolution of the Northern Ireland conflict. The Strand One dimension of the agreement will now consist of an Assembly made up of one hundred and eight members who will be elected by proportional representation by single transferable vote. Executive power will be exercised by a First Minister and Deputy First Minster with up to ten Ministers with Departmental responsibilities. The Strand Two institution will consist of a North/South Ministerial Council. The Council will be made up of representative of the Northern Ireland Assembly and the Irish Government. The Council's role will be to reach agreement on the adoption of common policies in areas where there is a mutual cross-border and all-island benefit, including agriculture, education, transport, tourism and the environment. Strand Three will consist of a British-Irish Council which will be made up of representatives of the British and Irish Governments and the devolved regional assemblies of Northern Ireland, Scotland and Wales. The function of the Council will be largely consultative with a view to reaching agreement on co-operation on matters of mutual interest in areas such as transport, education and EU issues.

Conclusion

Recent developments in the attempt to resolve the conflict in Northern Ireland have demonstrated a shift in official thinking in the Republic of Ireland on the territorial status of the six counties of Northern Ireland which remain under British rule. This softening in attitude is reflected in the Irish Government's willingness to amend Articles 2 and 3 of the Constitution. Moreover, it reflects a less monolithic model of Irish identity. The nation as encapsulated in contemporary political discourse has become more fluid reflecting a more complicated notion of Irish selfhood than that posited by the essentialist nationalist rhetoric of the founding elite. However, the position of northern nationalists has not shifted to any real extent from the hard-line irredentist stance of their forebears, despite the posturing of Sinn Fein. Beneath the shiny image of 'new' Sinn Fein lies a continuing allegiance to the notion of a thirty-two county Irish republic. Those elements of nationalist opinion who continue to remain steadfast in their quest for a united Ireland represent a major obstacle to progress on the road to a peaceful resolution of the conflict. Likewise, extreme unionist opinion has hardened into a deeper enmity for any settlement that would loosen their ties with the United Kingdom. The persistence of these seemingly intractable opinions do not augur well for an ultimate settlement.

Nonetheless, the latest constitutional initiative for settlement of the Northern Ireland problem has at least been agreed upon by the mainline political parties. An overwhelming majority of the electorate has supported the latest constitutional initiative. However, the refusal of the Democratic Unionist Party to back the process and the rumblings of discontent within the ranks of the IRA and the Loyalist paramilitary groups have placed a considerable strain on the process. The conduct of the main political parties in the new Northern Ireland Assembly will be the true test of their willingness to make this latest initiative work. It was once thought perhaps too optimistically that the longer the 'peace' persisted the greater would be the desire not to return to violent conflict. The holding of elections to a Northern Ireland Assembly may be of little value if the deeper psychological hatreds of the extremists on both sides are not first addressed. As Meron Benvenisti has noted in writing of another similar conflict, that between the PLO and Israel:

> ...years of violent conflict have left sediments of hatred, dehumanisation and brutalization of values. The mechanisms of violence, aggression and confrontation, inspired by destructive myths and mobilised indoctrination, duplicate themselves and the conflict (Benvenisti, 1996).

If the current peace process is to have any credibility or indeed success the deep-seated hatred, dehumanisation and brutalization must first be confronted. Otherwise this process may go the way of previous attempts at constitutionalising conflict resolution.

Notes

1. Article 2 states:

   > The national territory consists of the whole island of Ireland, its islands and territorial seas.

   Article 3 recognizes the political reality:

   > Pending the re-integration of the national territory, and without prejudice to the right of the Parliament and Government established by this Constitution to exercise jurisdiction over the whole of that territory, the laws enacted by that Parliament shall have the like area and extent of application as the laws of Saorstat Eireann and the like extra-territorial effect.

2. In interpreting Articles 2 and 3, Higgins CJ was of the view that these articles:

   can be understood only if their background of law and political theory is appreciated... One of the theories held in 1937 by a substantial number of citizens was that a nation, as distinct from a State, had rights; that the Irish people living in what is now called the Republic of Ireland and in Northern Ireland together formed the Irish Nation; that a Nation has a right to unity of territory in some form, be it as a unitary or federal State; that the *Government of Ireland Act 1920*, though legally binding, was a violation of that national right to unity which was superior to positive law. The national claim to unity exists not in the legal but in the political order and is one of the rights which are envisaged in Article 2; it is expressly saved by Article 3 which states the area to which the laws enacted by the Parliament established by the Constitution apply. The effect of Article 3 is that, until the division of the island of Ireland is ended, the laws enacted by the Parliament established by the Constitution are to apply to the same area and have the same extent of application as the laws of Saorstat

Eireann had. The area to which the laws of Saorstat Eireann applied was, having regard to the Articles of Agreement of 1921 and the Act of 1925, unquestionably the area known as the Republic of Ireland ([1977] I.R. 129, pp. 145-48).

6 Cultural Identity and Constitutional Reform: The Challenge of Northern Ireland[1]

DAMIAN O'LEARY

> Once we see the richness and complexity of social goods, once we appreciate the different ways in which different communities understand goods, value goods, and think various goods ought to be distributed, we will no longer imagine that it is possible to construct an adequate theory of justice without beginning from and returning to the actual practices of particular societies (Carens, 1995, p. 48).

The concept of community looms large in the politics of Northern Ireland. Northern Ireland comprises two traditions, each with its own community, constructing, defining, and moulding the identities of its members. Indeed, so much of the political space of Northern Ireland is consumed by considerations of community that, at times, there appears too little space for a more general or comprehensive form of political dialogue. On the surface it seems ironic that so much of the western world is trying to redefine the normative basis of its political institutions to accommodate demands for recognition by different cultural, social and other groups, while Northern Ireland seems to require a set of political institutions capable of transcending the particularities of each of its two traditions. There is a balance to be struck here, a balance between the recognition of cultural identities and practices that emanate from the constitutive attachments one has to one's community on the one hand, and the need to establish the basis for a common democratic political community with institutions and practices that provide spaces for political dialogue which respects cultural diversity on the other. The future of constitutional transformation in Northern Ireland has to operate between these two poles, between the recognition of cultural diversity and a common political community. Striking the right balance between issues of diversity and commonality is what confronts those concerned with Northern Ireland's future constitutional negotiations.

This chapter sketches out three broad routes to constitutional reform in Northern Ireland. I begin with the one most familiar to those in western societies who are used to thinking about constitutions as the corner stones of liberal democratic institutions. Archetypally, we could refer to this as liberal constitutionalism. Here the usual terms of discourse revolve around the concepts of democratic majorities, representative democracy, democratic consent, popular sovereignty, and so on, and reflect a conventional liberal stance to institutional design and function. The second route to constitutional transformation is proffered by advocates of consociationalism. Here, the focus is on principles of power-sharing, weighted majorities and group representation, as the means by which societies wracked by ethnic, religious and political conflicts can be managed if not reconciled completely. A third route to constitutional transformation is far less neat, does not admit of a grand design as in the previous two routes, and is concerned with the particularities of the practices that exist in Northern Ireland. I refer to this as substantive constitutionalism as it begins from an engaged, contextual perspective. From this engaged perspective I argue that constitutional transformation in Northern Ireland must take account of issues at the cultural as well as political level. Indeed, I argue that separating culture and politics in divided societies like Northern Ireland fails to appreciate the importance that recognition of diverse cultural identities has for political disputes. Therefore, I argue that the recognition of cultural diversity needs to be at the centre of constitutional considerations which aim to reconstruct the public sphere. I conclude with a brief look at some core features of the Belfast Agreement of 10 April 1998 - the latest attempt at constitutional reform in Northern Ireland.

Community, Cultural Identity and Constitutionalism

What significance does one's membership of a cultural community have for politics, and what relationship exists between cultural identity, political community and constitutional reform? In the first instance, our cultural attachments are primary in constructing our identity, our subjectivity. Something like this is expressed by Will Kymlicka when he suggests that our membership in a societal culture enables our capacity to grasp and revise our conception of the good (Kymlicka, 1995, pp. 82ff.). Our subjectivity is constructed against the backdrop of our location in a culture rich in frameworks of meaning and practice (Taylor, 1994; Tamir, 1993, chapter 2).

Failing to recognise the constitutive role culture plays in providing the frameworks against which one orients oneself in the world 'atomises' the subject. The subject becomes a fragmented, acultural, ahistorical being deprived of the moral and social frameworks necessary for everyday judgements of worth.

For many people the relationship between cultural identity and membership of a political community is unproblematic. Because states usually reflect the cultural attachments of the majority (or the most powerful) of its citizens, the relationship between the majority culture and the polity is relatively harmonious. In other words, there is a broad consensus amongst the population regarding the cultural institutions and practices of the state. However, in a number of cases, large numbers of people who belong to minority cultures are alienated from the institutions and practices of their political community. In some cases this is due to immigration movements, but often it has come about through unjust historical practices like colonisation (Kymlicka, 1995, pp. 101, 217n26). In such cases, there is a radical disjuncture between one's cultural identity and one's political membership. When political communities fail to recognise the presence of a diversity of cultural identities they often compel minorities to assimilate to the majority culture. Indeed, failing to recognise the diversity of citizens' cultural identities imposes an inferior status on those who fail to belong to the politically sanctioned culture and can lead to the internalisation of a sense of self as culturally and politically inferior (Taylor, 1994, p. 25).

The relationship between cultural identity, political membership and recognition of diversity is fundamental for constitutional reform in two ways. Firstly, constitutions reflect cultural identities as well as other community aspirations (Tully, 1995, pp. 5-6ff). Witness the difference in constitutions amongst countries that share a commitment to liberal democracy. These differences are a result of differences in cultural traditions and practices (See Carens, 1995; Russell, 1993). To the extent that constitutions do reflect cultural commitments, the challenge for those involved in the practice of constitutional reform is this: how do we ensure that the cultural frameworks of a constitutional process (and document) are not blind to the diversity of cultural identities present in a particular society? The problem is acute in respect of Northern Ireland, for how do we ensure that the diversity of cultural identities in the province are recognised as legitimate while simultaneously establishing a common political community? Recognition of cultural diversity, which does not reinforce sectarianism, must be at the centre of any attempt at constitutional reform in Northern Ireland.

A second point of connection between cultural identity, political membership and constitutional reform relates to issues of justice. Is it necessary, in terms of justice, for a constitution to include references to the diversity of its citizens? Or, rather, in the name of justice, are constitutions meant to offer a framework that transcends diversity in the quest for a common political community? Tully suggests 'that if the cultural ways of ... citizens were recognised and taken into account in reaching an agreement on a form of constitutional association, the constitutional order, and the world of everyday politics it constitutes, would be just' (Tully, 1995, p. 6). Implicit in Tully's claim is the need to establish a constitutional dialogue capable of recognising the cultural and political differences that exist between different traditions. Therefore, the legitimacy of the state and its related social, cultural and political institutions can only be brought about if the core features of citizens' identity are both recognised by the state and recognisable in the state.

Since cultural diversity has such relevance for constitutions, constitutional reform in Northern Ireland must take seriously the diversity of identities present within its boundaries. Constitutional negotiations need to acknowledge that the problem of cultural diversity cannot be procedurally severed from the practice of politics in the province. No matter what one regards as primary in the conflict in Northern Ireland - national identity, ethnicity, religion, historical injustice, imperialism and so on - it is absolutely crucial to recognise that political disputes of the kind in Northern Ireland are infused with cultural claims. Therefore, these dual forces of constitutional importance - politics and culture - cannot be neatly separated for means of political expediency. In parallel with contemporary political theoretical debates about justice, culture and politics are intertwined like the right and the good, they cannot be procedurally severed from one another for instrumental or pragmatic purposes (Beiner, 1995, chapter 4; Frazer and Lacey, 1993, pp. 113ff; Taylor, 1989, pp. 88-89; Sandel, 1982, chapter 4). Rather, challenges to commonality issued by claims of cultural difference must be embraced if the broader political goal is to construct a just and tolerant political community on the unstable foundations of communal conflict.

To drive this point home, let me turn to illustrate how the constitutional history of the province of Northern Ireland demonstrates the interconnections between culture and politics. I will argue that the two routes to constitutional reform tried in Northern Ireland - conventional liberal-majoritarian and consociational - demonstrate the weaknesses inherent in conceiving constitutional dialogue in overly narrow political categories.

Route One - Majoritarian Democracy, 1921-1972

One cannot say anything meaningful about the nature of the Northern Ireland problem without taking account of its political history. However, where one begins such an account might be seen to represent one's political affiliation and this, in itself, is demonstrative of the tangled web of political discourses that infuse in constructing Northern Ireland's history. On the two histories, John E. Finn puts it thus:

> Catholics begin their histories of brutal mistreatment by the British with the forcible settling of the Ulster plantation with Scottish colonists in 1607. Protestant histories begin with the savage Catholic uprising against the same plantation in 1641. When in 1689 King William's Protestant forces finally secured the plantation by defeating James's Catholic army, they inaugurated a conflict that has endured three centuries (Finn, 1991, p. 47).

It is symptomatic that the historical facts relevant to each community's historical narrative underlie the basis of their current political advocacy. Catholics lay claim to the invasion of Ulster by the Scots and Protestants lay claim to a defence of the Realm and their own place within it. This much, perhaps, is clear. For my present purposes, I want to concentrate on the constitutional history of Northern Ireland, whose contemporary constitutional 'problem' was shaped by the partition of Ireland in 1921 and the resultant creation of the devolved Government of Northern Ireland constituted under the auspices of Great Britain in the *Government of Ireland Act 1920.*

With the partition of Northern Ireland from the Irish Free State in 1921, the region was divided on religious-cultural-political grounds, which would mark the political terrain of the next 70 years. Under the *Government of Ireland Act*, Northern Ireland was constituted with conventional political, economic, social and legal institutions comparable to most independent states. As Claire Palley has noted:

> Put positively, the Northern Ireland Parliament [could] legislate on matters relating to law and order, to the police, to courts other than the

> Supreme Court, to civil and criminal law, to local government, to health and social services, to education, to planning and development, to commerce and industrial development and internal trade, to agriculture and to finance (Palley, 1972, pp. 368-369).

While Westminster reserved the right to make policy in foreign affairs, taxation, defence and other issues related to the maintenance of the Crown, the powers granted to the Northern Ireland parliament by the first Northern Ireland Constitution enabled the Protestant majority to rule on its own terms.

While the *Government of Ireland Act* did not contain an explicit bill of rights it did make reference to religious discrimination. For instance, Section 5 of the Act stated:

> The Parliament of Northern Ireland shall not make a law so as either directly or indirectly to establish or endow any religion, or prohibit or restrict the free exercise thereof, or give a preference, privilege, or advantage, or impose any disability or disadvantage, on account of religious belief or ecclesiastical status (Section 5(1)).

However, these references to liberal neutrality aside, the political reality of Northern Ireland was antithetical to the sentiment expressed above. As James Craig (Northern Ireland Prime Minister 1920-40) is reported to have said in 1934, Stormont was a 'Protestant Parliament for a Protestant people'. The constitutional limitations placed on the powers of Parliament were easily side-stepped by the Unionist majority. For instance, although the *Government of Ireland Act* instituted proportional representation and the single transferable vote (PR(STV)) it also made provision for Parliament to amend the voting system so long as it did not alter the number of MPs and that the changes in population were taken into consideration (Section 14(5); O'Leary and McGarry, 1993, pp. 119-25). Indeed 'Unionists argued that PR was not British, was undemocratic, prevented strong government, and contributed to indecisiveness and inefficiencies by enhancing the prospect of "hung parliaments"'(O'Leary and McGarry, 1993, p. 121). Thus the Unionist Government abolished the PR(STV) method prior to the 1929 Stormont election and replaced it with the plurality vote or the first-past-the-postmethod. The result was predictable. The Unionist Party formed a majority Government from 1921 until Stormont was prorogued and Westminster imposed 'direct rule' in 1972.

Fifty-one years of Unionist majority Government had several effects.

Firstly, and most obviously, liberal conceptions of state or political neutrality - evidenced in Section 5 of the *Government of Ireland Act* - appeared jaundiced in the face of the overwhelming evidence that Catholics suffered institutional discrimination in all areas of life. Indeed, Catholic perceptions of Protestant/unionist domination were well founded in light of the non-representative nature of Northern Ireland's most important institutions. For instance, the Protestant majority controlled the legal institutions of Northern Ireland. Of the seven High Court judges, six were Protestant and one Catholic, a pattern repeated at all levels of the Court down to Crown prosecutors, under sheriffs and clerks of the peace who were all Protestant (O'Leary and McGarry, 1993, p. 121). The security forces responsible for policing - The Royal Ulster Constabulary (RUC), A-, B- and C-specials - were all Protestant organisations. They had no legitimacy in the eyes of the nationalist community and were noted as being 'their' (the Protestants') police force (O'Leary and McGarry, 1993; O Connor, 1993, chapter 5; Ruane and Todd, 1996, pp. 120-121; Bardon, 1992, pp. 807-809). Moreover, the administrative arm of the state was also firmly controlled by Protestants. Senior administrative staff were between 92 and 98 percent Protestant while the occupational grade were 94 percent Protestant. What is crucial about these sorts of observations is not that over- or under-representations *necessarily* result in discrimination. Rather, in a situation of existing cultural and political conflict, such over-representations normally translate into prejudicial political outcomes for the minority community. In Northern Ireland, this meant that institutions that were supposed to be neutral with respect to political affiliations were servile to the interests of the governing UUP (Ulster Unionist Party). For instance, as O'Leary and McGarry (1993) point out, those responsible for the allocation of public housing, the locus of a great deal of political manoeuvring, were overwhelmingly servile to unionist interests.

> Housing-segregation maintained predictable electoral outcomes and prevented the development of mixed communities. Local authorities under UUP control west of the River Bann, where Catholics were far more likely to be the local majority of the electorate, were most zealous in using planning controls and allocation systems to maintain their political domination (O'Leary and McGarry, 1993, pp. 131-32).

UUP control of the institutions of Northern Ireland was made possible by one overarching factor: their ability to reconceive the idea of majoritarian democracy in line with their cultural and political aspirations.

The emergence of the Northern Ireland Civil Rights Association (NICRA) in 1967 brought to centre stage the nature and degree of Unionist dominance in Northern Ireland. The emergence of organisations whose sole aim was to expose the degree to which Catholics had been mistreated facilitated the dissemination of information about Northern Ireland on an international scale. Coupled with attempts by Northern Ireland's fourth Prime Minister Terence O'Neill (1963-69) to implement a more moderate Unionist line in response to the growing pressure from both internal and external sources, the situation reached boiling point. The reaction to the reform measures was symbolic of Northern Ireland's predicament at the time. While Catholics thought the reform measures did not go far enough, Protestant hard-liners viewed the reforms as capitulating to 'nationalist' political aspirations. O'Neill's resignation after the 1969 Stormont elections, the increasing militancy of both nationalists and loyalists, and the introduction of internment without trial in August 1971, all led inexorably to the mess that became known as Bloody Sunday. January 30th, 1972 laid witness to the dire straits of Northern Ireland's political landscape when British paratroopers fired on a civil rights march killing 14 protesters.

British Prime Minister Edward Heath prorogued Stormont and implemented direct rule under section 75 of the *Government of Ireland Act* on March 24th, 1972. This was the last nail in the coffin for the first attempt at conventional liberal constitutionalism in Northern Ireland. What ensued was a re-thinking of how conventional modes of political and institutional organisation might be made more malleable to the political demands of the minority community. Two instances stand out as foreshadowing the transition from majority rule to consociational constitutional arrangements, the 1973 power-sharing Assembly and the *Anglo-Irish Agreement 1985* (AIA).

The 1973 amendments to the *Government of Ireland Act*, which put forward a new plan for devolved government in the province, issued in a curious mixture of liberal democratic and consociational measures aimed at mitigating the political conflict in the province. The 1973 amendments outlined a new form of Assembly for the province which would consist of an unicameral house of representatives that would, in turn, be responsible for the creation of a power-sharing executive. However, the majority of Unionists withdrew their consent from the experiment over the role of the proposed Council of Ireland, which Unionists argued intimated a united Ireland. The Ulster Workers' Council strike over the ratification of the Sunningdale Agreement in May 1974 brought the province to a standstill which resulted in the collapse of the Assembly (Bardon, 1992, p. 703; Hadfield, 1989, pp. 110ff). The Assembly was prorogued in May 1974 and direct rule re-instated in July under the *Government of Ireland Act 1974* (Hadfield, 1989, pp. 116-17). What is important about the 1973 experiment is that it was the first attempt to implement some form of institutional arrangement which, by design, was meant to mitigate the power of the Protestant majority in the province. In a sense, this set the terms of reference for future proposals by making it clear that the wishes of the majority in the province were no longer going to be accounted for through the conventional channels of democratic politics. There would not be a return to majoritarian democracy in Northern Ireland.

The second instance in the experimental phase was absolutely crucial to the future of Northern Ireland. It initiated the other dimension or axis to government relations concerning Northern Ireland - and perhaps the most controversial - the relationship between Dublin and London. In important ways, the Dublin-London relationship is as crucial to political stability in Northern Ireland as the internal relations within the province and the relationship between Belfast and London. The AIA gave formal recognition that the Republic of Ireland had a stake in the future of Northern Ireland. This was a fundamental concession to the political difficulties of Northern Ireland. Let me explain.

The AIA is an international treaty where the governments of Great Britain and the Republic of Ireland agreed on the conditions whereby the status of Northern Ireland might be changed. Articles 1 and 2 of the AIA make it clear that the future of Northern Ireland was not merely a matter internal to Northern Ireland or Britain. Article 1 affirmed that:

> The two Governments
> (a) affirm that any change in the status of Northern Ireland would only come about with the consent of a majority of the people of Northern Ireland;
> (b) recognise that the present wish of a majority of the people of Northern Ireland is for no change in the status of Northern Ireland;
> (c) declare that, if in the future a majority of the people of Northern Ireland clearly wish for and formally consent to the establishment of a united Ireland, they will introduce and support in the respective Parliaments legislation to give effect to that wish.

Article 2 of the AIA established the 'Intergovernmental Conference [which was] concerned with Northern Ireland and with relations between the two parts of the island of Ireland, to deal ... on a regular basis with: (i) political matters; (ii) security and related matters; (iii) legal matters, including the administration of justice; (iv) the promotion of cross-border co-operation'(AIA, Article 2(a)). Article 2(b) went on to discuss the 'acceptance' by the British Government that the Irish Government was integral to any future political settlement in the province.

The creation of intergovernmental relations between London and Dublin confirmed what many outside Northern Ireland knew and what many inside Northern Ireland had been trying to avoid; namely, that the solution to the troubles in Northern Ireland would depend in large measure on relations between Great Britain and the Republic of Ireland. But the direct links between London and Dublin confirmed to unionist hard-liners that their community had to defend itself because the parliamentary representatives of the rest of Great Britain would not guarantee Northern Ireland's place in the Union. As for nationalist hard-liners, the AIA confirmed that a united Ireland would not be countenanced by the Republic of Ireland (*contra* Articles 2 & 3 of the Irish Constitution which lay territorial claim to Northern Ireland) while the Protestant majority desired to remain in the Union. On both sides then, the AIA represented a heavy blow to hard-line political aspirations.

The most important feature of the AIA is that it formally established that there will not be a return to the liberal-democratic form of majoritarian government in the province. Both British and Irish Governments affirmed the need for some form of devolved government for the province; that it be constructed so as to be representative of both communities and where the rights of each of the traditions in Northern Ireland are respected and given scope to flourish in the future. What this meant for the most die-hard unionists and nationalists is that neither a return to Stormont nor a united Ireland was a viable option. Put simply, future constitutional arrangements would be organised around concepts of power-sharing and 'coercive co-operation' (Lijphart, 1975; Lijphart, 1982; see also Barry, 1975a; Barry, 1975b.).

Route Two - The Consociational Alternative

One of the most important lessons learnt from the preceding fifty years of Northern Irish history was that constitutional proposals for change must be inclusive of both communities in the province. Northern Ireland's peculiar political predicament requires a different form of constitutional arrangement from that encountered in conventional majoritarian-ruled liberal democracies. Therefore, every serious proposal for constitutional change in Northern Ireland since 1973 has included some form of power-sharing or joint authority for the province in an attempt to overcome the legitimacy problems associated with the majoritarian rule approach. It is against this background that I want to examine briefly what has been suggested by way of consociationalism for Northern Ireland and then to go on to suggest why it is far more problematic as a political option than many of its advocates assume.

Leading consociational scholar Arend Lijphart lists four requirements of consociational politics. The first of these, a grand coalition or power-sharing is 'an executive in which the political leaders of all significant segments participate' (Lijphart, 1982, p. 166). This can take the form of a coalition in a cabinet within a parliamentary system or in a presidential system the offices of the executive could be distributed to include members from each of the political parties. These arrangements could be filtered down to all layers of administration so that all advisory and implementation staff are representative of the grand coalition of political parties. The second principle - autonomy for different groups - ensures that all decisions which effect major issues for the community should be made jointly by representatives of each of the political parties. Where a plethora of decisions do not affect the community in significant or important ways then each 'segment' of the population will be given the autonomy to deal with such decisions in their own way. The third element is that all appointments to public office and all funds are distributed on grounds proportional to each of the groups or segments of the population. Thus, any assembly or parliament must have its members elected by a proportional voting system so that minor parties are enfranchised and any form of majority rule is eliminated. The fourth principle, the minority veto, according to Lijphart, is the 'ultimate weapon that minorities need to protect their vital interests' (Lijphart, 1982, p. 166). This principle acknowledges that minority parties within a cabinet, assembly or parliament still need to be protected from the majority within such a body. The minority veto ensures that the majority within an executive or assembly cannot rule in their own interests without the assent of minority parties and interests.

There have been numerous proposals put forward as constitutional solutions to Northern Ireland's ills that have drawn on some or all of the principles outlined above. The most detailed account produced by the Institute for Public Policy Research (IPPR) (O'Leary et al., 1993) deserves our critical attention as an example of consociational constitutional design.

The IPPR proposal details the institutional arrangements of a new Northern Ireland. Article 1 of the proposed Northern Ireland Constitution elucidates the organisational nature of the province:

> Northern Ireland is an autonomous and democratic political region, part of the national territory of the United Kingdom and the Republic of Ireland. Its sovereignty is vested in its peoples and their respective states, which are the guardians and guarantors of its Constitution. Its citizens are entitled to full citizenship rights of either the Republic of Ireland or the United Kingdom, or both. Its government is organised according to co-operative principles, which guarantee the rights and fundamental freedoms of its constituent nationalities and religions, ensure the proportional representation of its constituent communities in public institutions, and protects their equality and security (O'Leary et al., 1993, p. 25).

This complete reworking of the province, which situates Northern Ireland as an autonomous region governed jointly by the Republic of Ireland and Great Britain, is about as macro a constitutional proposal as one could imagine. This is no less than a complete reconstruction of the province.

Under this proposal, the political decision-making institutions of the province would be organised around an executive council constructed on the principles of shared authority. (Hence its name - the Shared Authority Council of Northern Ireland - SACNI) The executive would consist of one member of the British cabinet, one member of the Irish Republic cabinet and three Northern Irish council members who would in turn appoint ministers. The SACNI would be responsible for all legislation relating to civil defence and security, citizenship, nationality, immigration and any other matter not delegated to other bodies. The executive would be responsible for enacting into law those bills proposed by a People's Assembly - the Assembly of the Peoples of Northern Ireland (APNI). The APNI would be elected on a proportional representation system and be divided into ministries equal to the number of ministries established by the SACNI. The central function of the APNI would be to satisfy the democratic element to the new constitutional formation of the province in giving the people a direct voice in electing members of their community to the Assembly as well as: (1) proposing bills to SACNI for enactment; (2) determining where all the major institutions of the province would be located; (3) compose a finance and justice ministry for review of the autonomous legal system of the province as well as a finance ministry. Northern Ireland would also have a Bill of Rights by incorporating into its

Constitution the European Convention on Human Rights, which would, in turn, be subject to interpretation and review by the Supreme Court of Northern Ireland.

These types of consociational solutions are, however, deeply flawed by their excessive formality and neglect of the substantive claims about cultural identity that both unionists and nationalists make. This neglect is fatal, since the most partisan members of each side of the conflict - and the paramilitary organisations they support - conceive of their interests in strong cultural as well as political terms.

Manifestations of the 'Cultural Conflict'[2]

One of the central ways in which this cultural conflict is played out is through the imagery and symbolism invoked by the advocates of the various paramilitary organisations in the province. The history or genealogy of the loyalist and nationalist paramilitary organisations bear the hallmarks of the cultural tags and symbols which have been instrumental in ensuring that the two communities remain divided on more than simply religious terms (See Bruce, 1994; O'Brien, 1995). The Ulster Volunteer Force (UVF) and the Ulster Defence Association (UDA) reinforce their 'Britishness' by staking their claims to legitimacy on the back of culturally significant moments in British history. For instance, the sacrifices made by the 36th Ulster Division at the Battle of the Somme in the First World War stand as testimony of Ulster's loyalty to the Union. Combining Northern Ireland's political narrative with significant moments in British history is meant to reinforce the 'Britishness' of Northern Ireland. Thus, loyalists who laid down their lives in the two World Wars for Britain believed themselves to be culturally 'British' and therefore 'defenders' of the 'Homeland'. The importance of the role of this sort of symbolism is writ large in the murals that decorate loyalist strongholds in the province. The paintings of soldiers in battle dress circa 1914 and 1939 are seen standing alongside paramilitaries clothed in balaklavas holding M-16s against a background of regimental insignias and decorations. The importance of this sort of lineage cannot be underestimated. Present day loyalist paramilitaries, despite being labelled terrorists and the like by the international community, as well as by the British Government, see themselves standing in a long line of patriots who, in defending 'Ulster' from the 'Irish', continue to defend the 'Realm' and the 'Union' from those who would abolish or obliterate it (i.e. the

Northern Nationalists and the Irish Republic).

Of course, loyalist paramilitaries are not alone in utilising cultural symbols as justifications for their role in the conflict. Nationalist paramilitaries are also adept at reinforcing their own forms of cultural symbolism, which are derived from centuries-old cultural narratives. The cultural and political claims symbolised in nationalist murals resonate with notions of cultural exclusivity. For example, the Irish Republican Army (IRA) utilises symbols of cultural difference, like their use of Gaelic, to reinforce their cultural 'otherness'. Other cultural symbols invoked in nationalist murals include extensive use of the Tricolour, Celtic visual images and the use of significant historical moments in Ireland's past like the Easter Rising in Dublin (1916). Thus, invoking images of cultural difference underpin nationalists' attempts to bolster their political claim as defenders of 'Irish' culture against the juggernaut of 'British' 'oppression' and 'domination'. In addition, it is also relatively easy for nationalists to point to the Republic to drive home the fact that there is a different cultural tradition alive and well on the island. This reinforces nationalists' arguments that aver that Ireland's independence can be won through British withdrawal - as it was in 1921. Like loyalist paramilitaries then, nationalist paramilitaries invoke a range of cultural symbols and narratives to legitimate their role in the political conflict. In this sense, cultural practices need to be regarded as thoroughly political. Indeed, driving a wedge between culture and politics serves to mystify rather than clarify the importance of the relationship between them. What must be realised is that culture and politics in Northern Ireland are often used to serve each other's purposes. That is, people from both communities use politics to demand protection for their culture, their 'way of life'. And they rely on their ability to articulate the substantive basis of their cultural difference - of the distinctive nature of their 'way of life' - to argue for distinct institutional recognition in the polity. It is, in part, because of their ability to invoke such a strong set of cultural narratives that the various paramilitary organisations have been able to rely on a steady flow of fresh recruits over the years.

What is important here is regardless of how others view paramilitary organisations they see themselves as defending their culture, their Britishness/Irishness, their cultural traditions of 'service for the Union/Republic', their 'way of life', their 'people' who are entrenched and clothed in British/Irish historical symbols. The present day conflict is thus legitimated through narratives that utilise cultural symbols defined in culturally exclusive ways. Consequently, notions of cultural difference are invoked to give political credibility to paramilitary action.

Against this crowded and complex political landscape, the idea of consociationalism, as a form of political organisation appears problematic. The limitations of this approach to political conflict are illustrated by its overly narrow and excessively formalistic conception of politics. Consociational approaches to political conflict limit the idea of political co-operation (and hence political and social order) to the leaders of various political parties, thereby suggesting that conflict is overcome through political leaders maximising pragmatic interests somehow divorced form their broader cultural interests. However, the history of Northern Ireland suggests that such an a-cultural approach to political conflict is inadequate. Although paramilitary organisations represent the most extreme views of both sides of the conflict, and are controversial organisations even within their own communities because of the violence they inflict, the cultural cast of their view of the conflict has deep resonance in the broader population.

The major flaw with consociationalism, and the IPPR proposal in particular, is its overly formalistic account of political practice underpinned by an instrumental conception of practical reason. That is, consociational approaches 'that the designers of social and political institutions are capable of working as culturally unencumbered actors, that it is possible to design institutions in a cultural vacuum' (N. Porter, 1996, p. 79). Instrumental approaches to political conflict fail on two counts: first, they fail to demonstrate how it is possible for political actors to 'step out' of their cultural locations and engage in substantive political dialogue, especially when the aim of that dialogue is to create a tolerant and inclusive public sphere; and secondly, they fail to recognise that claims against justice involve claims to cultural goods as much as they involve claims to political goods. Consequently, instrumental approaches fail to grasp that culture and politics are not mutually exclusive discourses capable of being separated at the political gate, as it were.

Route Three - Substantive Constitutionalism

I do not want to suggest that consociational principles have nothing to offer Northern Ireland. Indeed there does need to be some arrangement capable of securing a peace of long enough duration for more fundamental and pervasive reconciliation to occur. The Belfast Agreement of 10 April 1998 - the latest attempt at constitutional reform - should be welcomed with the proviso that it not be seen as 'the answer' to Northern Ireland's political and woes. The problem with constitutional proposals of the macro kind - large all-encompassing packages that re-shape and re-constitute political, social, legal and economic institutions evidenced in the Belfast Agreement - is that they fail to heed the fact that the province needs to be rebuilt from *within* as much as needs to be rebuilt from without. That is, it is not just the constitutional status or the nature and procedural form of Northern Ireland's institutions that are in need of reform. The attitudes, the perceptions, the political and cultural stances of the people within Northern Ireland are also in desperate need of critical attention. And this should be regarded in the ambit of political reform as much as issues of representation, security, education and so on. Issues of cultural identity and recognition need to be as much a part of political dialogue as constitutional arrangements that admit to more procedural and institutional forms. Toward the objective of admitting issues of cultural import into the broader political debate I want to suggest three terms of reference which speak to issues of justice by providing a framework for reconceiving constitutional dialogue in divided societies like Northern Ireland. I refer to these terms of reference as *just recognition*, *complex voices*, and *complex publics*.

The idea of *just recognition* is inspired by Charles Taylor's theoretical examination of the politics of recognition (Taylor, 1994; Taylor, 1991, chapter 5). Integral to recognition is the idea that we acknowledge the 'inherent worth' of those whose identity is defined in terms different from our own. In Northern Ireland, this would call for the immediate recognition of the minority community as bearing legitimate cultural identities that admit to legitimate political aspirations. Of course, there are limits to recognising the 'other' in any society. For instance, when the political aspirations of a cultural identity call for the political annihilation of the 'other' it fails to meet the 'inherent worth' principle inherent in just recognition. Consequently, nationalists in Northern Ireland who call for a united Ireland devoid of a unionist cultural and political presence fail to recognise the legitimacy of Protestant/unionist cultural and political identity. From the other side, unionists who deny that Irish/Catholic/nationalist symbols (like the Tricolour) have a legitimate place in the province of Northern Ireland fail to recognise the inherent worth of Northern Ireland's minority community. Both communities express rival national identities that admit to little common ground. However, this should not, by itself, preclude just recognition. The existence of an identity conceived in terms other to one's own does not, of itself, preclude recognition, as multicultural societies make clear. What does preclude recognition is whether one determines that the recognition of the other simultaneously detracts from one's own identity in unjust ways. To be sure, this is a complicated issue and neat answers are hard to find. But what I want to stress here is that there are some grounds for distinguishing between competing cultural and political identities. If the aspirations of one community depend upon the marginalisation, oppression and silencing of the other, then it fails to recognise the inherent worth of the other. This would violate the justice dimension to recognition of diverse cultural identities. To this extent, hard-line nationalist and hard-line unionist political aspirations are unjust to the extent that they fail to recognise the inherent worth of the 'other' in Northern Ireland.

Complex Voices refers to James Tully's notion that constitutional dialogue is just to the extent that it recognises the voice of the other. Tully argues that 'if the cultural ways of the citizens were recognised and taken into account in reaching an agreement on a form of constitutional association, the constitutional order, and the world of everyday politics it constitutes would be just with respect to this dimension of politics' (Tully, 1996, p. 6). The notion that constitutional dialogue takes place in a framework that gives minority cultural and political identities an *equal* voice is a novel suggestion. Even positing the possibility of equality between majority and minority identities, and the languages that accompany them, challenges those involved in constitutional dialogue to critically reflect on the theoretical and normative assumptions about political community inherent in their framework for discussion. Indeed, the notion that the language of constitutional dialogue itself be open to critical scrutiny - to ensure that it does not marginalise the 'other' by insisting on a comprehensive language that excludes minority perspectives - is challenging. For, how are we to determine whether the space created for minority voices allows them to speak in their own language? Moreover, how are we to deliberate about constitutional matters if minority voices operate with conflicting sets of normative assumptions regarding the political community? This latter question is all-important in the case of Northern Ireland. For instance, unionist conceptions of the political community (i.e. their defence of Northern Irish statehood) revolve around issues of consent measured by majority rule. Nationalist conceptions of political community revolve around notions of a united Ireland. Now, these two conceptions of political community each deny the 'other' a voice inasmuch as they leave no room for negotiation once they have established their 'first principles'. Thus, attempts to constitutionally embody concepts of citizenship, sovereignty, unity, and the like, such that they are synonymous with the symbols and language of just one of these conceptions of political community would be unjust because it denied an equal voice to a rival conception of political community. The challenges to conventional constitutionalism posed by conceiving constitutional dialogue as containing *complex voices* are fundamental for societies where political dialogue has been constructed by historical antagonisms. Challenges of this sort provide the impetus for reconceiving the terms of political dialogue to ensure a space for previously marginalised voices. Constitutionally recognising others means letting them speak in their complex voices - in languages that challenge majority or conventional assumptions regarding the nature of the political community.

Complex publics takes up the issue of recognising the voices of others by reconceiving the public sphere in sympathy with the complexity of citizens incorporated in divided societies. Iris Marion Young's conception of 'communicative democracy' (Young, 1997, chapter 3) provides us with a framework for thinking about democratic dialogue in a public sphere comprised of diverse voices. Young's emphasis on greeting, rhetoric and storytelling conveys the importance of reconstituting the public sphere to ensure the discourse of democratic societies takes full account of the 'plurality of perspectives, speaking styles, and ways of expressing the particularity of social situation as well as the general applicability of principles' (Young, 1997, p. 73). What Young offers those interested in constitutional transformation is a way of thinking about the public sphere when commonality is contested. The contested nature of community in Northern Ireland limits the possibility of conceiving the public sphere in terms of shared understandings and common meanings. On the contrary, Northern Ireland illustrates the problems associated with thinking about the public sphere in terms of unity or commonality. Consequently, what Northern Ireland requires is a public sphere which recognises cultural and political diversity as central to public discourse, where reaching 'understanding' calls for the 'acknowledgement of unshared meanings' (Young, 1997, p. 74) rather than shared ones. Recognising differences amongst a range of cultural, social, and political identities illuminates the complexity of discourses that constitute notions of 'the public'. The term *complex publics* is one way of recognising that the public sphere is constituted by a diversity of identities, not one shared or uncontested set of understandings that transcend cultural locations.

It is clear that Northern Ireland requires a public sphere capable of creating the space for an open, tolerant, and critical dialogue between rival political and cultural traditions. What I want to do now is reflect on some of the key proposals outlined in the Belfast Agreement and assess their ability to create a more tolerant and inclusive public sphere in Northern Ireland bearing in mind the three terms of reference that constitutional reform should follow.

There are six changes in the current organisational arrangements of Northern Ireland noted in the Belfast Agreement that most advocates of reform agree on. Firstly, the devolved Assembly in Northern Ireland elected by proportional representation and requiring weighted majorities is a positive step toward re-constituting public political dialogue in Northern Ireland. This reconstitutes Northern Ireland's political parties as significant players in the political process rather than mere respondents to various extraneous proposals. It forces them to go back to their constituencies with solid proposals for governance of the province. The requirement of weighted majorities as well as the proportional representation voting method achieves two further things: Firstly, it requires political parties from across the two communities to dialogue with one another as part of the 'normal' process of politics in the day to day running of the province; secondly, it is also the most effective way to give a voice to the people themselves. The ability of the people to elect representatives responsible to their constituencies is one way of reducing the impact, or marginalising the role, of paramilitary organisations.

Second, the proposed North/South Ministerial Council constructs a forum for co-operation where there is a clear common interest. Areas of common interest include such things as agriculture, education, transport, environment, waterways, social security/social welfare, tourism, EU programmes, fisheries, health and urban and rural development. It is important to remember that there are people in both Northern Ireland and the Republic who seek ties with one another but who wish these ties to be non-political.

Third, the British-Irish Council and the British-Irish Intergovernmental Conference reinforces the importance of the intergovernmental links between Dublin and London. It is crucial that these links remain in place to deal with the larger issues of political and economic significance, such as foreign policy and international economic agreements. Moreover, the British-Irish Intergovernmental Conference reinforces the importance of external voices in volatile situations that call for political dialogue across hostile political and cultural frontiers.

Fourth, incorporating the European Convention of Human Rights (ECHR) into Northern Ireland law, with the ability of individuals to bring cases against the Northern Ireland Government directly to the European Court, is a positive protective mechanism against political oppression. The power of the European Court to overturn Assembly legislation inconsistent with the ECHR also bolsters protection for Northern Ireland's minorities.

Fifth, it is essential that there be some space made in Northern Ireland for the symbols and practices of those who define themselves as Irish rather than British. The symbols expressing the cultural traditions of both communities need to be pruned of their exclusiveness to ensure that they cannot be used to incite hatred or vilification. But there needs to be some public expression of Ireland in the public institutions of the province if they are going to be able to command the allegiance of those within the minority Catholic/nationalist community. While the Belfast Agreement recognises the 'sensitivity of the use of symbols and emblems for public purposes' (Sect. 6 [Economic, Social and Cultural Issues]) the difficult task of changing symbols and emblems, of actually removing existing symbols of cultural exclusivity, remains a matter for later political negotiation by members of the new Assembly.

Sixth, it is fundamental that the process of reform, that is, the dialogue that accompanies these changes, be sensitive to the different cultural identities in the province. Therefore, the language of constitutionalism itself needs to be as diverse as the identities inherent in the province if the foundations of reformed institutions will be just in the eyes of cultural protagonists. The Belfast Agreement succeeds in giving a voice to members of the Catholic/nationalist community by recognising their different cultural heritage, and by recognising that nationalists have legitimate political and cultural aspirations politically opposed to the aspirations of the majority community. However, whether the structure of the new Assembly - and the public discourse it creates - is capable of accommodating divergent political and cultural identities is yet to be seen.

These six reforms to Northern Ireland's governance go some way toward fulfilling the conditions of a just yet diverse public sphere suggested by the terms *just recognition*, *complex voices* and *complex publics*. The proposed Assembly recognises the cultural diversity of the province by insisting on weighted majorities and proportional representation. The North/South Ministerial Council recognises that dialogue across political and cultural frontiers is necessary for a healthy and vibrant regional economy. The British-Irish Intergovernmental Conference makes it clear that the Republic of Ireland has a legitimate interest in Northern Ireland and leaves room for further constitutional negotiations should there be a desire to alter the current arrangements at a later date. As significant and important as these changes are, however, they focus entirely on institutional arrangements for governance. No doubt it is hoped that changing Northern Ireland's institutional structure will precipitate broader changes in the public sphere permitting exchanges across cultures in an atmosphere of trust and mutual recognition. What remains a matter of concern is the extent to which the Belfast Agreement assumes that participants in the new Assembly will be able to construct a dialogue across cultural and political differences. Perhaps we are beginning to see such a dialogue as the different political Parties from both communities rally in support of a Yes vote in the upcoming referendum - notable exclusion of Paisley's Democratic Unionist Party notwithstanding - we shall have to wait to see if there is any real progress towards a more inclusive, tolerant and respectful public dialogue between the two communities.

Conclusion

I began this chapter by positing important links between culture and politics. The interconnections between culture and politics demonstrate the need for rethinking strategies for constitutional transformation in Northern Ireland. I then went on to illustrate how the dual frameworks of culture and politics shaped political life in Northern Ireland from 1921 to the present. I also argued that consociational approaches to constitutional transformation assume what they set out to create - co-operation and tolerance. I argued that this assumption was unwarranted in a society wracked by cultural and political conflict. I have suggested an alternative path to constitutional transformation - substantive constitutionalism - which offers the hope of reconstituting public discourse in Northern Ireland capable of accommodating the diversity of identities that constitute the 'public'. This encapsulates and reinforces the importance of the passage I cited at the beginning of the chapter - once we understand the 'complexity of the social goods of different communities' as they appear in their everyday practices, 'we will no longer imagine that it is possible to construct an adequate theory of justice without beginning from and returning to the actual practices of particular societies' (Carens, 1995, p. 48). The idea of substantive constitutionalism, as I have conceived it, operates from this engaged, contextually sensitive, and critical perspective.

Notes

1. This chapter is based on an earlier paper written for a graduate course in the Department of Political Science at the University of Toronto in 1996. I am grateful to Professors Jennifer Nedelsky and Peter H. Russell for their critical comments on that paper. I am also grateful to Melissa Williams for critical comments and editorial advice.
2. I want to stress that I am not suggesting that the cultural conflicts or the cultural differences that do exist between unionists and nationalists are reducible to, or exclusively represented in, the paramilitary organisations. There are, of course, many different avenues through which the cultural differences between the two communities are expressed. For instance, the junior and secondary education system, the cultural festivals of the different regions, counties, neighbourhoods and blocks all express different conceptions of Northern Irish culture. Literature, visual art and political songs are also crucial elements, which express cultural perspectives in Northern Ireland. However, that notwithstanding, I think the paramilitary organisations happen to be particularly good at staking claims to cultural differences and are a very clear example of why the political landscape in Northern Ireland cannot be conceived in exclusively religious terms. For a critical discussion of cultural issues in Northern Ireland and Ireland see (Gallagher, 1995; Kearney, 1988; Longley, 1994; Porter, 1996, chapter 3; O'Connor, 1993; Porter, 1998).

7 'Race' and Language in American and Canadian Politics[1]

RICHARD ITON

> Canadian politics are a tilting ground for impassioned rivalries. An immemorial struggle persists between French and English, Catholics and Protestants... In this complex contest ... the whole future of Canada is at stake. In the first place, and above all, it is a racial problem (André Siegfried, Siegfried, 1907, p. 1).

Cultural and ethnic differences, constructed as language in Canadian politics and 'race' in American politics, promise to shape the futures, as they have the histories, of both nations.[2] Comparing the two cases, one might suggest, as did Pierre Vallières in *White Niggers of America*, that there are many interesting commonalities between the ethnicity-related tensions in both societies. In the final analysis, though, it is the differences that are striking, especially if one is concerned with the political challenges facing the two societies.

Although the capacity of key political processes and institutions, including the party system, to bridge the gap between various group interests is undoubtedly compromised by 'cultural politics' in both countries, because of the possibility of Quebec's separation, these issues receive much greater attention in Canada than in the United States. Specifically, in both contexts, cultural politics limit the ability of the parties of the left to maintain themselves as viable national parties and as effective counterweights to the parties of the right. Yet if a society's political health depends upon the ability of its political institutions to represent and mediate conflicting economic and cultural interests, Canada is and will remain much healthier than the United States. Even in the event that Quebec should separate, the basic capacity of Canadian political institutions to resolve conflicts in a peaceful manner is likely to endure. Despite the conventional wisdom that Canada is more deeply threatened by cultural politics than the United States, it would appear that the health of American political institutions is probably more profoundly at risk.

Vallières' analogy was based primarily on the suggestion that francophones in Quebec, and blacks in the United States, were both 'exploited ... second class citizens'. Continuing, he stated, 'The only difference between them [American blacks and Canadian francophones] is the color of their skin and the continent they came from' (Vallières, 1971, p. 21). To some extent, Vallières might have been correct in that the Canadian struggle to achieve linguistic/cultural peace, and the American effort to process 'race' used to be, at the most fundamental level, implicated with the class tensions and dynamics of the two societies. In the United States (see Table 1), this is still very much the case as blacks are roughly twice as likely to be unemployed as whites, black families are four times as likely to earn incomes that fall below the poverty line, and black families, overall, are more likely to be found in the lower income classes than their white counterparts (Hacker, 1992, p. 233). Furthermore, discussions regarding racial issues are in many instances, indirect (and arguably unconscious) considerations of class and class cleavages. Similarly, the inside Quebec 'negotiation' between francophones and anglophones (and more recently allophones) has historically been carried out against a broader backdrop of class tensions and economic differences.[3] Although this clearly was the case throughout the first part of this century, despite suggestions by former Quebec premier Jacques Parizeau that 'money and ethnics' have stifled the aspirations of francophone Quebec, no longer is the French/English divide as clearly a class divide, as it was twenty-eight years ago when Vallières was writing (see Table 2).[4]

Table 1 American Household Income by Race, 1967 and 1992 (in constant 1992 dollars; % making each amount)

	1967 - Black	1967 – White	1992 – Black	1992 - White
$0 – 15,000	45.6	23.4	42.7	21.6
$15 – 35,000	38.3	39.5	31.5	31.8
$35 – 50,000	10.2	19.8	12.8	17.7
Over $50,000	5.8	16.8	13.0	28.9

Source: Jennifer Hochschild, *Facing Up to the American Dream*, p. 44.

Table 2 Average Employment Income for Men and Women in Quebec in 1970, 1980 and 1985 ($ not adjusted for inflation)

	Women 1970	Women 1980	Women 1985	Men 1970	Men 1980	Men 1985
Unilingual Anglophone	$3,835	$10,271	$14,435	$8,171	$17,635	$23,924
Bilingual Anglophone	$3,956	$10,759	$14,449	$8,938	$19,562	$26,078
Unilingual Francophone	$3,097	$8,801	N/A	$5,136	$14,408	N/A
Bilingual Francophone	$3,842	$11,195	$14,718	$7,363	$19,547	$25,923

Source: André Raynauld, 'The Progress of Francophones', in *Canada, Adieu? Quebec Debates Its Future*, Richard Fidler, ed., p. 221, and François Vaillancourt, 'The Economic Status of the French Language and Francophones in Québec', in *Québec: State and Society*, 2nd edition, Alain-G. Gagnon, ed., p. 416.

Although the class subtext has waned in the Canadian instance, linguistic tensions in Canada, and racial dynamics in the United States have weakened the national lefts in the two societies significantly and the ability of working class and lower income constituencies to have their interests heard and acted upon in national politics.[5] In the United States, the left's inability to survive and thrive has been intimately connected to the strong association of class with race, of the left with blacks, and the consequent (and at times desperate) identification of many American whites, regardless of income status, with the middle class and status quo politics. As a study of the views of (objectively) working class Republican Party supporters in Michigan found, '[N]ot being black is what constitutes being middle class' (Greenberg, 1995, p. 39). While the left has traditionally been weak in the American South, contemporary developments have indicated that nationally (and at every level of government) the left - even when operationalised as the New Deal Democratic Party or even mere 'liberalism' - has been marginalised by the interaction of 'race' and class. This tendency for racial forces to undermine potential class alliances has affected American policy making (e.g., health care, income maintenance programmes, urban planning and support for public transportation), and some have suggested might be the underlying cause of American exceptionalism (i.e., the absence of the left in the United States compared to other Western, industrialised societies).[6]

In the Canadian case, it is clear that the inability of the New Democratic Party to present a strong challenge to the traditional and established parties (the Liberals and the Progressive Conservatives until recently), and the newer regional parties (the Bloc Quebecois - BQ - and Reform) is partially a result of the anglophone left's inability to break through in the province of Quebec and with francophone voters (See Young, 1969; Vallières, 1971; Olson, 1973; Trudeau, 1968). While Maurice Duplessis' conservative and nationalist Union Nationale administrations successfully locked out the left until the dawn of the Quiet Revolution and the rapid secularisation of Quebec society in the 1960s, the NDP has been no more successful in converting left-leaning Quebeckers to its cause over the course of the last thirty-odd years than its predecessor the Co-operative Commonwealth Federation (CCF).[7] Quebec has gone solidly Liberal, Progressive Conservative, at times slightly Creditiste, and more recently BQ, but it has yet (except for one hot minute, according to opinion polls, in November 1987) to give the NDP even the slightest bit of support. Although Quebecois nationalism, since the 1949 Asbestos strike and certainly since the 1960s, has had a clear social democratic component, and though the left has been relatively successful within Quebec, the NDP has not managed to speak the language of the left in tones and terms attractive to its 'natural' constituencies in Quebec.[8]

The impact of cultural tensions on the development of the Canadian welfare state, though, has been limited. Duplessis' regime did manage for a generation to restrict the development of a social welfare consensus at the national level, but since the Quiet Revolution, Quebec has supplied many of the architects of the Canadian welfare state, and has been at the forefront in terms of implementing progressive social welfare policies.[9] One of the major reasons why Canadian public policy has not been restricted by language debates, as the American state has been by race, is that federalism has functioned 'successfully' in the Canadian instance as a means of channelling and processing regional, and until recently, linguistic claims. In other words, whereas American state politics have been almost universally hamstrung by racial politics, the Canadian provinces have been able to circumvent the culture/class dynamic that has crippled the NDP as a national party by varying the scale of political activity. To the extent that Quebec has been the province of francophones, and the 'rest of Canada' the domain of English Canadians, provinces have been able to create public policy free of linguistic tensions, and in common, support national social welfare programmes.[10] The geographic concentration of the francophone minority has enabled Canadians to 'agree to disagree', a capacity which is embedded in the opt-out (or 'notwithstanding') clause which allows provinces to exempt themselves from some of the provisions of the federal Constitution. Canadian federalism, and the overlapping of provincial boundaries and linguistic group distributions, mean that language usually becomes a major issue only at the highest level of policy-making.

In the United States, in contrast, racial minorities are geographically dispersed and do not map neatly on to sub-unit boundaries. Blacks have been unable to exert the same degree of political influence that francophones have managed to as a consequence of their geographic concentration within the province of Quebec.[11] The redistricting that occurred in the United States subsequent to the 1990 census, as a consequence of the Justice Department's interpretation of the Voting Rights Act, was an attempt to secure a geographical foundation for the election of blacks, and hopefully the representation of black interests.[12] At the time when these efforts were at their peak - the early 1990s - the number of black representatives increased from 25 of the 435 seats in the House (5.7 percent) to 40 in 1992. These districts, concentrated overwhelmingly in the South, however, did not establish a sound geographical and political foundation for the expression and promotion of black political interests. The Supreme Court's questioning of the legitimacy of these efforts to increase the likelihood of the election of black (and Hispanic) representatives – beginning with the *Shaw v. Reno* case in 1993, and including the more recent *Miller v. Johnson* (1995), *Bush v. Vera* (1996), *Shaw v. Hunt* (1996) and *Abrams v. Johnson* (1997) decisions - has illustrated the tenuousness of these claims and highlighted the importance of geographical concentration to the promotion of the claims of minority groups (especially in political systems which have not institutionalised proportional representation).

Paradoxically, the dispersion of minority populations has reinforced the role of 'race' in American public policy making: since significant minority populations exist in most population centres, there is no escape from 'racial' conflict in any discrete policy area. Although public norms of discourse prohibit most political actors from appealing directly to 'race', it is clear that the discussion of key social policy issues is affected by such considerations.[13] In other words, the geographical dispersion of blacks throughout most of the United States has deprived the group of the same political strength that francophones take for granted in Canada. That same dispersion, though, has meant that politics throughout the United States, and at every level (municipal, state, federal), are affected by racial dynamics.

It is not surprising, then, that the most significant difference between Quebecois and African-American claims concern their attitudes towards federalism. American blacks have, on the whole, overwhelmingly supported a strong federal state and presence and have, justifiably, been wary of 'new federalisms' that promise to return power to the states (for example, the proposals offered throughout American history by individuals such as Thomas Jefferson, John C. Calhoun, Andrew Jackson, Ronald Reagan and Newt Gingrich). In contrast, Quebeckers have traditionally favoured a flexible and loose federation, and have since Confederation in 1867 - and certainly since the conscription battles over federal demands that Quebecois citizens should be required to fight in support of the British crown in the two world wars - been suspicious of a strong national government. One of the more interesting contrasts that the recent constitutional battles has produced is that between what is clearly Quebec's preferred mode of decentralisation and the model being offered, by the federal Liberals, and more strenuously by the Reform Party: whereas Quebec favours more power to the provinces while maintaining a comprehensive social welfare state, the latter advocate decentralisation and a scaled-back social welfare state.

While most of the provinces - except perhaps those in the Maritimes - support increased provincial power, few Quebeckers appear to support the fiscal conservatism now popular in Alberta, Ontario, and elsewhere. Indeed, attempts by Quebec's premier, Lucien Bouchard, to reduce the province's deficit have provoked particularly strong resistance from within the Parti Quebecois, Bouchard's own party, and the Quebec Federation of Labour, a long-time source of support for the PQ. Clement Godbout, the QFL's president, has recently stated, 'One of the main reasons we want Quebec sovereignty is that we think we would have a better Quebec. We think we'll have a Quebec more generous towards its people, with better living conditions for everyone in Quebec' (*The Toronto Star*, February 22, 1997, p. A8).[14]

Fiscal agendas aside, the decreasing class subtext associated with linguistic tensions in Canada, the geographical concentration of francophones in Quebec, and the ease with which federalism allows the tensions to be compartmentalised, indicate that the mechanisms for dealing with cultural/linguistic tensions in Canada should be able to process the issue relatively 'cleanly'. In contrast, racial/cultural tensions in the United States cannot be handled, limited or shaped by federal mechanisms, and are still quite imbued with class overtones and social welfare policy implications.

Wagering Cultural Futures

While the Canadian processing of linguistic tensions does not have to involve every other political decision or realm, in contrast, the American 'racial'/cultural story encompasses practically every aspect of American life.[15] For example, in clear contrast to the Canadian instance, the American obsession/fascination with race is not only a class phenomenon but also a sexual phenomenon that is anchored in issues of gender and sexual identity. American notions of 'the feminine', chivalry, machismo, and sexual liberation have always been, and continue to be, fundamentally racialised. This dynamic is apparent in many of the defining moments of American history: the battles over the 15th amendment (which gave black men the right to vote) and what would become the 19th amendment (enfranchising women), the interaction of racial and gender politics in the civil rights movement, and the manner in which misogynist and racist sentiments reinforced each other in the shaping and launching of the 'new right' in the 1970s and 1980s (See, e.g., David, 1983; Giddings, 1984; and Evans, 1980). As a result, the processing of racial issues in the United States will never be as 'compartmentalisable' as the treatment of linguistic tensions in Canada.

Not surprisingly, the broader philosophical contexts in which the two sets of issues are being addressed differ as well. The historical Canadian practices of cultural and linguistic accommodation have helped to create a political milieu in which issues of cultural pluralism can be openly discussed. The rhetoric of American assimilationism barely masks a racially polarised foundation. Although multiculturalism as government policy is hardly celebrated by all Canadians, and is regarded as suspect by Quebec sovereigntists, the perspective has not engendered nearly the hostility that the mere mention of the word generates in the United States (See Schlesinger, 1991). In a context where cultural pluralism is seen as a threat to the nation's security, it is not surprising that the processing of 'racial'/cultural issues, in the United States, continues to be arduous and painful.

One might also want to question Pierre Vallières' suggestion that there are broad similarities between francophone/anglophone tensions and the American racial saga on other grounds. The French/English divide is hardly that broad despite the 'two solitudes' rhetoric that underpins many of the analyses of Canadian history. There is not much of a basis upon which English and French Canadians can 'otherise' each other: i.e., see each other as the ultimate alien. The histories of the two peoples in Canada, and in Europe, have been too closely linked for such a relationship to develop although, it should be noted, in certain circumstances the smallest perceived differences can trigger the greatest conflicts. 'There appears to be a remarkable similarity throughout the country, and across the French/English difference', suggests Charles Taylor, 'when it comes to the things in life which are important.' Continuing, he contends that 'even when it comes to the values that specifically relate to political culture, there seems to be broad agreement' (Taylor, 1992, p. 53).[16] As class distinctions have receded, the relationship between the two linguistic groups has been based on mutual respect, equality, and to some extent, cultural kinship (e.g., though this clearly reflects the influence of class and religious factors as well, one could note the relatively easy relations between the Irish and francophone communities in Quebec).[17] While some writers might argue that a similar kinship connects 'black' and 'white' folk in the United States (e.g., Ralph Ellison and Stanley Crouch and most of the individuals in the 'American Negro' school or tradition), few Americans would suggest that the (perceived) differences between European and African Americans are as insignificant.[18] Again, American race relations have proceeded on the assumption that 'blacks' and 'whites' are the ultimate 'other' in relation to each other. This distancing, of course, relates to the historical construction of 'the West' and 'Africa', and the unresolved dialectic that links the two.

Arguably, one of the ironies connected to these two cases is that in Canada the debate about language is at some level a debate about culture. In other words, there is the assumption that the Canadian debate is not just about language but the preservation of francophone culture in the context of a largely anglophone nation (and indeed continent). The American struggle on the other hand is focussed on the more artificial realm of 'race', and only tangentially is it seen as a cultural issue or a matter of cultural difference, or preservation.

Even the investigations into school curricula, college canons, and values ('family' and otherwise) have tended to devolve into racial contests revolving around skin fetishes (See, e.g., Gates, 1992; Atlas, 1993; Schlesinger, 1991; and Asante, 1987).

The consciously cultural focus in Canada is ironic because the two cultural linguistic groups are so similar. It is hard, at this point, especially given the influences of globalisation and MTV, to imagine on what basis one would establish a long term difference between francophone and anglophone Canadian culture, except the relatively superficial realm of language.[19] One of the most striking developments over the last twenty-five years with regards to this issue, has been the decreasing distinctiveness of francophone cultural preferences (music, literature, theatre, and consumption patterns in general) in relation to those of anglophone Quebeckers and Canadians. Especially since the Quiet Revolution, the thorough secularisation of Quebecois society, and the elimination of the church as a focal point of francophone culture, the religious distinctions that gave weight to the cultural differences have dissipated. It is in this context that it is not surprising that Quebec is moving towards re-organising its school boards along linguistic lines, rather than on religious and linguistic bases. In contrast to the playwrights (e.g., Michel Tremblay), and musicians (e.g., Harmonium, Beau Dommage, Claude DuBois, Robert Charlebois, Les Seguins, etc.) and other distinctive cultural personalities that Quebec produced even a generation ago, contemporary Quebecois popular culture is not remarkably different from anglophone Canadian (or for that matter, anglophone American) popular culture. The most obvious example would be the singer Celine Dion.[20]

Overall, in contrast to the American case, it would seem that the politics of culture and language can be more easily compartmentalised, and the basis for cultural conflict and tension is not as significant in Canada.[21] Lastly, to the extent that cultural conflict persists, mechanisms (e.g., federalism) exist that should limit the possible consequences of the wrangling for policy making in general.

Political Cultures and Constitutions

While it is clear that the Canadian policy making process in general might be protected from most of the ramifications of anglophone/francophone conflict, fiscal conservatives have been able to exploit the dynamics put in motion by linguistic politics to marginalise the left. Indeed, in both the Canadian and American cases, the interaction of the forces of culture and class has weakened commitments to comprehensive public policy programmes and energised the right wing. The Reform Party is popular because it expresses the frustrations of some anglo-Canadians (particularly in the West) with the issue of Quebec's status in Canada. The actions of Reform leader Preston Manning during the months preceding the 1995 referendum, and the 1997 national election (as evidenced in the party's televised ads suggesting leaders from Quebec could not be trusted to resolve the national unity issue), seemed to indicate that the party believes it could become a majority party if Quebec separates, and that Reform is not sincerely supportive of a united Canada. Certainly in the short term, the Reform cause has been energised by the recent high stakes struggle over linguistic issues. The broader question of whether Reform becomes the Canadian party of the right, or whether the Progressive Conservatives can be resuscitated hinges on the Quebec issue. While there are some other platform differences between the two parties (Reform is further to the right on economics, and more willing to put immigration and broader cultural conflicts into play as partisan issues), the Conservatives' fate - as a party rooted in a functioning and united Canada - is implicated in the linguistic and cultural divisions that currently obsess the country. Whether the Conservatives prevail against Reform, the linguistic stalemate has contributed to the shifting of the axis of public debate to the right and brought about a change in public concerns and priorities that has empowered those forces opposed to a strong welfare state.[22] Inside Quebec, the extent to which class politics can be marginalised by linguistic and national unity concerns is reflected by the fact that Quebec's two major provincial parties, the Parti Quebecois and the Liberals, are led by former members of the right-of-centre, federal Progressive Conservatives (Lucien Bouchard and Jean Charest, respectively). While there has been no pronounced shift to the right as a result of the ascendancy of these two individuals, it is remarkable that the two figureheads of the pro- and anti-sovereignty movements within Quebec are both former Tories.[23] In the long term, it remains to be seen if the support linguistic conflicts have given to right wing politics will become a permanent feature of Canadian politics.[24]

Nevertheless, the partisan implications - for the left and for the overall health of the republic - are arguably more disturbing in the United States although there is nowhere near as strong a sense that the nation's survival is at stake. With regard to the processing of 'racial' issues, the American party system has settled into a basic equilibrium since the 1964 to 1972 period, from Barry Goldwater's significant loss to Richard Nixon's successful conversion of disaffected (white) Democrats to the Republican cause via the 'southern strategy'.[25] Since that period, when the realignment of the party system from the New Deal arrangements to the current configurations began, the Republicans have succeeded to some extent on the same basis as Reform in Canada: as the perceived most reliable opponents of change on the cultural front for 'threatened' constituencies. In contrast to Canada, where victory at the national level seems to depend upon winning a fair share of the seats in Quebec, a Reform-type of approach is a more reliable strategy for securing a majority in the US: i.e., either campaigning against blacks as the Republicans have done for the last 30-odd years, or at the very least, campaigning in such a way so as to signal to 'middle America' that one is not beholden to 'special interests' like blacks (to some extent the Clinton strategy which achieved plurality support in a three-way race in 1992 and in a two-way race in 1996).

The Reform/Republican parallel might work on another level if we consider the parties' respective behaviours with regard to the possibility of a Canada without Quebec, and the debate revolving around the constitutionality and desirability of increasing the number of black majority districts in the United States. As mentioned above, Reform's actions over the last two years might lead one to believe that Preston Manning wants to be prime minister of Canada: even if it means stoking Quebec separatist sentiments so as to empower Reform in a weakened (and possibly fractured) Canada. Reform, then, in the short term, and perhaps in the long term, benefits from the tensions that the Quebec issue has created (as Reform's battle with the BQ over which party would be the official opposition after the 1997 elections reflected on a symbolic level).[26] With regard to the issue of creating black majority Congressional districts, the Republican party has clearly supported these redistricting efforts because the resulting electoral maps have tended to create more solidly white - and Republican - seats as well as majority black and Democratic seats. The GOP has gone so far as supplying black groups with computer software that has made sophisticated challenges and proposals regarding these districts possible. Particularly in the South, these new districting plans have cost white Democratic members of the House their seats. On the other hand, the diminishing ranks of the white southern Democratic caucus must be considered in the broader context. The last thirty years have seen a gradual realignment that is only now really starting to sink in at the congressional and state legislature levels (See Davidson, 1994). In other words, the tide is already moving against white southern Democrats. Also, historically, white southern Democrats have been relatively conservative to the extent that they have weakened the progressive resolve of the party's national leadership. Yes, the recent redistricting has cost the Democratic Party support, but some might ask what kind of support? Either way, in much the same manner that it is alleged that the first Nixon administration supported affirmative action as a means of creating tensions between female and male, and black and white working class constituencies in the Democratic Party - and shaking the disaffected whites males loose to be picked up by the GOP - it is clear that the Republicans have a partisan interest in encouraging redistricting plans based on race.

In terms of the normative claims involved, one might also note that the claims underlying black support for black majority districts and Quebecois calls for a constitutional veto for Quebec are based on roughly similar logic. The effort to establish a veto for Quebec regarding any possible changes to the Canadian Constitution (and possibly any significant legislative re-orientations), and the interpretation of the Voting Rights Act that led to the initial establishment of a number of 'safe' districts for black and Hispanic candidates in the United States, both hinge on the notion that political decisions and outcomes are legitimate only if specific and identifiable constituencies have been formally involved in the decision-making process. In the Canadian case, the argument is that Quebec, as a proxy for the interests of French-speaking Quebeckers (and, at one time, French-speaking Canadians, roughly 20 percent of the population), must have the right to approve or veto any changes to the Canadian constitutional status quo based on a 'two nations' approach to Canadian constitutional history. According to this view, francophones and anglophones are the two groups who compacted to launch the Canadian project, and consequently, any amendments to that compact must be approved by a majority of the representatives of both 'founding peoples'.[27] The opposing view, in the contemporary context, would probably be the suggestion that Quebec is a province like all the others and can make no legitimate claims to a distinct status or society. More specifically, those disagreeing with the notion that Quebec should have a veto argue that Quebeckers, as Canadians, can influence policy as voters in proportion to their numbers within the current arrangements, and that recognition should not be extended formally to specific groups. The 'numbers' counterargument implicitly rejects the notion that francophones - as represented by Quebec - should have any special protections or recognition.

In the American case, the redistricting efforts have been based on the assumption that race is a significant factor in determining voting patterns, and that black interests - to paraphrase Carol Swain - are best represented by black faces.[28] These new districts certainly in no way represent a veto for black voters, and the various black voting constituencies, and are simply based on the premise that blacks are an identifiable and legitimate constituency that deserve formal representation by 'their own' whenever possible. The basic opposing arguments are similar to those raised against Quebec's claims to distinct society status and a veto: that government and the Constitution should not recognise 'race' as a basis for claims, that Americans should be seen as individuals competing in a neutral, open, and pluralistic bargaining process.[29]

The two claims to formal representation are not identical with regard to their potential impact upon their respective societies. While the debate surrounding Quebec's right to a veto is operating in the context of a broader discussion of Canada's future, and is seen by some as a step towards the end of the federation, at least for a brief period, the Justice Department did succeed in increasing the number of black majority districts and this was never perceived as endangering the survival of the United States as a political community.[30] Again, it should also be noted that francophones represent a more geographically concentrated and larger percentage of the Canadian population than blacks do in the US (roughly one-fifth versus one-tenth), and on the other hand, that French-speaking Quebeckers can hardly argue that they have not been represented in Ottawa in terms of prime ministers, cabinet positions, and real political power.

Both sets of claims have been raised in contexts that are in flux. In Quebec, the growing allophone population (particularly in the Montreal area) represents a threat to francophone supremacy even as the anglophone population in the province is depleted (see Table 3).[31] From a much longer historical perspective, the Canada established by the fusion of Upper Canada and Lower Canada has long been transcended geographically if not quite constitutionally (indeed, one can read Pierre Trudeau's project as an unsuccessful attempt to make the Canadian constitution reflective of the nation's late twentieth-century realities). Whatever the long-term prospects of Quebecois culture might be, the broader environment can only engender an understandable cultural insecurity.

For African-Americans, internal class and gender divisions threaten the continued viability of a singular black agenda. On an even more basic front, essentialist debates about the meaning and definition of 'blackness' might involve the abandonment of racially based definitions of identity (such as those traditionally used by the US Census Bureau). Lastly, at least in parts of the country, if not yet nationally, black claims have to be considered in the context of often competing claims raised by Hispanics in California and the West (primarily Mexican-Americans), in New York (primarily Puerto Rican and Dominican), and Florida (primarily Cuban-American), and Asian-Americans (concentrated primarily in the West).

Finally, both cases present clear challenges for the political institutions that might seek to integrate and bind their peoples together in a meaningful and constructive manner. Specifically, the ability of the party systems to reflect the broad range of existing interests effectively will continue to be limited as long as 'cultural' issues constitute the axis of political debate. In particular, the lefts in both societies are faced with very serious challenges. Nevertheless, one need not judge the legitimacy of these claims - the francophone attempts to secure distinct society status, enhanced

Table 3 Linguistic Groups (%) in the Province of Quebec and the City of Montreal

Province of Quebec	1981	1991
% Francophone	81.2	81.1
% Anglophone	9.7	8.7
% Allophone	6.7	7.5
% Multiple	2.4	2.6

The City of Montreal	1981	1991
% Francophone	65.6	61.3
% Anglophone	15.0	11.7
% Allophone	19.4	21.6
% Multiple	-	5.4

Source: Denis Monière and Roch Côté, eds. *Quebec 1996* (Montreal: Editions Fides, 1996), p.400.

powers, and a veto, and the African-American effort to maximise representation wherever possible - to recognise that the Canadian case, unlike the American, might be amenable to a solution of this sort (constitutional tinkering) while redistricting hardly represents a permanent or sufficient response to the American situation.[32]

Conclusions: Of Relative Leeway

From the perspective of those interested in the 'preservation' of their respective nations - and balanced, representative party systems (including a viable left) - one would have to argue that overall the Canadian project is in far better health, and less at risk in the long run, than the United States and its political processes. The absence of class, gender and broad policy implications in the Canadian instance mean that the stakes involved in the nation's linguistic and cultural struggles are really far lower. Furthermore, if one agrees that the cultural differences in question are smaller then it could be argued that Canada can afford to make a few mistakes (as one could argue it already has). While the absence of significant objective differences hardly prohibits the possibility of serious tension between seemingly quite similar groups - in certain contexts, the smallest perceived differences can become grounds for long-lasting and bitter conflict - even if the worst scenario should be realised, it is hard to believe that the relations between a truncated Canada and an independent Quebec would be all that bad: on what basis would hostilities be sustained, and for what purpose? One does not have to take a position on the legitimacy of granting Quebec a veto (and greater policy leeway), and recognising the province's distinct (or 'unique') status within Canada, to realise that either way potential changes would not cost the country all that much, and indeed might enhance its legitimacy in the eyes of a community that is insecure with regards to its future.

This is particularly so given that the most significant victims of Canada's linguistic wars have already been sacrificed: anglophones inside Quebec and francophones outside.

With regards to the United States and its 'race problem', the picture is really far more troubling. 'Race', as a complicating factor in American life, cannot be contained, as it cannot be compartmentalised. The stakes are quite high although an examination of the current analyses of American politics offers little hint that this is so. Class, gender, policy, and community are all caught up in the realm of race. One only has to walk through the nation's major cities to understand how reconstructed racial tensions are eating away at the nation's innards. In clear contrast to the Canadian case, the United States with its racial complexities is not a suitable candidate for simple constitutional reform: unlike those societies such as Canada where the relevant conflicts can be 'contained' within the parameters of constitutional debate, the racialisation of American politics and consequent immobilisation of the nation's social welfare policy process run too deep to be remedied by such means.[33]

Notes

1. I would like to thank Joseph Carens and Melissa Williams for their comments and suggestions regarding this article.
2. It should be noted that the American future inevitably will be influenced by linguistic conflicts (e.g., in Florida, Texas and California) as Canada finds itself increasingly embroiled in conflicts surrounding 'race' (especially if parties such as the Progressive Conservatives in Ontario, and the Reform Party, at the national level, dictate the public agenda). 'Race' is in quotation marks throughout the text simply to recognise that it is a construct.
3. The term 'allophone' is used to refer to those individuals whose mother tongue is neither French nor English.
4. Consequently, perhaps the most significant change that has occurred with regards to the language debate over the last generation has been the decreasing significance of the 'inside Quebec' debate (francophone versus anglophone), and the re-emergence of the significance of 'within Canada' negotiations (Quebec versus the rest of Canada). Vallières, a member of the Front de Liberation du Quebec (FLQ), had been arrested in New York City in September 1966 for allegedly entering the country illegally and 'disturbing the peace' while protesting outside of the United Nations. Indeed, he wrote *White Niggers of America* while sitting in the Manhattan House of Detention. At the request of Canadian authorities, Vallières and colleague Charles Gagnon were returned to Montreal to stand trial on charges of murder. They were convicted and sentenced to life imprisonment. Suggests André Raynauld, 'The "backwardness" of French Canadians that was the favourite theme of social studies for several decades is a thing of the past. It has been eradicated over the last 25 years through better education, mobility, access to management positions, notably in the federal public service, and much greater involvement in the business world' (Raynauld, 1991, p. 221). Jacques Parizeau made his comments regarding the role of 'money and ethnics' in his concession speech the night of the sovereignty referendum (October 30, 1995). He resigned his premiership shortly afterwards.

5. It should be noted that the strength of leftist politics inside the francophone and black communities has also been reduced by corporate notions of francophone identity and 'blackness' that have marginalised class (and gender) issues. Accordingly, the Bloc Quebecois draws membership and support from economic conservatives, social democrats, and former communists.
6. For a version of this argument, see (Quadagno, 1994).
7. The Quiet Revolution refers to the decade after Maurice Duplessis' death on September 7, 1959. As Pierre Trudeau has written, the period was characterised by a 'freedom of expression manifested in the press, on the radio, and on television, as well as in private conversations [that] was in sharp contrast to the timid thinking of the Duplessis era and the underground revolt that in those days had always led up a blind alley. Now revolt was coming up out of the catacombs, publishing reviews, building a "lay movement," and beginning to formulate the body of doctrine, still more or less confused, which was to give birth to separatism, the "quiet revolution," and the questioning of all of the traditional institutions and values of the French-Canadian nation.' See (Vallières, 1971, p. 178-79).
8. The extent to which the NDP has been marginalised by the language issue was illustrated once again in the debates among the party leaders in the 1997 national election campaign. The NDP's leader Alexa McDonough was effectively locked out of the French language debates because of her lack of facility with the language. Although Reform Party leader Preston Manning is no more fluent, he was confident enough about the relevance of his party to suggest that a debate be held to deal solely with the national unity question to which the NDP would not be invited (because the party, he contended, had nothing to say on the issue). Regarding the left's acceptance within Quebec, it is not surprising that the current leader of the nationalist Bloc Quebecois, Gilles Duceppe, is a former union leader and member of the Communist Party of Canada.
9. Quebec's role as a leader in developing social welfare policies was evident most recently in its move to institute a comprehensive child care programme.
10. Quebec's anglophone and allophone populations and the francophone populations in New Brunswick, Ontario and Manitoba represent partial exceptions to this pattern.
11. While francophones constitute over 80 percent of the population of the province of Quebec, none of the American states have populations that are even 40 percent black. Two of the southern states are in the 30 percent range (Mississippi at 35.4 percent and Louisiana at 30.8 percent), and three others are in the high twenties (South Carolina at 29.7 percent, Georgia at 26.8 percent, and Alabama at 25.2 percent). The American average is just over 13 percent while some states have very small black populations (e.g., Vermont, Montana, Idaho, South Dakota, Maine, North Dakota, Utah, New Hampshire, and Wyoming). See (Hacker, 1992, p. 228).

12. Carol Swain argues in *Black Faces, Black Interests* that the representation of black interests does not depend solely on the election of blacks to office. In fact, she suggests that the substantive representation of black interests can be achieved by a number of means. For a discussion of the relevant issues, see (Williams, 1998).
13. For an analysis of the ways in which 'race' can affect views of welfare policy, see (Gilens, 1996, pp. 593-604).
14. Continuing, Godbout suggests, 'Mr. Bouchard says we have to complete that exercise [public service cuts] in order to become sovereign. But if sovereignty means we're going to become collectively impoverished, that we're no longer going to have proper health and education programs, that the public service is going to be stripped to the bone, that private sector workers won't even have unions any more... I say, if that's what sovereignty is going to cost, we won't go for it.' *The Toronto Star*, February 22, 1997, p. A8.
15. Clearly in a period of high conflict and sensitivity - as Canadians are currently experiencing - most significant federal decisions have national unity implications.
16. See (Taylor, 1991, p. 53). Taylor suggests that the apparent convergence of francophone and anglophone political cultures is a recent phenomenon in many respects - and partly attributable to 'the prodigious effect of modern communications' - but notes (p. 54), 'Ironically, at the very moment when we agree upon so much, we are close to breakup.'
17. For an empirical analysis of Canadian and Quebecois views on issues of ethnicity, see (Kalin, 1995, pp. 28-44).
18. The American Negro school includes individuals such as Ralph Ellison, Albert Murray, Gerald Early, Stanley Crouch, Charles Johnson, and the musician Wynton Marsalis. The basic argument made by these individuals is that 'Negroes' should be understood as an American creation, and consequently that no sensible commonalities can be identified among different black populations in the diaspora (specifically that there is no 'African' component in African-American culture). Similarly, it is argued that all Americans are cultural mulattos and that American culture has been influenced by Negro-American folkways. For the clearest statement of these views, see (Ellison, 1964).
19. 'Globalisation' *can* trigger particularistic and preservationist responses. It is not clear that this has happened in Quebec in terms of popular culture (or for that matter, in Canada with regard to American influences).
20. One might go so far as to argue that the developments in Quebec over the course of the post-Quiet Revolution period suggest that indeed culture cannot be preserved by law or resuscitated by legislation. A distinctive francophone or Quebecois culture will maintain itself, survive and thrive, if the culture itself is viable and vital. Despite Bill 22, which was the first legislative attempt to try to increase French language education, and its successor Bill 101 which established the

French Language Charter in Quebec, the French language is not perceived to be any more secure than it was in 1974 (when Bill 22 was passed). According to a recent study released by Quebec's Office de la langue francaise, 'French has [not] become the language commonly used in public by Quebeckers.' Continuing, the report states, 'The trend toward francophones becoming a minority group on the island of Montreal appears inescapable. In fact, it is strongly possible, if not probable, that with francophones becoming a minority on the island of Montreal, this will not encourage members of other linguistic groups to adopt French as the commonly used language.' To the extent that the American racial conflicts are cultural conflicts - culture understood in the positive sense, not in terms of the sociological 'culture of poverty' approach - African-American culture (and the various African-American cultures) have survived despite the absence of state recognition and support, and indeed, despite the resistance of mainstream American institutions to acknowledging their existence and legitimacy. Again, the American case indicates that cultures emerge, perpetuate themselves, die, divide and/or multiply essentially regardless of government legislation. Given that various American governments have supported policies such as the 'black codes,' Jim Crow segregation, and variants of the 'one drop theory,' the resulting cultural realities would lead one to believe that attempts to categorise and/or legislate culture and ethnicity (and surely 'race') are inevitably prone to becoming - to borrow from Clarence Thomas - 'Kafkaesque.'

21. For some discussions of these cultural divisions, see Hacker, 1992; Hochschild, 1995; and Taylor, 1992.

22. There is some evidence that Reform has also pulled support from some of the NDP's traditional constituencies (particularly in the West).

23. In fact, Jean Charest did not abandon his affiliation with the federal Progressive Conservatives when he left the party's leadership to takeover the provincial Quebec Liberal party on March 26, 1998.

24. Perhaps ironically, the other party that might gain should Quebec separate would be the New Democratic Party. As mentioned earlier, the NDP has been weak because it has not been able to gain support in Quebec and because leftist constituencies in Quebec have been able to express themselves through the provincial Parti Quebecois, the Bloc Quebecois, and to a lesser extent, through the federal Liberals. The NDP, then, has suffered in terms of its ability to get votes inside Quebec, and consequently has been perceived as a less viable party, nationally, outside Quebec. To the degree that it has been perceived that the NDP cannot win, Canadians have been unwilling to 'waste' votes on it in national elections. Logically, a truncated Canada would provide the NDP with a new lease on life. On the other hand, the NDP's inability to get its message across in francophone Quebec might foreshadow a similar handicap in a nation where politics

are increasingly defined, and approached in terms of colour and ethnicity (i.e., beyond the traditional linguistic realm). One has to wonder if the NDP, and the left in general, will be any more successful promoting their causes in an increasingly multiethnic nation having failed to transcend a simple, binary linguistic divide. The developments in Ontario since 1995 would lead one to be a bit pessimistic about the left's ability to thrive in a multiethnic political culture.

25. For discussions of these developments, see Scammon and Wattenberg, 1970; Edsall and Edsall, 1990.

26. The Reform Party did win more seats than the Bloc Quebecois in the 1997 federal election and consequently won the right to form the official opposition which includes expanded rights to ask questions during question period and to set the public agenda. One other perk is the right of the opposition leader to live in Stornoway, a residence maintained by the public purse (and a perk, which the leaders of the BQ had pointedly rejected when they were the official opposition). This was a privilege that Reform Leader Preston Manning had previously promised to forsake. He changed his mind after the election.

27. Obviously, this approach marginalises the views of Canada's indigenous peoples.

28. Again, as mentioned above, Swain does not argue that black interests can only be represented by 'black faces'.

29. At this point, the Supreme Court's position on these districts is similar to its stance on affirmative action: race (or gender or language) cannot be the sole basis (for admission, hiring, promotion, or a particular electoral plan) but it can be a factor. A majority of the court might be open to even stricter limitations on the legitimacy of racial considerations in both areas. For a provocative discussion of alternate means of enhancing black political representation, see Guinier, 1994. For a discussion of the broader issues in the Canadian context, see Carens, 1996-97.

30. The similarity between the two sets of claims becomes stronger, perhaps, when one notes that many of the same arguments and issues have been raised with regards to affirmative action. Quebec's veto, black majority districts, and affirmative action programmes all relate to the question of whether cultural and ethnic groups can make legitimate claims for guaranteed access to the decision making process (understood in the broadest sense). The different claims suggest that the respective processes of the two societies might be illegitimate if the groups in question are not specifically and/or (roughly) proportionately represented.

31. For an analysis of Quebec's policies with regards to immigration, see (Carens, 1995).

32. For reasons discussed in greater depth by Carol Swain and Lani Guinier, one might even want to question whether these districts should be emphasised as the best means for blacks to enhance their representation in American politics and whether

these districts are even desirable - a scepticism that is certainly understandable from a leftist perspective. To the extent that such districts might limit or foreclose the possibility of cross-racial dialogue and coalitions, and specifically class-based alliances, they might be problematic. Also as Swain argues, the representation of 'black' interests (however defined) does not depend solely upon the presence of 'black faces'.

33. This suggestion that certain types of national conflicts are more amenable than others to resolution through constitutional means refers to the typology proposed in Robert Vipond's conference presentation.

8 Globalisation and Governance

JAN AART SCHOLTE

Introduction

'Globalisation' stands out for quite a large public, spread across the world, as one of the defining terms of contemporary social consciousness. Perhaps it is even, as one writer has suggested, 'the concept of the 1990s' (Waters, 1995, p.1). Discussions of globalisation tend at the same time to be explorations of social change. Many commentators have drawn causal connections between the spread of global relations and purported far-reaching transformations in structures of knowledge, authority, geography, community, ecology, time, and production.

The present chapter examines the implications of globalisation for governance. Like globalisation, 'governance' is a newly popular concept in social and political thought. Its increased currency since the 1980s has reflected a growing awareness that questions of authoritative regulation and the maintenance of social order are not reducible to government alone.

Indeed, contemporary globalisation has made it impossible - in relation to many policy issues - to conduct effective governance exclusively through the state. In other words, globalisation has made sovereign statehood impracticable. This is by no means to announce a demise of the state. On the contrary, across the continents state apparatuses are as large and active as ever. However, with globalisation world politics has moved to a post-sovereign condition where governance is dispersed across a multilayered public sector as well as numerous private-sector agencies.

The present chapter develops an argument regarding the shift from statism to post-sovereign governance in four sections.[1] The first section below outlines a working definition of globalisation as the rise of supraterritoriality. The second section delineates five altered features of statehood in the contemporary globalising world: namely, the end of sovereignty; service of supraterritorial as well as territorial constituencies; reduced provision of social security; disinclination towards interstate warfare; and increased involvement in multilateral regulatory arrangements. The third section describes the promotion by globalisation of a dispersion of many public regulatory competences 'downwards' to substate authorities (local and provincial) and 'upwards' to suprastate governance bodies (regional and transcontinental). The fourth section then indicates how globalisation has promoted the growth of various regulatory mechanisms through civic associations, giving governance a significant private as well as public character. The conclusion of the chapter notes that these various trends in governance have some worrying implications for democracy.

Globalisation

Any discussion of globalisation must indicate how that notion is being conceived. Much unnecessary confusion and acrimony has arisen in debates concerning globalisation because people have been insufficiently explicit, precise and consistent about definition. The conception employed here is but one of various available alternatives: in no way is it definitive.[2] Nonetheless, I do aim for clear and consistent usage.

In a word, globalisation is understood in the present context as the spread of supraterritoriality. From this perspective, globalisation involves a reorganisation of social space, a move away from a situation where geography is synonymous with territoriality. Social relations are supraterritorial when they are substantially detached from territorial space. Territorial location, territorial distance and territorial borders have at most a secondary relevance in respect of global circumstances like computer networks. Global conditions can extend anywhere in the world at the same time (e.g. the anthropogenic greenhouse effect) and can unite locations anywhere on the planet in effectively no time (e.g. a CNN broadcast). Global circumstances can and do surface simultaneously at any point on earth that is equipped to host them: e.g. companies like Nestlé or associations like Amnesty International. Global phenomena can and do move almost instantaneously across any distance: e.g. electronic foreign exchange markets.

When conceived in terms of supraterritoriality, global relations are qualitatively different from international relations. Internationality describes long-distance connections across borders between territorial units. In contrast, globality involves distanceless, transborder, supraterritorial relations in which topographical locations and country units lack determining influence. Internationality is embedded in territorial space; globality transcends it.

If we identify globality as supraterritoriality, then globalisation – the spread of supraterritoriality – has mainly transpired in the second half of the twentieth century. It is of course true that social relations have unfolded in a world context throughout recorded history. However, a 'world' context is not the same as a 'global' context. Ancient times did not experience transworld simultaneity and instantaneity of the kind found in telecommunications, global environmental changes, and so on. It is also true that the decades prior to 1914 witnessed high levels of cross-border migration, direct investment, finance and trade. However, as already emphasised, 'cross-border' transactions are not the same as 'transborder' relations. Global production, global finance and global markets have a qualitatively different spatial logic and were barely in evidence a hundred years ago.

The expansion of supraterritorial space has principally occurred during recent decades. In terms of transworld ecology, for example, climate change, the depletion of stratospheric ozone and the loss of biological diversity have all reached unprecedented levels in the late twentieth century. In relation to organisations, the numbers of transborder companies, transborder regulatory agencies and transborder civic associations each multiplied tenfold between 1960 and 1995. In respect of finance, the late twentieth century has seen exponential growth of transborder money flows, transborder bank deposits and loans, global securities markets, transworld dealing in financial derivatives, and so on (Scholte, 1997b). In regard to communications, only current generations (and not our nineteenth-century forebears) have witnessed the great expansion of air travel, rocketry, telephony, computer networks, radio and television. Transborder production chains (where different stages of manufacture are spread across several countries and connected through intrafirm trade) have appeared since the 1950s. Global markets (where products like Levi jeans and Duracell batteries are distributed and sold on a transworld basis) have likewise undergone most of their growth in the late twentieth century. Global consciousness, too, has but recently become a feature of everyday life. In earlier times only a narrow circle of intellectuals and businesspeople conceived of the world as a single place; yet today globality is firmly embedded in the popular imagination.

Before proceeding further, it is important to stress half a dozen qualifications concerning global relations. First, globality is not universality: to say that a circumstance is supraterritorial is not to say that it is everywhere. Second, globality is not homogeneity: phenomena that transcend territorial space do not necessarily erase diversity in the world.

Third, globality is not uniformity: transborder conditions do not affect everyone to the same extent and in the same ways. Fourth, globality does not eliminate territoriality: the two types of space coexist and interrelate. Fifth, globality does not spread in a predetermined and irreversible way: globalisation is neither foreordained or unstoppable. Sixth, globality is not inherently a good or a bad thing: supraterritorial spaces have been sites of both violence and emancipation.

While it is important not to draw false corollaries of the kind just mentioned, globalisation does in other ways have far-reaching implications for social structure. In a word, the contemporary accelerated growth of global networks and flows has broken the territorialist world order. Under conditions of territorialism, economy and society were organised in terms of territorial units (countries), culture and community were organised in a territorial framework (nations), and governance was organised on a territorial basis (states). Globalisation has in no way brought an end to territorial geography, communities and governments; however, the large-scale spread of supraterritoriality has meant that social relations today cannot be mapped in terms of countries, nations and states alone. In short, by moving outside a territorial mould, global relations call the whole of modern social organisation into question.

Reconstructions of the State[3]

Prima facie it is sensible to presume that globalisation poses a challenge to the state. Surely a proliferation of supraterritorial relations must create difficulties for a structure of governance that is quintessentially territorial? Indeed, as already noted, contemporary accelerated globalisation has ended the state's effective monopoly on governance. Numerous other sites of regulation have developed: substate and suprastate institutions; public and private agencies.

However, it is mistaken to speak - as many commentators have done - of a prospective demise or even an ongoing retreat of the state in the face of globalisation (cf. Ohmae, 1995; Strange, 1996). Whatever new world order might be emerging in the course of globalisation, for the moment the state remains a major part of it. Even in countries where neoliberal governments have ostensibly been committed to shrinking the public sector, states have often increased their payroll, budget, and scope of regulation. Shrinkage of the state in relation to privatisations (whose total value has run into hundreds of billions of dollars worldwide since the mid-1980s) and marketisation of social security has frequently been more than compensated by state expansion in other areas.

Some of this enlargement has been quite closely related to the spread of supraterritoriality. For instance, technologies of globalisation have given states surveillance tools and military equipment of unprecedented sophistication and destructive potential: e.g. nuclear missiles, spy satellites, computerised data banks, etc. The growth of global flows has encouraged many states to pursue greater environmental and consumer protection, to enact new data protection legislation, etc.

Indeed, states have often played an indispensable enabling role in respect of globalisation. For example, states have done much to further the application of universal technical standards. In addition, governments have facilitated the proliferation and growth of global firms with suitably constructed property laws, investment codes, tax regimes, etc. States have also provided much of the regulatory architecture for global finance (Helleiner, 1994; Kapstein, 1994). Moreover, states have created regional and transworld regulatory agencies (discussed below) which have further developed the legal infrastructure for globalisation.

True, some states have come under particular strain in the late twentieth century. For instance, recent years have witnessed some major implosions of government, with Somalia offering perhaps the most striking example. Furthermore, several states have divided during the decades of accelerated globalisation, including Ethiopia, Yugoslavia, ex-Czechoslovakia, and the former Soviet Union. Yet such developments hardly signal the end of the state. In most cases of threatened collapse, states have staged recoveries: Belgium, Uganda, etc. As for fragmentations, fusions, and other recompositions of states, such developments have been the stuff of world politics for centuries.

Rather than contracting or eliminating the state, the spread of supraterritoriality has tended to create a different kind of state. In the contemporary globalising world, states have: (a) lost sovereignty; (b) reoriented themselves to serve supraterritorial as well as territorial interests; (c) tended to reduce welfare guarantees; (d) redefined the use of warfare; and (e) turned increasingly to multilateral regulatory arrangements.

The End of Sovereignty

Prior to recent decades of accelerated globalisation, governance in the world - and at that time more distinctly international - system was constructed mainly around the principle of sovereign statehood. By conventional conceptions, sovereignty entails a claim by the state to supreme, comprehensive, unqualified and exclusive rule over its territorial jurisdiction. With supreme rule, the sovereign state answers to no higher authority; it always has the final say in respect of its territorial realm. With comprehensive rule, the sovereign state governs all aspects of social life: money supply, language, military affairs, sexual behaviour, formal education, etc. With unqualified rule, sovereign states respect a norm of nonintervention in one another's territorial jurisdictions. With exclusive rule, the sovereign state does not share authority over its realm with any other party.

True, in earlier times international relations practice sometimes fell short of the sovereignty norm. For example, most states at one time or another undertook military invasions and covert interventions in foreign jurisdictions. In addition, colonial administrations often exercised only limited control over peripheral districts of their claimed territory. Meanwhile weaker states often lacked the resources to make good their legal pretensions to sovereignty. However, sovereignty remained hypothetically realisable in the territorialist world of old. A state could, by strengthening its means, graduate from mere legal sovereignty to positive sovereignty. Moreover, the principle of sovereignty enjoyed largely unquestioning acceptance in these earlier times. Religious universalists, liberal cosmopolitans, and Marxist internationalists who rejected the norm constituted a small minority and were generally dismissed as utopians.

In the face of unprecedented globalisation in the late twentieth century, states can no longer be sovereign in the traditional sense of the word. For both physical and ideational reasons, a state cannot in contemporary globalising circumstances exercise ultimate, comprehensive, absolute and singular rule over a country. State sovereignty depends on territorialism, where all events occur at fixed locations: either within territorial jurisdictions; or at designated points across tightly patrolled borders. The end of territorialism therefore brings the end of sovereignty. Indeed, most new, post-colonial states (established in the time of accelerating globalisation) have never enjoyed sovereignty except in name.

Many material conditions in the current globalising world have transcended the territorialist geography which sovereignty presupposes. Computerised data transmissions, radio broadcasts, satellite remote sensing, and telephone calls do not halt at customs posts. Moreover, all occur: (a) at speeds that make it difficult for state surveillance to detect them in advance; and (b) in quantities that a state, even with greatly enhanced capabilities, cannot comprehensively track. Electronic mass media have also detracted from a state's dominion over language construction and education. Nor can a state exercise complete authority over transborder associations or global companies. Indeed, as detailed below, many regulations now come to the state from suprastate bodies rather than being formulated by that state itself. Likewise, governments intervene in, rather than control, global trade. With the development of global finance, states have also lost another former hallmark of sovereignty: namely, supreme and exclusive authority over money. Transworld ecological conditions such as ozone depletion and biodiversity loss have likewise contradicted the material preconditions of sovereignty.

In short, even where they are legally entitled to do so, contemporary states are quite unable singularly and fully to control the global flows that transcend their borders. To be sure, states have differential capacities to affect supraterritorial phenomena; hence the Japanese state can generally exert far more influence in global spaces than the Bolivian state. However, even the best endowed state does not have the means to assert sovereign control over transborder relations. Global circumstances cannot be fixed in a territorial space over which a state might aim to exercise supreme and exclusive jurisdiction. Indeed, on many occasions transworld phenomena influence circumstances in a country without ever directly touching its soil.

At the same time as overturning the material conditions of sovereignty, globalisation has also loosened crucial affective underpinnings of sovereignty. On the one hand, the new geography has advanced various nonterritorial identities and communities. Transborder loyalties on lines of religion, gender, race, class, sexual orientation, profession, etc. have diluted, rivalled and sometimes even overridden feelings of national solidarity that have lent so much legitimacy to state sovereignty (Scholte 1996b). At the same time, contemporary globalisation has also reinvigorated more localised solidarities. When faced with the vastness and seeming intangibility of globality, many people have turned away from the state to their local 'home' in order to nurture their possibilities of community and self-determination

(Scholte, 1996b). In addition, citizens and governors alike have in general become increasingly ready to give values such as economic growth, human rights, and ecological integrity – none of which is strictly bound to territory – a higher priority than sovereign statehood.

On a range of counts, then, globalisation has contradicted and subverted sovereign statehood. In this light, various authors have observed that the world has moved into 'the twilight of sovereignty' or 'beyond sovereignty' (Wriston, 1992; Soroos, 1986). It is said that 'sovereignty is no longer sacrosanct', even that sovereignty 'has lost much of its relevance' (Chopra and Weiss, 1992; Lapidoth, 1992, p. 345).

To be sure, the concept of sovereignty remains very much alive in contemporary political discourse. The idea continues to have important impacts insofar as people believe that sovereignty persists or ought to be retrieved. Government leaders in many countries regularly speak of 'defending sovereignty' even if - in the traditional understanding of the term - it is no longer in place to defend. Meanwhile, many citizens cling to the illusion of sovereignty insofar as they associate the principle with their cultural identity and broader security.

However, persistent rhetoric of sovereignty is quite different from persistent practice of sovereignty. Under contemporary conditions of globalisation, no amount of institution building will allow a state to achieve absolute, comprehensive, supreme and unilateral control of the global flows that affect its realm. At the same time, sovereignty has become discredited as the primary norm of world politics in substantial and influential circles of investors, managers, environmentalists, youth, feminists, human rights advocates, religious revivalists, and so on.

Turns towards Supraterritorial Constituencies

States have also changed in current times of globalisation with regard to the constituencies that they serve. The sovereign state of old generally represented so-called 'domestic' or 'national' interests. It sought to advance the pursuits of its citizens in the wider world and to defend them against harmful so-called 'external' or 'foreign' intrusions. To be sure, sovereign states often favoured the interests of certain sectors of their resident populace more than others: e.g. particular classes, religious denominations, or ethnic groups. However, such privileged constituencies almost always lay within the given state's territory.

Under the influence of contemporary globalisation, the state has become less consistent in holding a territorial line of defence of its 'inside' against its 'outside' and asserting 'domestic' interests against 'foreigners'. Instead, the post-sovereign state is more often an arena of collaboration and competition between a complex array of territorial and supraterritorial interests.

For example, today ministries from various states often engage in transgovernmental co-operation with each other - and sometimes in opposition to other sets of ministries. On these lines the United Nations Environment Programme has been a place where environment ministers from around the world have regularly complained about economics ministers. Likewise, finance ministries and central banks have tended to find more commonality of views amongst themselves than with other departments of their respective governments.

In addition, some contemporary states have occasionally served the cause of one or the other global social movement. For example, the Iranian state has since 1979 given extensive support to Islamicists worldwide. Other states have from time to time carried the banner for global environmentalism or for a human rights issue. For instance, in June 1995 the German, Danish, and Swedish states joined a transworld protest against the proposed sinking of the Brent Spar oil platform.

Most strikingly to date, however, post-sovereign states have served the interests of global capital in addition to (and on occasion instead of) national-territorial capital. (Needless to say, global capital includes not only 'foreign'-based enterprises, but also 'domestic'-based concerns with transborder operations.) Much contemporary state policy has thereby addressed the demands of global companies, transborder financial markets, transworld media and telecommunications, and so on. Many governments have feared that, if they do not provide sufficiently appealing taxation and regulation environments, footloose global capital will desert them. Indeed, some governments have reduced corporate tax rates in scarcely disguised interstate tax competition for mobile business. In this environment even governments with strong protectionist inclinations (like those of Cuba and Myanmar, for example) have tended to succumb to at least a partial accommodation of transborder capitalism. Robert Cox has in this light described contemporary states as 'transmission belts from the global to the national economic spheres' (1993, p. 260).

Cox exaggerates insofar as his metaphor could imply that the post-sovereign state has lost all sight of its 'internal', territorial constituency. In practice, the state has often been a site of struggle between territorial and supraterritorial capital. For example, even the radically neoliberal Thatcher Government prevaricated in the face of Nestlé's 1988 takeover of a 'British' institution, Rowntree Mackintosh. In the name of sustaining national competitiveness in global markets, many governments have sanctioned mergers and acquisitions that created oligopolies within their territorial jurisdictions. Especially in the more industrialised parts of the world, various states have responded to contemporary globalisation with intensified trade protectionism in respect of certain domestic economic sectors. Likewise, in the name of guarding domestic interests, immigration controls have rarely been as tight as they are at the end of the twentieth century, aided in particular by the new information technologies that have in other respects dissolved borders.

In short, it is not that globalisation has brought an end to territorial constituencies, but that the clientele of government has become partly globalised as well. *Raison d'état* has become more than *raison de la nation.* The state's service of both territorial and global interests can breed ambiguity and inconsistency in policy, particularly when the two conflict.

Retreats from Welfarism

The growth of supraterritorial capitalist constituencies also appears to have put significant downward pressures on state provisions of social security in the late twentieth century. Although data has yet to be fully assembled and systematically analysed (Bowles and Wagman, 1997), much evidence points to links between contemporary globalisation and the oft-proclaimed 'crisis of the welfare state'.

The history of states during the first three quarters of the twentieth century was in good part a story of growing cradle-to-the-grave public-sector guarantees of nutrition, health care, housing, education, minimum income, and other welfare needs. At the same time, regimes of progressive taxation were introduced to effect a substantial redistribution of wealth in many countries. A number of circumstances generated this expansion of social security programmes: the spread of universal suffrage; the Bolshevik challenge; and promises made by governing elites to suffering masses during the world wars and decolonisation struggles.

The growing power of global capital has contributed significantly to reversals of these trends during the last decades of the twentieth century. At a time when the financing of many social security systems was coming under strain in any case, the added pressure from transborder capital for reduced taxes and labour costs has also driven many governments to cut back social provisions in the name of 'global competitiveness'. Such shrinkages have been a cornerstone of many 'adjustment' packages in the South, 'reform' programmes in the North, and 'transition' policies in the former Soviet bloc.

Certain parts of the welfare state have usually come under more pressure than others. Governments have generally implemented the greatest cuts in respect of sunk costs such as unemployment benefits, old-age pensions, and untied official development assistance. In comparison, education and training budgets have often been less affected, particularly insofar as such spending is believed to enhance a country's position in global markets. That said, many economic restructuring programmes of the 1990s have incorporate so-called 'social safety nets' with the aim of reducing the worst pains for the poor and disadvantaged.

Yet almost no government anywhere today dares openly to pursue a programme of radical progressive redistribution of wealth. The world of the 1990s hosts many a would-be socialist who, as a statesperson facing global capitalism, has tempered or reversed programmes of redistribution. This roll call includes Blair in Britain, Murayama in Japan, Kok in the Netherlands, Kwasniewski in Poland, Mbeki in South Africa, Museveni in Uganda, and more. Meanwhile many other governments have unabashedly embraced neoliberalism, arguing that growing inequalities of wealth and income are unavoidable side effects of increased economic efficiency and viable public finances.

Yet it would be mistaken to conclude that globalisation and publicly provided social security are inherently in tension. Downward pressures have tended to arise when - as has been common in the late twentieth century - states have addressed social welfare individually and in the context of competition for global capital. However, other policy courses are available, including as yet underexplored multilateral arrangements. The current connection between globalisation and declining welfarism is historically contingent and could well prove to be temporary.

Altered Patterns of Warfare

Another by-product of widespread globalisation in the late twentieth century may be changes in the ways that states deploy armed forces. Preparation for and engagement in armed struggle was a major spur to the rise of the modern state and subsequently remained one of its chief preoccupations. However, the means and purposes of warfare have shifted over time, and the spread of supraterritoriality has arguably encouraged several such changes in the contemporary world.

For one thing, the expansion of supraterritorial interests would seem to have generally reduced incentives for interstate war, particularly in those countries and social circles where globalisation has proceeded the furthest. Interstate combat generally advances little purpose for - and sooner positively harms - global circulation of capital, transborder communities of religious, racial, and class solidarity, the management of global environmental degradation, and so on. Perhaps greater insight lies behind the flippant observation that no two countries with McDonald's outlets have ever entered into armed conflict with each other (Daily Telegraph, 21 December 1996). On similar lines Hans-Henrik Holm and Georg Sørensen have described an emergence of 'postmodern states' for whom warfare is unthinkable (1995, p. 204).

Yet contemporary accelerated globalisation has by no means created post-military states. On the contrary, the rise of transborder connectivity has occasioned considerable innovation in weapons: e.g. in the shape of fighter jets, missiles, spy satellites, etc. Computer networks were first developed in the armed forces and have remained a major tool of warfare. Transborder organisation has figured in the manufacture and marketing of much military equipment as well as in alliance structures, United Nations interventions, and paramilitary activities. Global finance largely paid for the Gulf War of 1990-91. In short, although the spread of supraterritoriality has in some ways contradicted the logics of interstate war, globalisation and militarisation have by no means been mutually exclusive.

Furthermore, globalisation has in other respects encouraged an increased inward application of officially sanctioned armed violence. For example, on various occasions contemporary police operations have aimed to secure the position of global companies, the implemention of structural adjustment programmes, or the privileges of an exploitative local elite who hold greater stakes in eurocurrency markets than in their purported 'homeland'. Many other times states have unleashed armed force to repress subnational ethnic movements or religious resurgence, both of which have often been fed by globalisation (Scholte, 1996b). In these respects, too, the post-sovereign state has not abjured militarisation so much as deployed armed force differently.

Indeed, it is conceivable that general warfare between major states could recur in spite - or even because - of globalisation. The pains of adjustment to global relations (e.g. in terms of poverty, job losses, ecological damage, cultural extinctions, heightened feelings of insecurity) might in certain circumstances encourage a return of widespread interstate warfare. A few decades of accelerated globalisation have not removed long-standing militarist political cultures in countries such as Britain, Japan, and the USA. On this count, too, liberalists' equations of globalisation and peace would appear to be dangerously complacent.

Increased Multilateralism

A fifth distinctive feature of post-sovereign states is their greater proclivity to enter into multilateral governance arrangements, to the point that various students of international relations have spoken of the development of multilateralism. In contrast to earlier generations, states in the late twentieth century have been less inclined to take unilateral initiatives in respect of world affairs. Foreign policy has since the 1950s come very often to involve collective arrangements of multiple states: e.g. regional integration schemes, the United Nations system, Group of Seven consultations, and so on. Also in contrast to traditional foreign policy, contemporary multilateral measures have frequently applied to 'internal affairs' as well as interstate relations: e.g. in relation to civil strife, labour policies, technology standards, industrial subsidies, local environmental protection schemes, and much more. Thus through multilateralism, as through so much else, globalisation has dissolved the distinctions between 'domestic' and 'foreign' affairs which marked international relations of old.

The growth of multilateralism is mainly discussed in the next section under the headings of regionalism and transworld governance. However, multilateral arrangements are an interstate as well as suprastate phenomenon. In other words, 'suprastate' does not mean 'nonstate'. Although multilateral regimes have acquired a certain life of their own, beyond that of the participating states, they remain integrally a matter of states, too. Multilateral mechanisms work through, shape, and sustain states at the same time that they are (substantially but not wholly) moulded by states.

The preceding section has indicated that globalisation shows no sign of erasing the state. On the contrary, states remain one of the principal agencies through which the consequences of globalisation can be addressed. However, the state in present times of globalisation is not the same state of the territorialist era. States in the late twentieth century are no longer sovereign. They look to supraterritorial as well as territorial constituents. They tend to reduce public provision of social security. They have less inclination towards interstate warfare. They are deeply enmeshed in multilateral governance arrangements. On all of these counts, contemporary globalisation has created a new kind of state.

Multifaceted Public Governance

In the post-sovereign condition that has arisen with accelerated globalisation during recent decades, states no longer stand at the pinnacle of governance. Rather, they are players - still very important players, to be sure - in networks of regulation that include also multiple substate and suprastate authorities. On the one hand, contemporary globalisation has encouraged a proliferation of direct transborder connections between local and provincial governments. At the same time, the expansion of supraterritoriality has promoted a major growth of regional and transworld governance mechanisms. As a result of this proliferation of substate and suprastate regulation alongside state activities, governance in the world system has become considerably more decentralised and fragmented in the late twentieth century. To this extent Hedley Bull was right to speculate in the mid-1970s about an emergent 'new mediævalism' in world politics with segmented and overlapping regulatory arrangements (1977, pp.254–55, 264–76).

Globalisation has furthered this dispersion of the public sector in three principal ways. First, as already discussed, the rapid contemporary spread of supraterritorial space has made sovereign statehood impracticable. Other institutions have moved to fill the many resultant gaps in effective regulation. Second, globalisation has introduced a number of problems (e.g. transborder capital flows, global environmental change, etc.) in which substate and suprastate agencies may hold a comparative advantage or at least a complementary role in relation to states. Third, the growth of global communication, global organisation, global finance and global consciousness has provided substate and suprastate authorities with the means to sustain world-scale networks, including many activities that bypass states.

Indeed, the various substate and suprastate authorities have acquired a relative autonomy from states. In other words, these bodies take their own initiatives and are not wholly subordinated to states. They can exert considerable power over weaker states in particular. However, this autonomy is but relative insofar as these local, provincial, regional and transworld bodies continue to interact with and be influenced by states. In short, largely on account of globalisation, the public sector has become increasingly multifaceted, with no 'level' holding systematic primacy over the others, in the way that the state did in the former age of sovereignty.

Substate Transborder Governance

The delegation of various areas of public policy from the state to substate authorities is hardly new to the present time of accelerated globalisation. However, in a notable departure from state-centred practices of the Westphalian system, many provincial, municipal and district governments have in the late twentieth century developed direct transborder contacts with each other (Duchacek, 1988; Hocking, 1993). These substate networks often do not directly involve central governments. Indeed, the policies pursued in this transstate diplomacy may run contrary to those prevailing at state level.

Much of this transborder governance has developed between municipalities. The trend is hardly surprising insofar as supraterritorial telecommunications webs, air corridors, capital flows and the like have connected so-called 'global cities' such as Los Angeles, Singapore, Johannesburg and Paris as much to one another as to their respective hinterlands. In small and medium-sized towns, too, local governments have taken transborder policy initiatives on matters such as development co-operation, control of crime, promotion of human rights, etc. For instance, by the late 1980s over 4200 town councils in 23 countries had declared themselves to be nuclear-free zones (Alger, 1990, p.511). In regard to global ecological issues, the International Council for Local Environmental

Initiatives, set up in 1990, eight years later connected over 240 members in 49 countries 'to achieve and monitor tangible improvements in global environmental conditions' (YIO, 1997; www.iclei.org).

Other transborder governance through substate institutions has developed at the level of provinces and federal states. In China, for example, the governments of Guangdong, Xinjiang, Shandong, and Yunnan Provinces have acquired sufficient autonomy in foreign policy from Beijing that some commentators have wondered whether the country can stay united in the longer term (Goodman and Segal, 1994; Segal, 1994). Tatarstan has similarly asserted its independence from Moscow in dealing with global capital. Meanwhile Andhra Pradesh has, in the interstate competition to attract transborder capital to India, negotiated its own structural adjustment loan with the World Bank in 1997, separately from the central government in New Delhi. In the USA, 41 federal states maintained a total of 151 offices in other countries by 1992. Two decades earlier only four of the fifty had had permanent representatives stationed abroad (Fry, 1995). In Europe, a Committee of the Regions established under the 1992 Maastricht Treaty has formalised direct consultation between suprastate institutions of the European Union and substate tiers of government in the member-states. The many other instances of transborder substate collaboration in Europe include the so-called 'Four Motors' network in operation since 1988 between Baden-Württemberg, Catalonia, Lombardy, and Rhône-Alpes.

To repeat a key qualification, however, this growth of substate initiatives in world politics does not signal the end of states as significant sites of regulation. Transstate activities of local and provincial governments signal the impracticability of sovereignty, but not the imminent demise of states. The European Commission's Director of Science and Technology almost certainly exaggerated upon declaring in 1994 that:

> ...in just a few decades, nation-states ... will no longer be so relevant. Instead, rich regions built around cities such as Osaka, San Francisco and the four motors of Europe will acquire effective power (quoted in Runyan, 1996, p. 242).

Regionalisation

Concurrently with the developments at substate levels just described, recent times of accelerated globalisation have also witnessed a proliferation of multilateral regional regulatory schemes. More than a hundred such arrangements have appeared during the past half-century, including two score in the 1990s. To be sure, some regional initiatives are paper agreements. However, others have promoted substantial growth of transstate laws and institutions, transborder production and markets, and transterritorial identities.

Regionalisation has transpired across the world. The most far-reaching instances have occurred in Europe, where fifty years of progressive widening and deepening of regional integration has culminated in the European Union (EU) of the 1990s. Other major regional governance projects have appeared in Central America (1960), East Africa (1967 - relaunched in 1991), South East Asia (1968), the Caribbean (1973), West Africa (1975 and 1994), Southern Africa (1980 and 1993), the Persian Gulf (1981), Central Asia (1984), South Asia (1985), Central Europe (1989), the Black Sea area (1993), North America (1994), and South America (1995).

Projecting current trends forward, some commentators have speculated that governance in the twenty-first century could involve a new multilateralism of regions in place of the old multilateralism of states (Hettne, 1997). Already transpacific Asia-Pacific Economic Cooperation (APEC) has been pursued since 1989. The EU and the Association of South East Asian Nations have held summit meetings in 1996 and 1998. Other proposals have suggested that coordination amongst the EU, the North American Free Trade Area, and East Asia could supplant and extend the present activities of the Group of Seven.

Like substate agencies with transborder relations, a number of regional institutions have also acquired a degree of autonomy from states in postsovereign world politics. It is of course quite true that states have instigated regional projects and remained the principal participants in them. However, in some ways states have also been constrained to 'go regional': e.g. in order adequately to respond to global capital, transborder ecological problems, etc. Moreover, regional governance has in a number of cases developed to a point that the regimes have authority over member states as well as vice versa. The EU in particular has gone beyond an interstate arrangement to suprastate governance as well, with its own Commission, Parliament and Court of Justice, together with some 20,000 regulatory measures generated to date.

Regionalisation can at first blush seem to contradict globalisation.

After all, regions are territorial units, and regionalisation entails a reconfiguration of territorial borders. In at least five other respects, however, regionalisation and globalisation have been complementary and interconnected. For one thing, technologies of global transportation and communication have made possible a tight coordination of activities on large regional scales. Second, regional common markets have provided convenience and economies of scale for the distribution and sale of global products. Third, regional customs unions have facilitated the development of transborder production processes. Fourth, regional governance arrangements have often proved to be an effective mechanism for the administration of global norms: e.g. in areas such as human rights, technical standardisation, etc. Fifth, the growth of transborder consciousness has prepared people intellectually for the construction of suprastate regional frameworks. Indeed, various observers have suggested that regional integration constitutes an intermediate stage towards full-scale globalism, that regional initiatives are building blocks rather than stumbling blocks for globalisation (Tober, 1993, p.101; Hettne, 1994).

On the other hand, in some respects regionalisation can also be connected to globalisation in a negative sense. Regionalism can be a reaction against globalism, as a macronationalist, neoprotectionist defence against the turbulence of globalising capitalism, the imposition of global cultures, and so on. Some EU controls on external trade and ever-tightening restrictions on immigration into the region well illustrate this reactive dynamic.

To be sure, globalisation has not been the only force propelling the proliferation and growth of suprastate regional projects in the late twentieth century. Local, national and region-specific circumstances have also determined where regionalisation has taken place, in what forms, at what speeds, and so on. However, it seems unlikely that so many regional schemes would have appeared in recent decades - and developed as far as they have – in the absence of the contemporary large-scale growth of supraterritorial relations.

Transworld Governance

Even the most cursory glance at contemporary world politics reveals that there is more to suprastate governance than regional arrangements. Institutions like the United Nations system, the World Trade Organisation

(WTO), the Bank for International Settlements (BIS), the Organisation for Economic Cooperation and Development (OECD) and more have regulatory authority that extends across regions. Although a few of these bodies were established in the second half of the nineteenth century and early twentieth century, the greatest proliferation of transworld institutions and legal instruments has occurred in recent decades.

Agencies like the United Nations Environment Programme (UNEP) and the International Monetary Fund (IMF) embody veritable global governance. For one thing, they formulate and administer rules through transworld networks of instantaneous communications. Moreover, many of these regulations apply to the world as a single place, irrespective of distances and borders. Indeed, supraterritorial governance institutions have (together with states and regional bodies) established many regulatory frameworks that have responded to and/or facilitated accelerated globalisation in the late twentieth century.

For example, much recently developed global regulation has served to promote the growth of transborder production and markets. The Uruguay Round of trade liberalisation (1986–94) and subsequent negotiations through the newly established WTO have greatly reduced state-imposed inhibitions to cross-border trade. WTO rules have applied to 90 percent of current account transactions, whereas the earlier General Agreement on Tariffs and Trade covered only 7 percent (ul Haq, 1995, p.5). Other negotiations of the 1990s through the WTO and the OECD have aimed to realise a 'free flow of investment' principle, under which states would normally have no right to deny entry to transborder capital. The World Intellectual Property Organisation (WIPO) and trade-related intellectual property rights (TRIPs) administered through the WTO have strengthened global protection of patents, marks, industrial designs, trade secrets and copyrights.

Other growth of public transworld governance has responded to large-scale globalisation of finance in the late twentieth century. For instance, the IMF has undertaken various initiatives since the early 1980s to restore stability to transborder financial flows. To the extent that the Fund has begun to act as a lender of last resort and to address questions concerning the supervision of global capital markets, it has become something of a suprastate central bank. Meanwhile, the BIS has since 1974 developed some general principles for the supervision of transworld banking (on matters such as capital adequacy, payment and settlement systems, etc.).

The acceleration of global ecological degradation has also prompted a significant expansion of transworld governance. Since the 1970s most of the principal global governance agencies have created special organs and programmes to address environmental issues. The many initiatives of this kind include the OECD Environment Committee (1970), the UN Commission on Sustainable Development (1993), the WTO Committee on Trade and Environment (1995), and so on. In addition, multiple global treaties have been concluded in respect of supraterritorial environmental problems such as transboundary air pollution (1979), depletion of stratospheric ozone (1985), and climate change (1992).

In respect of global communications, meanwhile, the International Telecommunication Union handbook of technical standards now runs to some 10,000 pages. The United Nations Educational, Scientific and Cultural Organisation (UNESCO) has promoted the global circulation of written, visual and auditory materials, including through new electronic media. For its part the OECD has since the 1980s taken important initiatives in the formulation of transborder principles to govern digital information technologies.

Finally, contemporary growth of transworld governance has gone some way to institutionalise growing global consciousness, including elements of transborder morality. For example, on the principle that armed conflict between (or even within) states is a matter of global concern, the United Nations has undertaken multiple peacekeeping operations since 1956 and several humanitarian interventions in the 1990s. In a further unprecedented initiative of suprastate conflict management, the UN provided assistance and supervision in some ninety elections between 1990 and 1994 (Findlay, 1995, p.49). The second half of the twentieth century has also witnessed unprecedented growth of suprastate regimes in the area of human rights. Several global conventions on human rights now have supervisory committees made up of experts who act in their personal capacity rather than as representatives of states. Meanwhile the International Labour Organisation has built up a transworld labour code encompassing (as of 1994) 174 Conventions and 181 Recommendations (Cunniah, 1995).

Thus the various aspects of globalisation have combined to encourage a rapid growth of transworld regulation in recent decades. This development does not signal the demise of the state - any more than does regionalisation or the expansion of transborder relations by substate authorities. However, the trend demonstrates - once again - the end of sovereign statehood. Although it is states that have created global governance institutions, they have done so at least partly in response to pressures of globalisation. Nor have states fully controlled the further actions and development of transworld authorities. For example, governments can do little to overturn the findings of a WTO Panel of Experts regarding violations of global trade rules. The IMF has since the late 1970s undertaken systematic authoritative surveillance of the macroeconomic policies of all member states. Client governments have limited bargaining room with the IMF and World Bank in respect of structural adjustment programmes. Hardly any government now invokes (as Myanmar did in 1996) the 'domestic jurisdiction' clause of the Charter to deny entry to a UN human rights mission. Even the sovereignty-obsessed government of China has endorsed the concept of UN peacekeeping and has since 1989 moreover participated in these activities (Kim, 1994, pp.49–53). The 1990s have seen a subtle move beyond humanitarian assistance (at the request of the afflicted state) to humanitarian intervention (at the behest of the world community).

However, whatever its precise relationship with the state, transworld regulation has become a significant part of contemporary governance. Of course, this growth has had many limitations in respect of neglected issues, double standards, limited enforcement, frequent poor coordination between agencies, pervasive understaffing, widespread underfunding, and fragile legitimacy in the eyes of many citizens. Yet these omissions and shortcomings do not negate the crucial point that postsovereign governance involves a notable transworld dimension.

In sum, then, globalisation has fostered a dispersal of regulatory competences, as the post-sovereign state has come to share tasks of governance with relatively autonomous substate offices on the one hand and with relatively autonomous suprastate agencies on the other. Daniel Bell has described the situation by arguing that 'the nation-state is becoming too small for the big problems of life, and too big for the small problems of life' (1987, pp.13–14). In the resulting multilayered public sector, governance tends to lack a clear centre of command and control in the manner previously provided by the sovereign state.

Notes

1. An earlier version of this argument has been published as (Scholte, 1997c).
2. I have discussed diverse conceptions of 'globalisation' in (Scholte, 1996a) and (Scholte, 1997a).
3. I have previously presented a number of points in this section in (Scholte, 1997a).

9 Regional Integration and Restrictive Constitutionalism in North America and Western Europe

ROBERT O'BRIEN

Introduction

This chapter develops some thoughts about the relationship between regional integration and constitutional democracy. It brings together analysis from the political economy of regional integration and a rudimentary understanding of constitutionalism. The primary question addressed is: 'What are the implications of regional integration in Western Europe and North America for constitutional democracy?' The answer is by no means clear cut, but several suggestions for further consideration and research will be advanced. The primary argument is that formalized regional integration leads to a shift in emphasis to the constitutional side of the constitutional - democracy balance. Moreover, this shift is consistent with a view of democracy as a restrictive rather than an enabling practice (Held, 1987). Regional integration is thus contributing to a form of restrictive constitutionalism which defends the rights of commercial interests and reduces the scope for citizen influence over economic and social policy.

The examples of North America and Western Europe will be used to illustrate the main argument and to demonstrate variations on the general theme. It will also be suggested that one of the explanations for this shift in constitutional and democratic orders can be found in the varying levels of political community within the regions. A late and incipient continental political community at the mass level facilitates the adoption of an order based upon restrictive principles. The degree to which this mass community might develop will help to determine the ultimate nature of regional constitutional orders and may shift the balance to a more inclusive form of democracy.

The chapter unfolds in six sections. Initially, the concept of constitutional democracy is outlined. The second section provides an overview of the NAFTA and EU regional constitutions. The third section relates how these developments have highlighted the shortcoming of national and regional democratic practice. The fourth section discusses the problem of the disjuncture between legal frameworks and political communities, focusing upon workers in North America. Section five broadens the chapter's horizons to the multilateral level to illustrate how similar problems are being created at the World Trade Organization. The final section revisits the argument concerning transnational communities and restrictive democracy.

Constitutional Democracy

The starting point for this investigation is the term 'constitutional democracy' and Walter F. Murphy's (1993) work on the relationship between constitutions and democracy. He claims that a constitutional democracy blends elements of two theories and practices - the constitutionalist and the democratic. The constitutional strategy is to protect individual rights through institutional restraints on the powers of government. In contrast, democratic theory is concerned with ensuring that government bends to the will of the people. Constitutional democracy is a hybrid system which attempts to both subject governmental policy to popular influence and restrict government power through institutional means such as division of powers, bills of rights and judicial review. Murphy's definitional exercise seems reasonable, but it contains three assumptions that will prove problematic later in the paper. The first assumption is that representative democracy is democracy. We shall see that an increasing number of citizens is questioning whether representative forms of democracy are sufficient to ensure democratic practice. The second assumption is that democracy should be thought of in national terms. Increasing concerns are being expressed about the relationship between democracy at the regional and multilateral levels. The third assumption is that constitutions are about protecting the rights of individuals or citizens. Regional constitutions are equally if not more concerned about protecting corporate or commercial rights. These assumptions reflect recent (post 1945) practice, but they may be poor guides to the future. The way in which regional integration challenges these assumptions is outlined below.

The Regional Frameworks

The 1980s saw the second wave of regional integration of the post-1945 era. Although the specific forms of regional integration arrangements varied, they were motivated by similar structural pressures (O'Brien, 1995). Firms sought economies of scale and access to larger markets while states were anxious to attract investment and assist nationally based production in gaining access to larger markets. A compact between state and corporate elites drove the attempt to liberalize markets and create new regulatory frameworks to guide their operation.

In the European case, regional integration dates back to the 1950s with the founding of the European Steel and Coal Community and the European Economic Community (EEC). The EEC was, as the British often referred to it, a common market. It attempted to liberalize trade amongst member countries and erected a common external barrier to the outside world. Such a project required a degree of supranationality to coordinate common policy and settle disputes. West European states interested in economic liberalization, but threatened by such institutionalized integration formed the European Free Trade Area (EFTA). However, by 1972 the British and Irish governments decided that the benefits of EEC membership outweighed those of the looser association.

The European Union, as it is now called, is a distinctive political arrangement which goes further in establishing regional authorities than any other regional agreement. Some have made the argument that it is even an example of integrative federalism. Similar to the United States and Switzerland, it is a 'constitutional order that strives at unity in diversity among previously independent or confederally related component entities. The goal of establishing an effective central government with direct operation on the people inside its sphere of powers is pursued under respect of the powers of the component entities . . .' (Lenaerts, 1990, p.206). Sovereignty is divided, but guaranteed by a common legal order and adjudicated by a supreme court. The Treaty of Rome serves as the European Community's constitution. European Community law takes precedence over national law, binding Member States (Sipkov, 1988). The European Court of Justice arbitrates disputes by delineating the specific, implied, and non-specific powers of the EC with regard to its members.

In contrast to the European Union, regional integration in North America has taken the form of free trade agreements. The 1988 Canada – United States Free Trade Agreement was soon followed by the North American Free Trade Agreement which brought Mexico into a trilateral relationship with Canada and the United States. This agreement eliminated tariffs between the countries and attempted to liberalize trade in a large number of economic sectors from agriculture to energy to services to investment. It did not require a common external tariff. The three countries are free to set their own tariffs towards outside countries. For example, the United States can continue to protect its domestic sugar industry by placing tariffs against Caribbean sugar, while Canadians import it duty free.

The NAFTA made no provisions for a Parliament, an activist bureaucracy such as the European Commission or a North American court. There were no commitments to developing common Research and Development policies, nor is there a continental regional development fund or a common agricultural policy. The greatest degree of continental institutional building was in the area of dispute settlement. A system of dispute settlement panels were created to mediate disputes concerning the various provisions of the agreement.

The Democracy Problem

The North American and Western European regional integration projects have highlighted the gap between elites and the public over regional integration and demonstrated the ability of representative democracy to insulate political and economic elites from the will of the people. In some cases it provided a clear illustration of the distorting power of financial interests in the democratic process and how a spectrum of political parties could adopt a common front against majority opinion. It is clear that in many of the states involved in NAFTA and the Maastricht Treaty, these agreements were implemented against the will of a majority of the population. The movement of elites to change basic rules of social organization against their constituents' wishes raises serious questions about the legitimacy of these institutions from a democratic perspective. Let us examine some of the more prominent examples.

In Canada, the Canada-United States Free Trade agreement was the subject of intensive dispute and was only settled through a general election. There are two aspects of Canada's entry into the Free Trade Agreement (FTA) relevant to this study. The first is that the government pursued such a policy despite the objections of many of its citizens. The Canadian electoral system ensured that the free trade agreement was ratified despite a majority of the citizens voting for anti-free trade parties (Caplan, Kirby and Segal, 1989). The second aspect was the prominent role that money played in swinging the final result. Transnational corporations spent over $5.2 million on Free Trade propaganda over two years and approximately $2.1 million during the election campaign itself.[1] Business intervention in the final weeks of the campaign proved essential to reversing the tide of anti-FTA opinion.

Several years later the United States' decision to proceed with a North American Free Trade Agreement caused a similar level of turmoil. The existence of an American Democratic deficit was illustrated during the NAFTA debate.[2] The ratification of NAFTA turned out to be an intense political struggle pitting labor, most environmental groups and the populist Ross Perot against big business. The class nature and division between transnational elites and less integrated groups was striking as President Clinton was able to draw upon the support of former Presidents, Nobel laureate economists and Fortune 500 business leaders. In order to get NAFTA through the House of Representatives, President Clinton abandoned his core constituency and relied upon otherwise hostile conservative Republicans to ensure NAFTA passage. The wealthier, more educated, more white collar a district was, the more likely the Representative voted in favor of NAFTA.[3] An incredible series of specific arrangements were agreed by the United States administration to swing votes including the promise to secure the extradition of an accused Mexican rapist and a fund raising appearance by the Vice-President to assist an indebted member of the House of Representatives.[4]

In most European countries the Maastricht Treaty caused a great deal of concern. The Treaty appeared to be a solid agreement between member states, but ran into trouble as some governments submitted it directly to the people for ratification. Despite the overwhelming support of political and economic elites backing the integration process large sections of national opinion, in some cases the majority, rejected their advice. On 2 June 1992 the Danes rejected the treaty by a margin of 50.7 percent to 49.3 percent.[5] It is significant that although 80 percent of Parliamentarians backed the treaty, less than 50 percent of the population agreed. In France, the referendum passed with the slimmest of majorities, 51 to 49 percent.[6] Luckily for the progress of the Treaty in Britain the establishment of the two major parties, Labour and the Conservatives, stood firm against calls for a referendum. Although arguments were phrased in terms of Parliament's role in decision-making the primary motivation probably had more to do with polling results such as the mid November (1992) poll suggesting that 43 percent of the British electorate were against the Treaty, only 26 percent in favor and 31 percent undecided.[7]

This brief review of the domestic politics surrounding regional integration in North America and Western Europe gives rise to a number of conclusions. The first is the existence of a persistent and wide gulf between elites and the majority of national populations concerning future plans for regional integration. The second is the striking division within the public resulting from class differences. This is accompanied by a scrambling of traditional political alignments as elements on the right and left oppose integration projects. The third is a lingering dissatisfaction with the political process which handles integration issues. The process favored elite and wealthy interests over public unease. Equally important, opposition to elite projects were restricted to frustrating existing projects rather than proposing more favorable alternatives.

It should come as no surprise that the political process is imperfect or that it favors some interests over others. What is particularly important about its operation in this case is that regional integration debates are not simply about specific issues, but are similar to constitutional amendments. They create new political structures and centres of authority above states. They change the political architecture and determine the rules for future political and economic interaction. Because of the sense that regional integration agreements are about long term decision-making structures, citizens desire to have a direct voice is greater than in other issues. However, whereas domestic constitutional amendments often require a 2/3rds majority of public or legislative support, regional integration projects have, at times, been implemented with less than 50 per cent public support. It is because of the constitution like qualities of regional arrangements that national democratic shortcomings take on more significance.

Not only did regional integration pose problems for domestic democracy there was disquiet about how the regional institutions themselves would operate. In the European Union there was a sustained critique concerning the functioning of the primary institutions - Council of Ministers, Parliament and Commission. It was alleged that while power had been transferred to these institutions, they were less accountable than national institutions (Williams, 1990). In North America, debate centred around whether institutions would be created and to what degree they would be subject to pressure from non-elite social forces.

A recent text comparing six constitutions suggested that 'Constitutions are codes of norms which aspire to regulate the allocation of powers, functions and duties among various agencies and officers of government, and to define the relationship between these and the public.' (Finer, Bogdanor and Rudden, 1995, p.1). Interestingly, this collection included the Treaty of European Union, even though Europe is not a state. Adopting a loose definition, one might suggest that a constitution is a set of principles setting out fundamental law which governs the conduct of relations within a community, state or organization. There is some sense that a constitution lies outside the regular legislative process, setting out the ground rules upon which activity takes place. Adopting a wide definition, it is possible to consider the process of regional integration in Western Europe and North America as evidence of a movement to a new constitutionalism. (Gill, 1992). This new constitutionalism is marked by two distinctive features. The first is that although it deals with economic issues, its implications also lie in the political field as it enshrines a particular form of democracy. The second feature is that the constitution-making takes place at a supra or international level, beyond the reach of large sections of the national polity.

The new constitutionalism attempts to institutionalize a classical liberal view of the role of government. This revival of classical liberalism, as seen in the Conservative governments of Britain and Canada and the Republican Party in the United States, tries to restore the economic foundation of liberalism -- namely restricting government intervention in the economy (Hayek, 1960; Friedmann, 1982). As John Gray (1986, p.79) explains 'Common to all contemporary classical liberalism is the goal of a form of limited government under the rule of law in which . . . the central economic powers of government - powers of taxation, spending and the issuance of money - are subject to rules no less stringent than those which protect the basic personal liberties.' The ultimate goal is to constitutionalize economic policies that are, or were, the subject of political debate.

Two national policy areas can serve as an example of this trend. The first is the move to institutionalize the role and duties of central banks. By making central banks independent of political authorities and requiring them to pursue a goal of zero inflation, the political debate about levels of growth and employment is marginalized, because the rules of the economic game state that in all cases control of inflation takes priority. Subsequent discussion must take place in this limiting context. A second example is the desire to have balanced budget requirements inserted into constitutions. These would stipulate that in any given time period governments would be forbidden from spending more than they collect in revenue. Such a measure would prevent governments from borrowing money to fund projects that might otherwise be deemed desirable through the political process.

In the balance between democracy and constitutionalism outlined by Murphy, this trend is a sharp turn to the constitutionalism side. It seeks to greatly reduce the number of policy levers available to governments. It is an attempt to restrict the legitimate purview of political action through constitutional means. Questions of resource distribution and equality are downgraded in favor of economic liberty. Not only is this an attempt to frame the rules under which politics is conducted, but it is also an attempt to redefine what politics is. It removes particular actions from the realm of the possible (e.g. screening of foreign investment, nationalization, subsidies).

An interesting aspect of this new constitutionalism is that while some attempts are being made to establish it at a national level, the focus of attention is at the inter or supranational level. The strategy is to create agreements between states which limit domestic policy initiatives. This is an effective strategy for two reasons. Firstly, as indicated in the previous section, it is easier to reach agreement with another state than to amend the domestic constitution. National parliaments tend to be dominated by the executive and foreign policy is relatively insulated from public pressure. Indeed, part of the key to success for such a strategy of constitutionalism is the ability to guide the required measures past mechanisms and institutions subject to popular pressure. In the US system this is the House of Representatives, in the European Union, it is the threat of a referendum. At the moment we see such a struggle being played out in Britain and Germany over the question of referenda and monetary union.

Secondly, even though these agreements take the form of international treaties or reform of domestic legislation to comply with such agreements, they hold out the promise of having constitutional durability. They are more likely to discipline future national legislation and less likely to be challenged than other elements of the legislative agenda. This can be attributed to the practice of bundling and the discipline of financial markets. Specific legislation and issues are bundled into a large agreement so that any attempt to change an individual element of the agreement risks unraveling the whole package. This raises the costs of any individual change so high, that it is unlikely to take place. The cost is raised further by the pressure of international financial markets. An effort to amend or withdraw from the whole package signals a weakening in the government's desire to remain committed to liberal principles. Such a weakening sends danger signals to the financial markets and risks capital flight.

These regional arrangements share one common factor with national constitutions -- their prime objective is to restrain the powers of government. The difference is that whereas national constitutions tend to focus on protecting civil liberties (and property rights) of the citizens, the regional arrangements are more interested in protecting private economic rights. The rights being protected are not those of the average citizen, but those of private enterprise and corporate interests. The freedoms protected are: the freedom to invest, freedom to move capital, freedom from government restrictions with regard to performance requirements, freedom from onerous government intervention in the market.

In the case of the FTA and NAFTA, it was clear that a primary purpose was to encase liberal reforms internationally so that future governments would have great difficulty in changing policy. Writing about the FTA, one of the Canadian negotiators noted that the most important, but least publicized objectives was to implement domestic reforms (Hart, 1989, p.73). Key provisions included chapter nine on energy and sixteen on investment. The energy provisions enshrined a continental energy market, preventing the return of nationalistic energy development. The investment section provided for compensation in the event of governments deciding to create public industries such as auto insurance. US economist Paul Krugman argued that the NAFTA had little to do with economic gain, but a great deal to do with locking in policies of a friendly Mexican government (Krugman, 1993, p.13).

The drive for a single market in Europe has been accompanied by a host of measures eliminating government barriers to economic activity. One of the most interesting developments has been the invigoration of competition policy to restrict state expenditure. This has primarily taken place in the form of restriction on the subsidies that member states can provide to specific industries. The Treaty based commitment dating from the 1950s was largely unused until the single market initiative generated the political will for increased enforcement. This enforcement has led to a shift in national policy instruments and a change in the understanding of legitimate government intervention in the economy (O'Brien, 1997).

Just as national constitutions can be compared with regard to role of the judiciary, division of powers, and protection of rights, so can the institutional arrangements in the EU and NAFTA. The EU arrangement is far more elaborate, with a strong court and attention to rights that fall outside of a strictly liberal constitutional view (e.g. social chapter). Its similarity to domestic constitutions has been noted in the literature. The most notable quality is its supranational element which allows a court to enforce law that has made its way through the European Union legal process.

NAFTA less clearly resembles a national constitution, as there is a limited role for transnational judicial review, few common rules, and an effort to restrict jurisdiction to purely economic matters. There are no institutions between which power is divided as in the European case. The legislative oversight provided for in the Agreement often is meant only to ensure that governments live up to the spirit of their national legislation. The international, as opposed to supranational, elements of the North American arrangements are clear. These traits reflect the more general problem of creating any international regulatory framework or constitution which binds the United States. Nevertheless, for a wide range of economic activity, the North American Free Trade Agreement may now serve as a constitution and appeals can be lodged to the trilateral framework if particular parties or governments feel their economic rights have been violated.

The Community Problem

This chapter has argued that regional integration is taking on the form of a constitutional arrangement which is meant to safeguard the interests of the regions largest firms and is relatively less concerned with social regulation. This is more pronounced in North America than in Western Europe. It is also argued that this effort at new constitutionalism has highlighted the degree to which domestic and regional political structures lack broad support and democratic credentials. Again the difficulties are more pronounced on the western side of the Atlantic.

One of the main difficulties is that a form of political community which might balance the interests of transnational business has not yet developed in either region. Whereas capitalist interests have been gradually internationalizing since the establishment of postwar Keynsian welfare states (Sklair, 1997) other elements have been slower to respond. Elements of civil society such as social welfare and labor groups have tended to remain focused upon the local and national level. This is not surprising as the creation of regional civil society on a mass level is an immense task (Drainville, 1997). However, the labor movement is one area where clear changes can be seen as a North American labor entity seems to be slowly taking shape.

Women's groups and women's labor organizations have been at the forefront of creating a new North American community. Gabriel and Macdonald (1995) have outlined how NAFTA has led to increasing contact between women's organizations in Canada and Mexico. Although extensive differences arise from different social conditions, attempts are being made to develop strategies that will benefit women in both countries. This grass roots activity is starting to bring together groups of women who formerly had no contact. An interesting example both of the internationalization and the cooperation between social movements is the Maquila Solidarity Network. It has been established to support vulnerable workers in free trade zones such as the Mexican Maquiladora border regions with the United States and in Central America.[8] With the onset of NAFTA, the organization is concerned with Mexican working conditions as a whole. It brings together Solidarity Works, a Canadian labor education group with a continental women's network, Mujer a Mujer (Woman to Woman). Since the vast majority of workers in the Maquilas are women, the project is concerned both with women's and workers' issues in general and the plight of women workers in particular. The Network attempts to distribute information, lobby corporations and governments and bring community activists together. A key element of this project is to demonstrate the common interests between Canadian and Mexican women and workers.

Canadian labor unions have also been increasingly active in internationalizing their activity. Indeed, North American issues are increasingly seen as domestic issues by the labor movement. Whereas Canadian unions' previous internationalism may have been practiced at a distance, today's 'international' activity is seen to be immediately relevant to national workers. An interesting organizational point is that within the Canadian Labour Congress, the primary researcher on NAFTA works in the Canadian section rather than the international office. The CLC has outlined a major priority as the establishment of continental workers rights and a social charter for North Americans.[9] To this end it has been trying to influence discussions about any arrangements which might enable Chile to join NAFTA.

There are also signs that the US labor movement has undergone significant transformation and is undertaking an new form of internationalism. In the US context, Rupert (1995) has argued that the NAFTA debate may be a watershed in organized labor's acceptance of the dominant brand of liberalism. Not only did labor break with US corporations over the issue of linking workers rights to regional trade agreements, but it also openly opposed a Democratic Party leadership and a sitting Democratic President. A second notable change in the policies of organized labor was the attempt to work with environmental and consumer groups to forge a common position on this element of economic policy. Finally, the AFL-CIO was forced to cultivate relations with the emerging independent Mexican unions rather than rely on the Mexican government sponsored CMT union. The CMT proved adequate for US workers' interest in the Cold War when the fight was against Communism, but allies in the fight against transnational exploitation would have to be found in unions controlled by their members.

Noticeable changes are also taking place in the relationship between US and Mexican labor organizations. In Mexico, the government's neoliberal reforms have undercut its traditional labor base and opened the door to independent labor organizations. While the challenges are great, there is some indication that new labor movements are more ready to work in transnational North American alliances (Cook, 1995). As mentioned earlier, large parts of the US labor movement have been shifted out of their national complacency by NAFTA. Multinationals are creating a continental working class and labor is beginning to respond (Moody, 1995). One prominent example is the strategic alliance between the United Electrical, Radio & Machine Workers of America (UE) and the Mexican Authentic Labor Front (FAT). UE and FAT have agreed to target the same firms in Mexico and the US with the northern union providing additional financing for Mexican organizing (Alexander and Gilmore, 1994). While one might object that this is little more than national cooperation, it marks a considerable shift from the postwar nationalist position typical of US labor (Herod, 1997).

The activity outlined above is evidence of a change in political activity in some sections of the North American community. It reveals increasing cooperation between social movements and between movements from each country. It signals the possible expansion of the notion of political community past national boundaries. It is particularly revealing that the left and right in North America are starting to change their views on the institutionalization of North American agreement. Environmental and labor groups which initially opposed continental institutions as a dilution of national sovereignty now push for institutions to enforce labor and environmental standards. Business organizations so eager to establish legal frameworks for expanded economic activity now struggle to prevent the growth of institutions which might be able to regulate their activity on a continental basis. They are resisting the attempt at neoliberal constitutionalism.

It should be remembered, however, that these social movements still remain on the margins of political power, vastly under funded and under resourced in comparison to their political and economic opponents. They have been engaged in a frantic attempt to catch up with transnational business which has had the privilege of designing the existing North American integration project. The social movements have intensified cooperation, but must still bridge differences emerging from divergent class positions, gender roles and linguistic backgrounds. Their importance lies in their implications for future political activity and institution building rather than in their accomplishments to date. At the most optimistic one could claim that the notion of political community may be in the process of redefinition, as the activity of social movements catches up with the international business civilization and globalization from below transforms traditional political categories and alliances.

The Multilateral Level

The regional issue serves as a bridge between the national and international or global democracy discussions. It has had the dual effect of highlighting dissatisfaction and opening up consideration of new democratic arrangements. Similar to the international level it serves as an illustration of the global economic pressures forcing a restructuring of economic and political relationships in the attempt to maintain competitiveness. It emphasizes many of the shortcomings of national representative democracy as citizens views are brushed aside. This feeds a sense that popular control is not achieved through existing institutions and that it is time to reconsider democracy's original meaning and new forms of practice. Yet, unlike the larger world international arena, the regional area offers opportunities to rebuild democratic mechanisms within a limited geographic space. Reforms impossible at an international level because of size, resource or cultural diversity may be feasible on a more limited regional scale.

The movement to regional integration in North America and Western Europe in the last decade and a half has sparked a reconsideration of the nature of democracy in the relevant states. This review is part of a broader questioning of democratic theory and practice at a number of levels - global, regional and national. A number of commentators have highlighted the dissatisfaction in national liberal democracies. For example, Charles Maier (1994) recently identified a moral crisis in Western democracies. A different interpretation has been offered by Ikenberry (1995) who has suggested that the Western malaise is due to the inability of states to fulfil citizen expectations in a time of slow economic growth and global competition. At a superficial level one could attribute the morass to weak leadership in the face of difficult conditions. For example, the international news magazine *Time* diagnosed the general disquiet by concentrating on the particular attributes of leaders.[10]

Other investigations have pointed to the need to rethink national theories of democracy in the face of globalization. David Held, has pointed to the existence of international organizations, international law, large military powers and a world economy as evidence that the international now impinges upon national democratic practice.[11] Democracy cannot function solely on a national basis and must be reconstituted on an international level. He labels his democratic approach as 'Cosmopolitan' and stresses the need to build democratic international institutions (Held, 1993, pp.13-52).[12] Other scholars, such as R.B.J. Walker (1993, pp.141-158), have argued that these postmodern times violate traditional understandings of sovereignty and democracy to such an extent that new forms of democracy are required. The dilemma is that structures of power and issues of concern are firmly rooted in a global context, but participation, representation and legitimacy are fixed at the state level (Connoly, 1991). Rather than stressing the rebuilding of state like institutions at an international level, new social movements are put forward as the hope for global democratic practice. One of the primary tasks of such movements and the way in which they might contribute to increasing democracy is by creating a global political community which has a sense of common problems (Thiele, 1993; Brecher, Childs and Culter, 1993).

Regional Constitutions as Restrictive Democracy

After examining the case closely we are left with the continuation of an old debate in a new environment. The old debate concerns the preferred version of democracy - restrictive (protective) or developmental. One strain of the democratic tradition, sometimes referred to as protective democracy, stresses traditional liberal concerns such as the protection against arbitrary state power through the rule of law and a system of representative government. The modern strain of such thought is the neoliberal program as espoused by Hayek (1960), Nozick (1974) and their political advocates. David Held has characterized this recent model as 'legal democracy,' (Held, 1987, pp.245-54) but the description 'restrictive democracy' may be more appropriate as it captures the normative thrust of limiting the powers of government and the extent of mass participation and influence. In the balancing of values the stress is very much on the liberal at the expense of the democratic in liberal democracy. A minimal state that grants protection to private property and civil liberties is the utopia envisaged by such theorists. In the context of our discussion, this strain is represented by those forces seeking to build continental liberal economic zones with the minimum of state or regional regulation. It is an attempt to encase restrictive democracy in a regional constitutional framework.

The second strand is sometimes called 'developmental democracy' because it views democratic participation as being of value for its positive contribution to people's lives and natures (Macpherson, 1976, pp.44-76; Held, 1987, pp.72-104). It is justified on the basis of assisting in the developmental possibilities of its citizens. The developmental tradition has stressed the desirability both of having a more active participation by citizens in the democratic process and ensuring that citizens have the resources enabling equal participation. In recent decades the demand has been for a form of participatory democracy in which economic institutions would be democratized and political institutions would be more susceptible to control by the mass of the population (Pateman 1989; Macpherson 1976). Feminist critiques of liberal democracy have consistently argued that its promise is undermined by the unequal resources of people and the subordinate position of women in particular (Wollstonecraft 1792/1982; Pateman 1983). The developmental tradition is represented by the social movements in North America, the attempts at securing a Social Charter in Western Europe and efforts to build a European wide democracy. Its aim is to broaden restrictive constitutions to encompass or facilitate the development of social rights.

This struggle over the content of constitutions and democracy may be familiar, but it is taking place in a new and more complicated environment. Rather than being confined to the state, it is also being waged at the regional and world or global level. There is an attempt to democratize national states, regional institutions and global organizations. This is a complicated task because the boundaries of the political community are similarly fluctuating. In some cases it may be confined to those within a state, in others it may be the inhabitants of a region, while in other instances it may extend world-wide to all those affected by the functioning of particular institutions. This chapter has highlighted organized labor's attempt to forge a new North American community. However, this is but one of a variety of responses and institutions developed in the struggle to define democratic practice. While North America and Western Europe both face regional democratic issues, the specific policies and institutions they develop are different. Variations in the regions such as the extent of institutionalization, size of states, and dominant political forces suggests different political and economic arrangements.

Whereas five years ago the possibility of increased regional integration contributing to increased developmental democratic practice seemed unlikely, it now appears that new opportunities have been created. The slowing of the momentum of integration in the EU and the need for European elites to recruit the public to their cause offers hope for institutional reform. The increased politicization of trade issues in North America and the formation of extensive grass roots coalitions to counter the business agenda indicates that democratic mechanisms and democratizing policies will continue to be on the agenda.

Conclusion

This chapter argued that economic regionalization and the institutions created to manage that process are complicating our stable notions of constitutional democracy as embodied in the opening use of Murphy. More specifically, we can point to three unsettling developments. Firstly, the adequacy of representative democracy has been called into question. The democratic content of societies in North America and Western Europe is under scrutiny as the gap between elites and the public seems to be widening. This may be contributing to the pressure for extra-parliamentary politics in addition to, or as a substitute for, traditional political institutions (parties, parliaments). Although there are a number of causes, it appears that representative democracy is under pressure to democratize.

Secondly, it is no longer sufficient to think only in terms of national constitutions. It is time to acknowledge a layering of constitutional restraints upon government policy. The study of national constitutions could be supplemented or even challenged by further consideration of international or supranational constitutions and their interaction with national structures. The challenge here is two-fold. The first challenge is to consider the relationship between the national and international constitutions and the second is to ponder the implications of a new restrictive constitutionalism for our understanding of politics itself. Restrictive constituionalism is in the process of narrowing the scope of issues located in the political realm.

Thirdly, the formation of emerging political communities in response to regional integration suggests that the balance between restrictive and enabling forms of democracy is not yet fixed. The struggle continues over whether constitutionalism will increasingly be synonymous with corporate interest and restrictive democracy or whether there is room for an enabling form of constitutionalism at the regional level. Will it be possible for emerging political communities such as the labor movement to push for arrangements which facilitate the pursuit of social rights? The ineffectiveness of the NAFTA side accord on labor rights suggests that it will be a difficult task. On the optimistic side one can point to the fact the battle has only recently begun.

Notes

1. 'Four Giants Disclose Pro-Free-Trade Donations', *Toronto Star*, 11 April 1989.
2. Although this paper stresses the links between regional integration and democratic shortfalls, discussion of the American democratic deficit can, and often does, proceed without reference to NAFTA or the global economy. For an example see Durant (1995).
3. See 'Clinton Forms New Coalition to Win NAFTA's Approval', *Congressional Quarterly Weekly*, 20 November 1993, pp. 3181-3185.
4. Last minute horsetrading needed to get NAFTA through the House is catalogued in 'NAFTA's Bizarre Bazaar', Public Citizen, Washington, DC:, 1993.
5. *The Independent on Sunday*, 7 June 1992. *The Independent*, 18 and 20 June 1992.
6. *Le Monde*, 22 September 1992.
7. *The Independent*, 14 November 1992.
8. 'Solidarity with Maquila Workers', Maquila Solidarity Network, Toronto.
9. 'CLC Views on NAFTA and Its Expansion in the Hemisphere', Policy Statement, Ottawa, May 1995.
10. 'What's Happened to Leadership?' *Time*, 12 July 1993.
11. Dahl (1994) has also recently turned his attention to the difficulties of internationalization for democracy. For much of the world outside of the major Western powers the international imposing upon domestic political arrangements is not new. The history of colonialism is one example. What may be new is that the strongest states and their citizens are also encountering limits to domestic democracy.
12. Gester (1992) suggests how the IMF could be made more democratic.

10 Constitutionalism as a Form of Conflict Resolution

ROBERT VIPOND

Introduction

In the vast literature on international relations, there is a special place reserved for those volumes that seek to understand the relationship between human rights and interstate conflict. Even the non-expert will instantly recognise the possibilities. The violation of human rights can sometimes be the proximate cause of international tension and conflict (as, for instance, in international reaction to the suppression of dissent in Tiananmen Square). The violation of human rights can often be the by-product of international conflict (as in the former Yugoslavia and Rwanda). And, more hopefully, it is possible that a renewed recognition of the importance of human rights may follow from international conflict (the formulation of the United Nations' Universal Declaration of Human Rights, enacted in response to the horrors of the Second World War, is here the more celebrated example).

Now, what characterises much of the impressive work in the area of conflict resolution and human rights is the attempt to identify a set of universal norms or practices that can be applied, deductively as it were, to specific politico/military and geographic contexts. This is, after all, why it is called the *Universal* Declaration of Human Rights. And, as Alan Cairns notes in his chapter in this volume, there is at least some evidence to suggest that the demonstration effect has worked as intended. In Canada, for instance, it is clear that the example established by the UN Declaration helped mobilise support for a domestic charter of rights just as, in the United States, the promulgation of international norms of justice was an important trigger for the civil rights movement. Indeed, as Vivien Hart argues in her essay, constitutions have become 'badges of legitimacy for regimes seeking acceptance from their own citizens and in the eyes of the world'; and within these constitutions, 'rights are ubiquitous'.

But this pattern hardly seems to exhaust the possibilities. I begin, therefore, with something of a thought experiment: What would happen if we were to begin where most of the literature on international norms and human rights ends, that is with the domestic intersection between rights and conflict? What, in other words, if we were to begin to think about the relation between conflict and human rights inductively, that is from an account of domestic constitutional politics and law rather than deductively, from a set of universal norms mediated by international agencies and law? And what if we were to systematise and extend the lessons of indigenous constitutional practice rather than build on the apparatus already established by international law? The argument I want to advance here, based in part on the evidence provided by the chapters in this volume, is that the work of using domestic constitutionalism to create a theory of international conflict resolution has already begun. My goal is to categorise and assess several of the examples that have been discussed here in order to create a typology of constitutional strategies for resolving conflict.

In the interests of truth in advertising, however, allow me to insert a disclaimer at the outset. The typology developed here is intended to be suggestive, not exhaustive. I do not want for a minute to claim that the configuration I am about to present is definitive. I do hope, however, that it will provide some evidence for those interested in the large question of conflict resolution to realise that, though they have been trained in different academic disciplines and sub-disciplines, there exists common ground to build upon.

Constitutional Stigmatisation

Alan Cairns' idea of 'constitutional stigmatisation' is so striking because it would appear at first blush to pose an oxymoron. Yet, as he shows in detail, using the law to codify, systematise and deepen exclusion from the usual benefits of citizenship is far more common than most constitutionalists will care to acknowledge. Actually, the news is perhaps even worse than Cairns reports, for if one pursues the history of constitutional stigmatisation a step further, one stumbles upon another apparent oxymoron - constitutional violence. The fact is that the history of constitutional stigmatisation has typically been interwoven with patterns of conflict and violence; stigmatisation and violence are, indeed, constitutional twins.

If one extrapolates from Cairns' account of constitutional stigmatisation, three basic patterns of constitutional violence emerge. There is, first, the case in which constitutional stigmatisation occurs as a direct consequence of violence. In the case of European imperialism, for instance, the stigmatisation of which Cairns speaks followed, often directly, from military victory or conquest. The imperial mentality assumed the cultural and/or racial superiority of the imperial overlord and the concomitant inferiority of the subject people, the evidence for which was said to consist precisely in the fact that the one had defeated the other militarily. And while, as Cairns emphasises, the imperial mentality was often internalised psychologically in a complex form of behavioural deference that replaced muskets with manners, it is important to remember that the legacy of violence and the promise of renewed violence was never too far from the surface. In this sense, constitutional stigmatisation was not simply an outgrowth of an imperial mentality; it was, more bluntly, the institutionalisation of imperial military policy.

Note, though, that constitutional stigmatisation can also occur as an attempt to reverse, rather than solidify, the effects of military action. This is what is so interesting about the example of the American South after the Civil War. Having lost the Civil War on the battlefields, most southern legislatures attempted to reverse that military defeat through a sort of constitutional counter-attack. Thus, the rapid and breathtakingly successful growth of Jim Crow laws throughout the South recreated the very sort of constitutional stigmatisation that the abolition of slavery and the adoption of the 13th, 14th and 15th Amendments were intended to overcome. In the memorable words of US Supreme Court Justice Harlan who dissented from the majority view that Jim Crow laws were actually consistent with the Constitution, legally mandated racial separation was 'a badge of inferiority' (*Plessy v. Ferguson*, 1896). And here again, the connection between constitutional stigmatisation and constitutional violence was blunt and very real. Quoting C. Vann Woodward, Cairns notes that Jim Crow laws 'gave free rein and the majesty of the law to mass aggressions that might otherwise have been curbed, blunted or deflected.'

This leads to the second major connection between constitutional stigmatisation and constitutional violence. The modern Anglo-American understanding of Constitutionalism is almost synonymous with the idea of limited government. Although there are many disagreements about what powers need to be limited and by whom, the idea that unrestricted, arbitrary or untrammelled state power is fundamentally inconsistent with human liberty is pretty much bedrock. What is so striking about Cairns' account, therefore, and what deepens the oxymoronic quality of the term constitutional stigmatisation, is the realisation that this sort of codified exclusion not only follows from violence, it legitimises it. Indeed, one of the things that unites Cairns' five cases is that all of them, to one extent or another, not only tolerated but actually legitimated violence. This is clear, as the example of lynchings suggests, in the American example. It was true, although widely variable in practice, in the imperial constitution as well. The shocking history of the way in which Indian residential schools in Canada tolerated the physical and sexual abuse of children they were supposed to be educating is now just coming to light. The very need to create something called the Truth and Reconciliation Commission in South Africa speaks to the legacy of violence left by apartheid. And most horrible of all, the legalised annihilation of Jews by the Third Reich demonstrates how one of the central functions of a constitution - defining or ordering the rights and responsibilities of citizenship - can actually become the vehicle of genocide.

Finally, it is clear from Cairns' account that the process of constitutional stigmatisation can, at least sometimes and under certain conditions, provoke a backlash on the part of those most deeply injured by the stigmatisation. The process of African decolonisation, for instance, while not uniformly violent, had moments of significant conflict. The American Revolution was fought against the background of a 'train of abuses', many of which stemmed from the basic grievance that Americans were in some sense second-class citizens, that is that they did not enjoy the basic rights enjoyed by other 'Englishmen'. Several of the most important and violent confrontations between Canada's aboriginal peoples and the Canadian state, most notably the Riel Rebellion, can really only be understood in the context of constitutional stigmatisation. And it is easy to see how one might interpret the culture of violence in present-day South Africa as one strand in the enduring legacy of apartheid.

Let me state my point directly: One might argue that constitutional stigmatisation is one way, favoured by some elites, to 'resolve' conflict in the sense of solidifying, institutionalising, codifying, or reversing the results of (military) conflict. In this sense, the story of constitutional stigmatisation is the story of how victors have defined by law who belongs and who does not belong to a given community in a way that integrates the lessons of military conquest without having constantly to resort to military means to maintain their (victorious) superiority.

Quite apart from any moral or philosophic objections one might have to these forms of stigmatisation, Cairns' account is particularly useful because it demonstrates that, judged as a political strategy, constitutional stigmatisation fails on its own terms because it ultimately undermines itself. Constitutional stigmatisation may solidify the results of military conquest. But it appears no less likely that constitutional stigmatisation may be used to reverse the effects of conflict, legitimise constitutional violence and, ultimately, incite opposition and rebellion against the very stigmas that the strategy is meant to entrench. In this sense, constitutional stigmatisation appears irrational. If constitutional stigmatisation looks like an oxymoron and sounds like an oxymoron, perhaps it really is just that.

The American Constitutional Model

At first glance, it may seem odd to think of the American Constitution as a vehicle for resolving conflict but, in fact, it is impossible to understand the framing of the US Constitution apart from this strategy. Not only was the nation forged through a conflict, a War of Independence, in which constitutional issues powerfully propelled both sides; more importantly, and much to the surprise of many Americans, victory over the British did not put an end to conflict. Indeed, as Gordon Wood and others have argued, the intra-American conflicts that dominated the 1780s - ranging from border wars to taxpayer revolts - made thoughtful Americans realise that the sources of conflict were as much internal as external, as much connected to domestic causes as foreign powers (Wood, 1969). If the Declaration of Independence was the product of the 'long train of abuses' visited by British rule, the need to create a constitution a decade later was produced, in the words of James Madison, by the 'unsteadiness and injustice, with which a factious spirit has tainted *our* public administration' (Madison *et al*, 1982, 43; emphasis added).

In Madison's account, 'the various and unequal distribution of property' (Madison *et al*, 1982, 44) was the most common source of factional violence. His solution to the problem of faction - to liberate commerce and extend the political boundaries of the Union in a way that would defy any simple and enduring identification between property and political power - is, of course, well known. It is sometimes forgotten, however, that Madison's factions argument was based on an analogy to religious factionalism, and here, I think, one approaches the essence of the American constitutional experiment (Madison *et al*, 1982, 264). In a nutshell, the American approach to religion encompasses two fundamental and related principles. One is religious liberty, protected constitutionally as the individual's right to the free exercise of religion. The other is the principle, again constitutionally enshrined, that prohibits the establishment of religion, that is the use of state power to privilege one religion at the expense of another or others. Where Europe had been riven by religious wars and religious persecution, the Americans constructed an alternative approach to religion that was built around the fundamental ideas of constitutionally protected individual rights and limited, neutral government. The American approach to religion meant to limit religious conflict by in effect privatising it, by setting down the basic principle that religious belief should not be a criterion or test by which to confer a benefit or impose a burden. So far as the Constitution is concerned, there is neither Protestant nor Catholic nor atheist - there are only rights-bearing individuals. What unites Americans, by this account, is not therefore their religious beliefs, their ethnic origins nor their class status. Indeed, to a very large extent, the goal is to make those characteristics constitutionally meaningless. What unites them is their dedication to what Michael Ignatieff calls the ideal of the 'civic nation'- to the idea that they are 'a community of equal, rights-bearing citizens, united in patriotic attachment to a shared set of political practices and values' (Ignatieff, 1993, 7-8). In the language of Seymour Martin Lipset, this is the 'American Creed', and it stands as a powerful experiment in using constitutions as a means of resolving or forestalling conflict (Lipset, 1996).

Over the years, this model of liberal constitutionalism has become the industry standard as it were, and numerous attempts have been made to export and adapt the American model of individual rights-based politics throughout the world. A decade or two ago, conferences such as the one that gave birth to this volume almost certainly would have used the American model as an implicit or explicit guide to constitutional norms, especially if the analytic lens were trained on other Anglo-American democracies. The American model travels less well now, even though there has been something of a renaissance in comparative constitutional studies. The Sussex-Toronto conference demonstrated clearly that there is enormous and growing interest in the sub-discipline of comparative constitutionalism. Yet, at the conference, the American model was very much in the background - when it was present at all.

There are, I think, two basic reasons for this eclipse. As Bernard Yack has noted, one problem with idealising the American constitutional model in this way is that 'it all seems a little too good to be true, a little too close to what we would believe about the world' (Yack, 1996, 195). The history of slavery and racism in the US, to state the obvious, throws into question the extent to which the liberal model of rights has actually dominated American politics. Of course, one might reply, as many have, that slavery is the great exception to American liberalism, the great 'dilemma' as Myrdal put it, yet maintain one's optimism that liberal values will ultimately prevail - even in matters of race. But the problem actually goes deeper than this. In a magisterial new study, Rogers Smith argues that, in fact, racism was just one of a series of world views that have informed American political and debate throughout its history (Smith, 1998). By Smith's reading, it is not that the dominant idea of liberalism has from time to time been challenged by illiberal ideologies. Rather, his argument is that one must read American political history as a series of contests among competing ideologies in which none - liberalism included - is clearly dominant and overmatched.

Along the same lines, Will Kymlicka argues that, far from living up to the ideal of neutrality, American law has frequently grafted cultural considerations onto its liberal jurisprudence of individual rights. To those Americans who argue that the idea of 'multicultural citizenship' simply cannot be applied to the United States, Kymlicka shows in detail just how far American law has travelled from the purely liberal foundation of a neutral state protecting uncluttered individual rights (Kymlicka, 1995). And, as Yack argues, even to talk about America as the civic nation *par excellence* or to engage the language of American exceptionalism is already to accept the idea that the United States 'comes loaded with inherited cultural baggage' since the point of such arguments is that liberalism grew in the United States in a way that it could not, or at least did not, elsewhere (Yack, 1996, p. 196).

This leads to the second reason why the American constitutional model these days seems to travel less well than it used to. Here the argument is not so much that individual rights-based constitutionalism has failed to live up to its billing and so suffers from the charge that rights-based constitutionalism is unrealistic, inconsistent or hypocritical. The argument, rather, is that American constitutionalism has succeeded all too well at implanting the idea of individual rights applied neutrally or impartially but that the very ideal leaves something to be desired. This is really the point of departure for Melissa Williams and the literature on which she draws. As Williams suggests, what lies at the heart of most standard accounts of liberal justice in the United States is the notion of difference-blindness. The idea that considerations of social difference should be excluded from decision-making applies with equal force to the work of theorists like John Rawls and Ronald Dworkin who want to define a liberal conception of justice and to the work of constitutional courts that bear the responsibility of applying them. Thus, in its approach to cases dealing with patterns of racial discrimination in education, the US Supreme Court early on concluded that it had authority to strike down statutes that violated, as a matter of law, the principle of neutrality by discriminating *de jure* between black and white children. At the same time, however, it concluded that it had no power to address claims of racially-based inequality in education as long as the law was neutral on its face, arguing that in such cases, the patterns of unequal education were merely *de facto* in nature and hence beyond constitutional remedy.

Such devotion to uniformity and neutrality has a number of advantages, not the least being that it has helped courts in the US define a role for themselves that does not overwhelm either their institutional capacity or their legitimacy. But from another perspective, this approach is deeply problematic. As Williams points out, 'by defining justice through a process of reasoning which totally abstracts from social particularity, liberals have inadvertently built bias in their principles of justice themselves'. Liberal justice may, in other words, live up to its ideal of applying individual rights neutrally, but can we call it justice when under this definition blacks are significantly under-represented in legislatures and well-paying jobs, significantly over-represented in prisons and on death row, and where in many parts of the country, public education remains largely segregated as a matter of fact? If one of the tests of constitutionalism is the extent to which it preempts, resolves and heals the scars created by conflict, then it is not so clear that the American model is the runaway preferred choice. As Richard Iton shows very well in his essay in this volume, the US remains a deeply divided society, whether in spite of or because of its deep commitment to a difference-blind conception of justice and constitutionalism.

The Culturalised Constitution

The alternative to the difference-blind constitution represented by the American model is, of course, in some sense to read cultural particularity into the constitution. I say 'in some sense' because there are several quite different approaches available. Let me mention three. First, there is what Canadians tend to call the 'citizen plus' model of constitutionalism in which cultural particularity achieves constitutional status which grafts cultural recognition onto a liberal constitutional foundation. Thus, while Canada's *Charter of Rights* (1982) is essentially a liberal document directed to the identification and exposition of fundamental freedoms that are enjoyed by every citizen, the Charter also includes a clause which states explicitly that it 'shall be interpreted in a manner consistent with the preservation and enhancement of the multicultural heritage of Canadians' (Canada, 1982, sec. 27). Similarly, while the Charter directs that 'everyone' should enjoy 'freedom of conscience and religion', the provision of public funds for denominational schools is selectively, not universally, applied so as to keep a bargain made in the original Confederation settlement of 1867. There is no need here to multiply the examples. The point simply is that the Canadian Constitution, like many others, grants legal recognition to cultural difference even while maintaining its liberal core. If in the US there is only one uniform category of citizenship, it might be said that the Canadian *Charter* creates a regime of 'citizens plus'.

Whether such a regime mitigates conflict or feeds it is, of course, hotly debated in Canada. Nowhere is this more evident than in the ongoing debate over Quebec's constitutional status in (or out of) Canada. In response to the growth of Quebec nationalism, several national governments and political parties have attempted to find a way to recognise Quebec's cultural distinctiveness. For the most part, this has been quite explicitly a strategy of reconciliation in which (largely) English-Canadian political elites have attempted to staunch the growing popularity of the sovereignty movement within Quebec by providing some form of constitutional recognition that would make Quebeckers feel as if they were fully accepted within the Canadian Confederation. The various attempts that have been made, however, have all had to confront the problem that any constitutional recognition of Quebec's distinctiveness would seem to violate the core liberal presumption that equality does not permit a form of constitutional favouritism. And that, as it turns out, has proven to be a powerful rallying point (Vipond, 1995). However one assigns the blame in this case, what does seem clear is that attempting to recognise cultural particularity through what Peter Russell calls 'mega-constitutionalism' is a high risk strategy that threatens, if unsuccessful, to produce the very conflict it is meant to banish (Russell, 1992).

As the name suggests, the 'citizen plus' constitution remains very much anchored to the principles of liberal individualism. This is both its great strength and its most signal weakness. A more wholesale approach to culturalising the constitution follows from the work on consociational democracy, pioneered and authoritatively elaborated by Arend Lijphart. Although there are numerous variants on the consociational model, the basic principle is to develop constitutional and institutional mechanisms that explicitly represent cultural communities in the hopes that one can both recognise the importance of cultural autonomy and provide an institutional forum for working together in a way that will preempt conflict.

As Damian O'Leary argues in his essay in this volume, almost every organised effort to rethink and resolve the Irish problem has turned to some form of consociationalism for inspiration. The most recent attempt, the 1998 Irish Accord, is a striking case in point. Set against the backdrop of seventy years of conflict, the Accord is built on a consociational foundation. At the heart of the Accord is the creation of a democratic assembly in Northern Ireland which, first, would be configured through a system of proportional representation (to ensure adequate minority representation) and second, which would operate according to a complex system of weighted majorities, double or parallel majorities on culturally sensitive matters, and cross-community coalitions at the executive level to ensure that the goals of 'partnership, equality and mutual respect' are achieved (Belfast Agreement, 1998). In such a system, there is no attempt whatsoever to hide or mask cultural identity for constitutional purposes. Quite the opposite. According to the Agreement, individuals elected to the Northern Irish Assembly would be required to designate their identity - 'nationalist, unionist, or other' - for the purposes of measuring and calculating cross-community support for those votes that require defined levels of cross-community support (Belfast Agreement, 1998). In this case, cultural identity is more than an add-on to an otherwise de-cultured liberal order. It is utterly central to the constitutional architecture.

At the same time, it is important to understand that the Irish Accord does not abandon what I have called the 'American' commitment to constitutional neutrality. In a section devoted to describing the 'safeguards' put in place, the agreement makes it clear that the Assembly's decisions will be governed by the European Convention on Human Rights and 'any Bill of

Rights for Northern Ireland supplementing it' (Belfast Agreement, 1998). Yet, even here, the emphasis is on neutrality between individuals and communities that are culturally defined and situated. As the Accord puts it, sovereign power shall be exercised 'with rigorous impartiality on behalf of all the people *in the diversity of their identities and traditions*' (emphasis added). Government 'shall be founded on the principles of full respect for, and equality of, civil, political, social and cultural rights, of freedom from discrimination for all citizens'. And there should be 'just and equal treatment for the identity, ethos, and aspirations of both communities'. In short, this is to be a fully culturalised constitutional arrangement.

If the proposed assembly for Northern Ireland is a good example of consociational constitution-making, it also underscores the usefulness of federalism as an institutional strategy for conflict resolution. Where consociational arrangements typically aim to pacify by creating some sort of partnership or power-sharing among groups, federalism is designed to remove contentious subjects from the public agenda by dividing power between geographically distinct and constitutionally autonomous units. In the Irish case, the new assembly in Northern Ireland will have much the same proto-federal relation to Westminster that the new Scottish assembly will have. That is, it will have the authority to legislate on specified matters considered to be local in nature, mechanisms for coordination with Westminster will be developed (as in Scotland), and judicial review will be established to settle 'disputes over legislative competence' (Belfast Agreement, 1998). And in both cases, Northern Ireland and Scotland, the essential constitutional calculation is the same: to its supporters, devolution has the virtue both of democratising politics by providing for real self-government at the local level and of domesticating cultural conflict by confining it to a territory or jurisdiction in which conflict is less likely to occur because the population is culturally more homogeneous.

The Irish and Scottish cases are illustrative, not isolated. Federalism is enjoying a renaissance among constitution-makers intent on finding ways to blunt or defuse cultural, ethnic or religious conflict, and it has been recently taken up with interest in polities as diverse as Spain, Belgium and South Africa - not to mention the European Union itself. Nor is this the only reason that federalism is attractive. In their quite different ways, Robert O'Brien and Jan Aart Scholte point to the growing political importance of federal structures and regional governance, the one in response to the emergence of regional trading blocs; the other to globalisation. Whatever the model, the important question is whether federal structures actually perform the stabilising function they are meant to perform or whether, alternatively, they actually exacerbate the conflict they are meant to contain.

This is, needless to say, an enormously difficult question on which to generalise. To some extent, the proof is necessarily in the pudding; the success of federalism as a tool for controlling conflict needs to be measured by its ability to create and sustain durable and longstanding accommodation between and among groups rather than providing the means for escalating conflict. This, I think, is one of the chief virtues of the Canadian case in comparative politics, for here one finds one of the world's oldest functioning federations yet one that is (apparently constantly) vulnerable to threats of federal self-destruction. Actually, it has served as model, both favourable and unfavourable, virtually since the Confederation settlement was consummated in 1867. The way in which the Canadian federal system accommodated Quebec's religious, linguistic and legal distinctiveness was widely used in the 1890s in Britain, for instance, as a model for Irish home rule. And since then, the growth of Quebec nationalism and sovereignism has been held up as a cautionary example in a number of federal states. The real difficulty, however, is not just in inferring the 'right' lessons from the Canadian case. The larger problem is in generalising from one culturally and historically specific case to another, distinguishing those institutional or constitutional commitments that are useful comparators from those that are not. Even a cursory glance at the literature on comparative federalism suggests that on this score much work remains to be done.

Approaches from Below: The Importance of Civil Society

I have wanted to establish here not simply that constitutionalism needs to be understood as an attempt, ultimately anchored to the idea of rights, to resolve conflict. Rather, I have wanted to show that this way of thinking about constitutionalism is so pervasive, diverse and underappreciated that we really need to establish a typology of its various forms. Yet if my theme is diversity and complexity, I should note as well that all three of the basic constitutional types I have discussed thus far - constitutional stigmatisation, the American model and the culturalised constitution - share one important characteristic, namely that they are all elite-driven initiatives. However popular such things as Nazism and the treatment of Canadian Indians may have been in the general population, there is no question that political, social and/or economic elites invested most heavily in them, perfected them, and perpetuated them. Despite its popular ratification state by state, there is broad agreement that the US Constitution took the shape it did and appeared at the time it did because of the fear that the unpropertied many would tyrannise over the propertied few. And most of the attempts to culturalise the Constitution - especially consociational models - begin from the explicit goal to foster elite accommodation.

Yet as Damian O'Leary and Patrick Hanafin argue in the Irish case, any constitutional strategy that does not understand the importance of building from below, that is amidst the institutions of civil society, is profoundly short-sighted. This point resonates to the Canadian ear because of the way in which popular dissatisfaction, expressed through legislative and referendum defeats, derailed two successive attempts at wholesale elite-driven constitutional reform in Canada. What surprised many observers in those cases was the way in which form and substance converged, that distaste for the 'top-down' process by which the constitutional proposals had been negotiated was as important as any substantive misgivings about the constitutional provisions themselves.

The arguments in this volume go deeper, however. It is not enough to 'add the people and stir' through popular ratification of what are bound to be controversial constitutional proposals. The Irish case suggests that simple changes of strategy - like holding a referendum soon after the elite bargaining is over rather than, as in the Canadian case, carrying out ratification over a prolonged period - may be tactically shrewd. The fact remains, however, that, even with its successful ratification, the Irish attempt at constitutional reform remains deeply fraught because the sources of conflict are so deeply embedded in Irish history and politics.

To put the point slightly differently, one might say (with Robert O'Brien) that to be successfully employed as a vehicle for conflict resolution, constitution-makers must pay attention to the need both to 'restrict' and 'enable' political activity. The constitution-maker's first response to conflict may be to establish rules and limits on the sort of behaviour that produces aggression. Thus, to the extent that personal security is threatened by the use of land mines (internationally) or arbitrary police power (domestically), the first instinct of liberal constitutionalists is, quite properly, to want to find ways to control or limit those actions. But it is insufficient to rest satisfied with these restrictive measures. It is equally important to enable citizens to find the constitutional space in which to work out, blunt and resolve conflict - especially those that follow from significant differences of ethnicity, religion and race. And, to do that, it is crucial that civil society be considered a positive resource for constitutional politics rather than being treated as something of an alien force - relegated to the other side of the brightly-lit boundaries that separate public from private, state from society, legal from political, and constitutional from non-constitutional.

It may seem at first odd to place this challenge on the constitutionalist's plate since, if conflict resolution is usually cast as a subfield of international relations, civil society is typically the bailiwick of sociologists and anthropologists. In fact, however, the essays in this volume, taken together, demonstrate eloquently that there is much for the constitutionalist to contribute to the new effort to build theories and develop practices that are 'enabling' in this sense. Melissa Williams' reflections on reforming the institutions of deliberative democracy, Damian O'Leary's emphasis on the need for 'substantive constitutionalism' in Ireland, Robert O'Brien's analysis of the place of civil society in a globalised economy, and Vivien Hart's insights on the power of constitutions and 'rights talk' to instil conceptions of identity - all speak to the growing view that constitutionalism is far from obsolete in both theory and practice. The challenge, both intellectually and politically, is daunting. But it is a challenge, I hope I have persuaded you, that is both central to the idea of constitutionalism and in urgent need of careful refinement.

Bibliography

Adam, H. (1996), 'Anti-Semitism and Anti-Black Racism: Nazi Germany and Apartheid in South Africa', *Telos*, no. 108, pp. 25-46.

Ajzenstat, J. (1988), *The Political Thought of Lord Durham*, McGill-Queen's University Press, Kingston and Montreal.

Alexander, R. and Gilmore, P. (1994), 'The Emergence of Cross-Border Labor Solidarity', *NACLA Report on the Americas*, vol. XXVII, pp. 42-48.

Alger, C.F. (1990), 'The World Relations of Cities: Closing the Gap between Social Science Paradigms and Everyday Human Experience', *International Studies Quarterly*, vol. 34, pp. 493-518.

Andre R. (1991), 'The Progress of Francophones', in R. Fidler (ed), *Canada, Adieu? Quebec Debates Its Future*, The Institute for Research on Public Policy, Halifax.

Asante, M. K. (1987), *The Afrocentric Idea,* Temple University Press, Philadelphia.

Atlas, J. (1993), *Battle of the Books*, W. W. Norton, New York.

Awolowo, O. (1966), *Thoughts on the Nigerian Constitution*, Oxford University Press, Ibadan.

Bardon, J. (1992), *A History of Ulster*, The Blackstaff Press, Belfast.

Bazilli, S. (1991), *Putting Women on the Agenda*, Ravan Press, Cape Town.

Beiner, R. (1995), *What's the Matter with Liberalism*? University of California Press, Berkeley.

Bell, D. (1987), 'The World and the United States in 2013', *Daedalus*, vol. 116, pp. 1-32.

Benvenisti, M. (1996), *City of Stone*: *The Hidden History of Jerusalem*, University of California Press, Berkeley, cited in Elon, A. (1997), 'Jerusalem Blues', *New York Review of Books*, Vol. XLIV, pp. 4-9.

Boldt, M. (1993), *Surviving as Indians*: *The Challenge of Self-Government*, University of Toronto Press, Toronto.

Bowles, P. and Wagman, B. (1997), 'Globalization and the Welfare State: Four Hypotheses and Some Empirical Evidence'. Paper presented to the Annual Convention of the International Studies Association, Toronto.

Brannigan, J. (1996), 'Writing DeTermiNation: Reading Death in(to) Irish National Identity', in J. Brannigan, R. Robbins and J. Wolfreys (eds), *Applying: To Derrida*, Macmillan, Basingstoke, pp.55-70.

Brecher, J., Childs J. B. and Culter, J. (eds) (1993), *Global Visions: Beyond the New World Order*, South End Press, Boston.

Breton, R. (1984), 'The production and allocation of symbolic resources: an analysis of the linguistic and ethnocultural fields in Canada', *Canadian Review of Sociology and Anthropology*, vol. 21, pp. 123-44.

Browne, V. (1995), 'Accept peace-then work hard to keep it', *Sunday Times*, 9 July, p.10.

Bruce, S. (1994), *The Edge of the Union: The Ulster Loyalist Political Vision*, Oxford University Press, Oxford.

Bull, H. (1977), *The Anarchial Society: A Study of Order in World Politics*. London: Macmillan.

Canada (1982), *Constitution Act*.

Canada, Government of (1969), *Statement of the Government of Canada on Indian Policy*, Presented to the 28th Parliament, 1st Sess., by the Honourable Jean Chrétien, Minister of Indian Affairs and Northern Development, Department of Indian Affairs and Northern Development, Ottawa.

Caplan, G., Kirby M. and Segal, H. (1989), *Election: The Issues, The Strategies, The Aftermath*, Prentice Hall: Ontario.

Carens, J. H. (1995), 'Complex Justice, Cultural Difference, and Political Community', in David Miller and Michael Walzer (eds), *Pluralism, Justice and Equality*, Oxford University Press, Oxford, pp. 45-66.

Carens, J. H. (1995), 'Immigration, Political Community and the Transformation of Identity: Quebec's Immigration Policies in Critical Perspective', in J. H. Carens (ed), *Is Quebec Nationalism Just? Perspectives From Anglophone Canada*, McGill-Queens University Press, Montreal.

Carens, J. H. (1996), 'Dimensions of Citizenship and National Identity in Canada', *The Philosophical Forum*, vol. XXVIII, pp.111-42.

Cell, J. W. (1982), The *Highest Stage of White Supremacy: The Origins of Segregation in South Africa and the American South*, Cambridge University Press, Cambridge.

Chopra, J. and T. G. Weiss (1992), 'Sovereignty Is No Longer Sacrosanct: Codifying Humanitarian Intervention', *Ethics and International Affairs*, vol. 6, pp.95-117.

Cohen, J. (1989), ' Deliberation and Democratic Legitimacy', in A. Hamlin and P. Petit (eds), *The Good Polity: Normative Analysis of the State*, Basil Blackwell, Oxford.

Cohen, J. (1996), 'Procedure and Substance in Deliberative Democracy', in S. Benhabib (ed), *Democracy and Difference*, Princeton University Press, Princeton.

Collins, E. and Meehan, E. (1994), 'Women's Rights in Employment and Related Areas', in C. McCrudden and G. Chambers (eds), *Individual Rights and the Law in Britain*, Clarendon Press, Oxford.

Connolly, W. (1991), 'Democracy and Territoriality', *Millennium*, vol. 20, pp.463-84.

Cook, L. M. (1995), 'Mexican State-Labor Relations and the Political Implications of Free Trade', *Latin American Perspectives*, 84 vol. 22, pp. 77-94.

Cook, R. J. (ed). (1994). *Human Rights of Women: National and International Perspectives*, University of Pennsylvania Press, Philadelphia.

Cowen, D. V. (1961), *The Foundations of Freedom: With Special Reference to Southern Africa*, Oxford University Press, Cape Town.

Cox, R. W. (1993), 'Structural Issues of Global Governance', in S. Gill (ed), *Gramsci, Historical Materialism, and International Relations,* Cambridge University Press, Cambridge, pp. 259-89.

Cruise O'Brien, C. (1994). *Ancestral Voices: Religion and Nationalism in Ireland*, Poolbeg, Dublin.

Cunniah, D. (1995), 'How to Use the ILO's Supervisory System', *Free Labour World* (January), p.8.

Cutrufelli, M. R. (1983), *Women of Africa*, Zed Press, London.

Dahl, R. (1994). 'A Democratic Dilemma: System Effectiveness versus Citizen Participation', *Political Science Quarterly*, vol. 109, pp. 23-34.

Davenport, T. R. H. (1991), *South Africa: A Modern History*, 4th ed. University of Toronto Press, Toronto.

Davidson, C. (ed) (1994), *The Quiet Revolution in the South*, Princeton University Press, Princeton.

Davis, A. (1983), *Women, Race and Class*, Vintage, New York.

Dawidowicz, L. S. (1986), *The War Against the Jews, 1933-1945*, 10th anniversary edition, Bantam Books, Toronto.

de Smith, S. A. (1964), *The New Commonwealth and its Constitutions*, Stevens, London.

de Vos, P. (1997), 'The Role of International Human Rights Law in the Drafting of the Social and Economic Rights in South Africa's 1996 Constitution', Paper Presented at Conference on *Constitutional Transition: Hong Kong 1997 and Global Perspectives*, Hong Kong, May 29-June 1 1997.

Dickason, O. P. (1992), *Canada's First Nations: A History of Founding Peoples from Earliest Times*, McClelland and Stewart, Toronto.

Drainville, A. (1997), 'Continental Integration and Civil Society in the Americas', *Social Justice*, vol. 24, pp. 120-47.

Drakulic, S. (1994), *The Balkan Express*, Harper Collins, New York.

Duchacek, I. D. *et al* (eds) (1988), *Perforated Sovereignties and International Relations: Trans-Sovereign Contacts of Subnational Governments,*: Greenwood, Westport, CT.

Dugard, J. (1995), ' International Human Rights', in D. van Wyk *et al* (eds), *Rights and Constitutionalism: The New South African Legal Order*, Clarendon Press, Oxford.

Durant, R. F. (1995), 'The Democratic Deficit in America', *Political Science Quarterly*, vol. 110, pp. 25-47.

Dyck, N. (1991), *What is the Indian 'Problem': Tutelage and Resistance in Canadian Indian Administration* Institute of Social and Economic Research, Memorial University of Newfoundland, St. John's.

Eastland, T. and Bennett, W. J. (1979), *Counting By Race: Equality from the Founding Fathers to Bakke and Weber*, Basic Books, New York.

Edsall, T. and Edsall, M. (1990), *Chain Reaction*, W. W. Norton, New York.

Egyptian Society of International Law. (1953), *Documents on Sudan, 1899-1953*, Brochure no. 14.

El Hamamsy, L. S. (1959), 'General Report: The Political Role of Women in Tropical and Sub-tropical Countries', in *Women's Role in the Development of Tropical and Sub-Tropical Countries*, INCIDI, Brussels.

Ellis, W., (1995), 'Last Twist of the Orange Card?', *Sunday Times*, 10 September, p.5.

Ellison, R. (1964), *Shadow and Act*, Vintage, New York.

Elster, J. (1995), 'Strategic Uses of Argument', in K. Arrow, *et al.* (eds), *Barriers to Conflict Resolution*,. W. W. Norton, New York.

Evans, S. (1980), *Personal Politics*, Vintage, New York.

Fawzi, S. (1959), 'Sudan', in *Women's Role in the Development of Tropical and Sub-Tropical Countries*, INCIDI, Brussels.

Fidler, R. (ed) (1991), *Canada, Adieu? Quebec Debates Its Future*, The Institute for Research on Public Policy, Halifax.

Findlay, T. (1995), 'Armed Conflict Prevention, Management and Resolution', in *SIPRI Yearbook 1995*, Oxford University Press, Oxford, pp. 37-82.

Finer, S. E. Bogdanor, V. and Rudden, B. (1995), *Comparing Constitutions*, Clarendon Press, Oxford.

Frazer, E. and Lacey, N. (1993), *The Politics of Community: A Feminist Critique of the Liberal-Communitarian Debate*, University of Toronto Press, Toronto.

Fredrickson, G. M. (1971), *The Black Image in the White Mind: The Debate on Afro-American Character and Destiny, 1817-1914*, Harper & Row, New York.

Fredrickson, G. M. (1981), *White Supremacy: A Comparative Study in American and South African History*, Oxford University Press, New York.

Friedländer, S. (1997), *Nazi Germany and the Jews: Volume 1, The Years of Persecution, 1933-1939*, HarperCollins, New York.

Friedmann, M. (1982), *Capitalism and Freedom*, University of Chicago Press, Chicago.

Fry, E. H. (1995), 'The Vincibility of Modern Nation-States: Challenges from the International and Subnational Arenas', Paper to the Annual Convention of the International Studies Association, Chicago.

Gabriel, C. and Macdonald, L. (1994), 'NAFTA, Women and Organising in Canada and Mexico: Forging a Feminist Internationality', *Millennium*, vol. 23, pp. 535-62.

Gallagher, M. (1995), 'How many nations are there in Ireland?', *Ethnic and Racial Studies,* vol. 18, pp. 715-39.

Gates, H. L., Jr. (1992), *Loose Canons*, Oxford University Press, New York.

Gester, R. (1993), 'Proposal for Voting Reform', *Journal of World Trade*, vol. 27, pp. 121-36.

Ghai, Y. P. (1967), 'Independence and Safeguards in Kenya', *East African Law Journal,* vol. 3, pp. 177-217.

Ghai, Y. P. (1993), 'The Theory of the State in the Third World and the Problematics of Constitutionalism', in Douglas Greenberg *et al* (eds), *Constitutionalism and Democracy: Transitions in the Contemporary World,* Oxford University Press, New York.

Giddings, P. (1984), *When and Where I Enter*, Bantam Books, New York.

Gilens, M. (1996), ' "Race Coding" and White Opposition to Welfare', *American Political Science Review*, vol. 90, pp. 593-604.

Giliomee, H. and Schlemmer, L. (1989), *From Apartheid to Nation-Building*, Oxford University Press, Cape Town.

Gill, S. (1992), 'The Emerging World Order and European Change', in R. Miliband and L. Panitch (eds), *The Socialist Register 1992*, Merlin Press, London, pp. 157-96.

Goldsworthy, D. (ed). (1994), *The Conservative Government and the End of Empire, 1951-1957, Part II, Politics and Administration*, British Documents on the End of Empire, Series A, Vol. 3, HMSO, London.

Gong, G. W. (1984), *The Standard of 'Civilization' in International Society*, Clarendon Press, Oxford.

Goodman, D. S. G. and Segal, G. (eds) (1994), *China Deconstructs: Politics, Trade and Regionalism*, Routledge, lONDON.

Gray, J. (1986), *Liberalism,* University of Minnesota Press, Minneapolis.

Greenberg, S. (1995), *Middle Class Dreams*, Times Books, New York.

Guinier, L. (1994), *The Tyranny of the Majority*, The Free Press, New York.

Habermas, J. (1990), 'Discourse Ethics: Notes on a Program of Philosophical Justification' in *Moral Consciousness and Communicative Action*, MIT Press, Cambridge.

Hacker, A. (1992), *Two Nations*, Ballantine Books, New York.

Hadfield, B. (1989), *The Constitution of Northern Ireland,* SLS Legal Publications, Belfast.

Hanafin, P. (1996) 'Reproductive Rights and the Irish Constitution: From the Sanctity of Life to the Sanctity of Autonomy?', *European Journal of Health Law,* vol. 3, pp. 179-88.

Hanafin, P. (1997a), 'Defying the Female: The Irish Constitutional Text as Phallocentric Manifesto', *Textual Practice*, vol. 11, pp. 249-73.

Hanafin, P. (1997b), *Last Rights: Death, Dying and the Law in Ireland,* Cork University Press, Cork.

Hart, M. (1989), 'The Future on the Table: The Continuing Negotiating Agenda Under the Canada-United States Free Trade Agreement', in R. Dearden, M. Hart and D. Steger (eds), *Living with Free Trade*, Institute for Research on Public Policy, Ottawa.

Hawthorn, H. B. (ed) (1967), *A Survey of the Contemporary Indians of Canada,* vol.1, The Queen's Printer, Ottawa.

Hay, M. J. and Stichter, S. (1990), *African Women-South of the Sahara*, Longmans, London.

Hayek, F. A. (1960), *The Constitution of Liberty*, University of Chicago Press, Chicago.

Held, D. (1987), *Models of Democracy*, Cambridge University Press, Cambridge.

Held, D. (1993), 'Democracy: From City-States to A Cosmopolitan Order?' in D Held, *Prospects for Democracy*, Polity Press, Cambridge, pp. 13-52.

Helleiner, E. (1994), *States and the Reemergence of Global Finance: From Bretton Woods to the 1990s*, Cornell University Press, Ithaca, NY.

Herod, A. (1997), 'Labor as an Agent of Globalization and as Global Agent', in K. Cox (ed), *Spaces of Globalization*, Guilford, New York, pp. 167-200.

Hettne, B. (1994), 'The Regional Factor in the Formation of a New World Order', in Y. Sakamoto (ed.), *Global Transformation: Challenges to the State System*, United Nations University Press, Tokyo, pp.134-66.

Hettne, B. (1997), 'The Double Movement: Global Market versus Regionalism', in R. W. Cox (ed.), *The New Realism: Perspectives on Multilateralism and World Order,* United Nations University Press, Tokyo, pp. 223-42.

Heyns, C. (1995), 'African Human Rights Law and the European Convention'. *South African Journal on Human Rights*, vol. 11, pp. 252-63.

Hobsbawm, E. J. (1987), *The Age of Empire, 1875-1914*, Weidenfeld and Nicolson, London.

Hochschild, J. (1995), *Facing Up to the American Dream: Race, Class, and the Soul of the American Nation*, Princeton University Press, Princeton.

Hocking, B. (1993), *Localizing Foreign Policy: Non-Central Governments and Multilayered Diplomacy,* Macmillan, Basingstoke.

Holland, D. C. (1962), 'Human Rights in Nigeria', *Current Legal Problems*, vol.15, pp. 145-58.

Holm, H. H. and S□renson, G. (1995), 'International Relations Theory in A World of Variation', in *Whose World Order? Uneven Globalization and the End of the Cold War*, Westview, Boulder, pp. 187-206.

Howard, R. E. (1986), *Human Rights in Commonwealth Africa*, Rowman and Littlefield, Totowa, N.J.

Ignatieff, M. (1993), *Blood and Belonging: Journeys into the New Nationalism,* Farrar, Strauss and Giroux, New York.

Ikenberry, G. (1995), 'Funk de Siecle: Impasse of Western Industrial Society at Century's End', *Millennium*, vol. 24, pp. 113-28.

Jackson, R. H. (1990), *Quasi-States: Sovereignty, International Relations, and the Third World*, Cambridge University Press, Cambridge.

Jamieson, K. (1978), *Indian Women and the Law in Canada: Citizens Minus*, Minister of Supply and Services, Ottawa.

Johnson, C. (1986), 'Class and Gender: Yoruba Women in the Colonial Period', in C. Robertson and I. Berger (eds), *Women and Class in Africa*, Africana Publishing Company, New York.

Johnson, J. (1998), 'Arguing for Deliberation: Some Skeptical Considerations', in J. Elster (ed), *Deliberative Democracy*, Cambridge University Press, Cambridge.

Kadalie, R. (1995), 'Constitutional Equality: The Implications for Women in South Africa', *Social Politics*, vol. 2, pp. 208-224.

Kaganas, F and Murray, C. (1994), 'The Contest between Culture and Gender Equality Under South Africa's Interim Constitution', *Journal of Law and Society*, vol. 21, pp. 409-33.

Kalin, R. (1995), 'Ethnicity and Citizenship Attitudes in Canada: Analyses of a 1991 National Survey', *Nationalism and Ethnic Politics*, vol. 3, pp. 28-44.

Kapstein, E. B. (1994), *Governing the Global Economy: International Finance and the State*, Harvard University Press, Cambridge, MA.

Kearney, R. (1988), *Transitions: Narratives in Modern Irish Culture*, Manchester University Press, Manchester.

Kendle, J. (1997), *Federal Britain: A History*, Routledge, London.

Kentridge, S. (1996), 'Bills of Rights-the South African Experiment', *Law Quarterly Review*, vol. 112, pp. 237-60.

Kenya Constitutional Conference, 1960: Report (1960), Cmnd. 960, HMSO, London.

Kershaw, I. (1993), *The Nazi Dictatorship: Problems and Perspectives of Interpretation*, 3d ed., Edward Arnold, London.

Kershaw, I. (1995), 'The Extinction of Human Rights in Nazi Germany', in O. Hufton (ed), *Historical Change and Human Rights: The Oxford Amnesty Lectures*, 1994, Basic Books, New York.

Kiernan, V. G. (1972), *The Lords of Human Kind: European Attitudes to the Outside World in the Imperial Age*, Penguin Books, Harmondsworth.

Kim, S. S. (1994), 'Chinese Perspectives on World Order', in D. Jacobsen (ed.) *Old Nations, New World: Conceptions of World Order*, Westview, Boulder, pp. 37-74.

Krugman, P. (1993) 'The Uncomfortable Truth About NAFTA' , *Foreign Affairs*, vol. 72, pp. 13-19.

Kymlicka, W. (1995), *Multicultural Citizenship: A Liberal Theory of Minority Rights,* Clarendon Press, Oxford.

Lapidoth, R. (1992), 'Sovereignty in Transition', *Journal of International Affairs*, vol. 45, pp. 325-46.

Lenaerts, K. (1990), 'Constitutionalism and the Many Faces of Federalism', *The American Journal of Comparative Law*, vol.38, pp. 205-263.

Lester, A. (1984), 'Fundamental Rights: The United Kingdom Isolated', *Public Law*, vol. 100, pp. 46-72.

Lijphart, A. (1982), 'Consociation: The Model and its Application in Divided Societies', in D. Rea (ed), *Political Co-operation in Divided Societies: A Series of Papers Relevant to the Conflict in Northern Ireland*, Gill and Macmillan, Dublin.

Linton, M. (1996) 'Most Catholics in north reject united Ireland', *The Guardian*, February 28, p.5.

Lipset, S. M. (1996) *American Exceptionalism*, Norton, New York.

Longley, E. (1994), 'From Cathleen to Anorexia - The Breakdown of Irelands', in E. Longley *The Living Stream: Literature and Revisionism in Ireland*, Bloodaxe Books, Newcastle upon Tyne.

Longley, E. (1994), *The Living Stream: Literature and Revisionism in Ireland*, Bloodaxe Books, Newcastle upon Tyne.

Loury, G. C. (1995), *One by One from the Inside Out: Essays and Reviews on Race and Responsibility in America*, Free Press, New York.

Macpherson, C. B. (1976), *The Life and Times of Liberal Democracy*, Oxford University Press, Oxford.

Madison, J. *et al* (1982), *The Federalist Papers*, Bantam, New York.

Maier, C. (1994), 'Democracy and its Discontents', *Foreign Affairs*, July/August, pp. 48-64.

Mamdani, M. (1996), *Citizen and Subject: Contemporary Africa and the Legacy of Late Colonialism*, Princeton University Press, Princeton.

Manin, B. (1987), 'On Legitimacy and Deliberation', *Political Theory*, vol. 15, pp. 338-68.

Marks, S. and Trapido, S. (1987), 'The politics of race, class and nationalism', in S. Marks and S. Trapido (eds), *The Politics of Race, Class and Nationalism in Twentieth-Century South Africa*, Longman, London.

Marrus, M. R. (1987), *The Holocaust in History*, Lester & Opren Dennys Ltd., Toronto.

Marston, G. (1993), 'The United Kingdom's Part in the Preparation of the European Convention on Human Rights', *International and Comparative Law Quarterly*, vol. 42, pp. 796-826.

McGarry, J. and O'Leary, B. (1995), *Explaining Northern Ireland: Broken Images*, Blackwell, Oxford

McLiam Wilson, R. (1989), *Ripley Bogle*, Deutsch, London.

Minow, M. (1990), *Making All the Difference*, Cornell University Press, Ithaca.

Moniére, D. and Côté, R. (eds) (1996), *Quebec 1996*, Editions Fides, Montreal.

Moody, K. (1995), 'NAFTA and the Corporate Redesign of North America', *Latin American Perspectives*, vol. 22, pp. 95-106.

Müller, I. (1991), *Hitler's Justice: The Courts of the Third Reich*, Harvard University Press, Cambridge.

Mullin, J. (1998) 'Everyone's a winner, bar Sinn Fein', *The Guardian*, January 13, p. 4.

Murphy, W. F. (1993), 'Constitutions, Constitutionalism, and Democracy', in Greenberg, D. *et al*, (eds), *Constitutionalism and Democracy*, Oxford University Press, Oxford, pp. 3-25.

Mydans, Seth (1998), 'When Friends Rebel, A Reign Ends Quickly', *New York Times,* May 24, p. A8.

Myrdal, G. (1944), *An American Dilemma: The Negro Problem and Modern Democracy*, 2 vols., Harper, New York.

Ndegwa, S. N. (1997), 'Citizenship and Ethnicity: An Examination of Two Transition Moments in Kenyan Politics', *American Political Science Review,* vol. 91, pp. 599-616.

Nieman, D. G. (1991), *Promises to Keep: African Americans and the Constitutional Order, 1776 to the Present*, Oxford University Press, New York.

Noakes, J. and Pridham, G. (eds) (1974), *Documents on Nazism, 1919-1945*, Jonathan Cape, London.

Northern Ireland Office, (1995a), *A Framework For Accountable Government in Northern Ireland*, Her Majesty's Stationery Office, Belfast.

Northern Ireland Office, (1995b), *A New Framework For Agreement: A Shared Understanding Between The British And Irish Governments To Assist Discussion And Negotiation Involving The Northern Irish Parties*, Her Majesty's Stationery Office, Belfast and Government Stationery Office, Dublin.

Norton, A. (1988) *Reflections on Political Identity*, The Johns Hopkins University Press, Baltimore.

Nozick, R. (1974), *Anarchy, State and Utopia*, Basil Blackwell, Oxford.

Nyerere, J. (1993), 'Reflections on Constitutions and African Experience', in T. J. Barron *et al* (eds), *Constitutions and National Identity*, Quadriga, Edinburgh.

O'Brien, B. (1995), *The Long War: The IRA and Sinn Féin from Armed Struggle to Peace Talks*, The O'Brien Press, Dublin.

O'Brien, R. (1995), 'North American Integration and International Relations Theory', *Canadian Journal of Political Science*, vol. XXVIII, pp. 693-724.

O'Brien, R. (1997), *Subsidy Regulation and State Transformation in North America, GATT and the EU,* Macmillan, Basingstoke.

O Connor, F. (1993), *In Search of a State: Catholics in Northern Ireland*, The Blackstaff Press, Belfast.

Odumoso, O.I. (1963), *The Nigerian Constitution*, Sweet and Maxwell, London.

Ohmae, K. (1995), *The End of the Nation State: The Rise of Regional Economies*. Free Press, New York.

Okin, S. M. (1989), *Justice, Gender and the Family*, Basic Books, New York.

Okoth-Ogendo, H.W.O. (1993), 'Constitutions without Constitutionalism: Reflections on an African Political Paradox', in D. Greenberg *et al* (eds), *Constitutionalism and Democracy: Transitions in the Contemporary World*, Oxford University Press, New York.

O'Leary, B. (1989), 'The limits of coercive consociationalism in Northern Ireland', *Political Studies*, vol. 37, pp. 452-68.

O'Leary, B. and McGarry, J. (1993), *The Politics of Antagonism: Understanding Northern Ireland*, Athlone Press, London and Atlantic Highlands, NJ.

Olson, A. L. (1973), *The Canadian Left in Quebec During the Great Depression*, Duke University Press, Durham.

Pateman, C. (1983), 'Feminism and Democracy', in Duncan, G. (ed), *Democratic Theory and Practice*, Cambridge University Press, Cambridge, pp. 204-17.

Pateman, C. (1989), *Participation and Democratic Theory*, Cambridge University Press, Cambridge.

Patterson, O. (1982), *Slavery and Social Death*, Harvard University Press, Cambridge.

Perham, M. (1970), *Colonial Sequence 1949 to 1969*, Methuen, London.

Phillips, A. (1993), *Democracy & Difference*, Pennsylvania State University Press, University Park, Pennsylvania.

Plessy v Ferguson (1896), 163 U.S. 537.

Porter, E. (1998), 'Identity, location, plurality: Women, nationalism and Northern Ireland', in R. Wilford and B. Miller (eds), *Women, Ethnicity and Nationalism: The Politics of Divided Societies*, Routledge, London.

Porter, N. (1996), *Rethinking Unionism: An Alternative Vision for Northern Ireland*, The Blackstaff Press, Belfast.

Posel, D. (1987), 'The language of domination, 1978-1983', in S. Marks and S. Trapido (eds), *The Politics of Race, Class and Nationalism in Twentieth Century South Africa*, Longman, London.

Pulzer, P. (1992), *Jews and the German State: The Political History of a Minority, 1848-1933*, Blackwell, Oxford.

Pulzer, P. (1997), 'Psychopaths and Conformists, Adventurers and Moral Cowards', *London Review of Books*, January 23, p. 20.

Quadagno, J. (1994), *The Color of Welfare*, Oxford University Press, New York.

Quansah, E. K. (1992), 'Unity Dow v Attorney-General of Botswana: One More Relic of a Woman's Servitude Removed', *African Journal of International and Comparative Law*, vol. 4, pp. 195-204.

Rawls, J. (1971), *A Theory of Justice*, Harvard University Press, Cambridge.

Report of the Advisory Commission on the Review of the Constitution of Rhodesia and Nyasaland, (1960), Cmnd 1148, HMSO, London.

Rose, A.M. (1944), 'Postscript', in G. Myrdal, *An American Dilemma: The Negro Problem and Modern Democracy*, 2 vols., Harper, New York.

Rousseau, J- J. (1978), *On the Social Contract*, ed. R. D. Masters, trans. J. R. Masters, St. Martin's Press, New York.

Royal Commission on Aboriginal Peoples (1996), *Final Report*, 5 vols., Canada Communication Group, Ottawa.

Ruane, J. and Todd, J. (1996), *The Dynamics of Conflict in Northern Ireland: Power, Conflict and Emancipation*, Cambridge University Press, Cambridge.

Runyan, A. S. (1996), 'The Places of Women in Trading Places: Gendered Global/Regional Regimes and Inter-nationalized Feminist Resistance', in E. Kofman and G. Youngs (eds), *Globalization: Theory and Practice*, Pinter, London, pp. 238-52.

Rupert, M. (1995), '(Re) Politicizing in the Global Economy: Liberal Common Sense and Ideological Struggle in the US NAFTA Debate', *Review of International Political Economy*, vol. 2, pp. 658-92.

Russell, P. (1992) *Constitutional Odyssey*, University of Toronto Press, Toronto.

Russell, P. H. (1993), 'Canada's Mega Constitutional Politics in Comparative Perspective', Institut für Politikwissenschaft der Phillips-Universität.

Said, E. W. (1993), *Culture and Imperialism*, Knopf, New York.

Sandel, M. J. (1982), *Liberalism and the Limits of Justice,* Cambridge University Press, Cambridge.

Scammon, R. and Wattenberg , B. (1970), *The Real Majority*, Coward-McCann, New York.

Scanlon, T. M. (1982), 'Contractualism and Utilarianism', in A. Sen and B. Williams (eds), *Utilitarianism and Beyond*, Cambridge University Press, Cambridge.

Schlesinger, A. (1991), *The Disuniting of America*, Norton, New York.

Scholte, J. A. (1996a), 'Beyond the Buzzword: Towards a Critical Theory of Globalisation', in E. Kofman and G. Youngs (eds), *Globalization: Theory and Practice*, Pinter, London, pp.43-57.

Scholte, J. A. (1996b), 'The Geography of Collective Identities in a Globalizing World', *Review of International Political Economy*, vol. 3, pp. 565-607.

Scholte, J. A. (1997a), 'Global Capitalism and the State', *International Affairs*, vol. 73, pp. 427-52.

Scholte, J. A. (1997b), 'Global Trade and Finance', in J. Baylis and S. Smith (eds), *The Globalization of World Politics: An Introduction to International Relations,* Oxford University Press, Oxford, pp. 429-47.

Scholte, J. A. (1997c), 'The Globalization of World Politics', in J. Bayliss and S. Smith (eds), *The Globalization of World Politics: An Introduction to International Relations*, Oxford University Press, Oxford, pp. 13-30.

Segal, G. (1994), *China Changes Shape: Regionalism and Foreign Policy*, International Institute of Strategic Studies, London.

Siegfried, A. (1907), *The Race Question in Canada*, Everleigh Nash, London.

Silver, A. I. (1982), *The French-Canadian Idea of Confederation, 1864-1900*, University of Toronto Press, Toronto.

Sipkov, I. (1988). 'The European Economic Community: A Sovereign Entity Under Its Own Legal Order', *International Journal of Legal Information*, vol. 16, pp. 177-89.

Sklair, L. (1997), 'Transnational Social Movements for Global Capitalism', *Review of International Political Economy*, vol. 4, pp. 514-38.

Smith, A. D. (1971), *Theories of Nationalism*, Penguin, Harmondsworth.

Smith, R. M. (1997), *Civic Ideals: Conflicting Visions of Citizenship in U.S. History*, Yale University Press, New Haven.

Soroos, M. J. (1986), *Beyond Sovereignity: The Challenge of Global Policy*, University of South Carolina Press, Columbia.

Spivak, Gayatri Chakravorty (1976) 'Preface', in J. Derrida, *Of Grammatology*, Johns Hopkins University Press, Baltimore.

Stamatopoulou, E. (1995), 'Women's Rights and the United Nations', in J. Peters and A. Wolper (eds), *Women's Rights, Human Rights: International Feminist Perspectives*, Routledge, New York.

Stamp, P. (1995), 'Burying Otieno: The Politics of Gender and Ethnicity in Kenya', in B. Laslett, J. Brenner and Y. Arat (eds), *Rethinking the Political: Gender, Resistance and the State*, University of Chicago Press, Chicago.

Steiner, H. J. and Alston, P. (eds), (1996), *International Human Rights in Context: Law, Politics, Morals*, Clarendon Press, Oxford.

Strange, S. (1996), *The Retreat of the State: The Diffusion of Power in the World Economy*, Cambridge University Press, Cambridge.

Strobel, M. (1976), 'From *Lelemama* to Lobbying: Women's Associations in Mombasa, Kenya', in N. J. Hafkin and E. G. Bay (eds), *Women in Africa*, Stanford University Press, Stanford.

Swain, C. (1993), *Black Faces, Black Interest*, Harvard University Press, Cambridge.

Tamir, Y. (1993), *Liberal Nationalism*, Princeton University Press, Princeton.

Taylor, C. (1989), *Sources of the Self: The Making of the Modern Identity*, Harvard University Press, Cambridge.

Taylor, C. (1991), 'Shared and Divergent Values', in R. L. Watts and D. M. Brown (eds), *Options for a New Canada*, University of Toronto Press, Toronto.

Taylor, C. (1992), 'The Politics of Recognition', in Amy Gutmann (ed), *Multiculturalism and 'The Politics of Recognition: An Essay by Charles Taylor*, Princeton University Press, Princeton.

Taylor, C. (1992), *Multiculturalism and 'The Politics of Recognition'*, Princeton University Press, Princeton.

Taylor, C. (1994) 'The Politics of Recognition', in Amy Gutmann (ed) *Multiculturalism: Examining the Politics of Recognition* Princeton University Press, Princeton.

Thiele, L. (1993), 'Making Democracy Safe for the World: Social Movements and Global Politics', *Alternatives,* vol. 18, pp. 273-305.

Thornton, A. P. (1965), *The Doctrine of Imperialism*, John Wiley and Sons, Inc., New York.

Thornton, A. P. (1978), *Imperialism in the Twentieth Century*, Macmillan, London.

Tober, D. (1993), 'One World - One Vision for Business', in S. Bushrui *et al* (eds), *Transition to a Global Society,* Oneworld, Oxford, pp. 98-107.

Todd, J. (1995), 'Equality, plurality and democracy: justifications of proposed constitutional settlements of the Northern Ireland Conflict', *Ethnic and Racial Studies*, vol. 18, pp. 818-36.

Tully, J. (1995), *Strange Multiplicity: Constitutionalism in an Age of Diversity* Cambridge University Press, Cambridge.

ul Haq, M. *et al.* (eds), (1995), *The UN and the Bretton Woods Institutions: New Challenges for the Twenty-First Century,* Macmillan, Basingstoke.

Vaillancourt, F. (1993), 'The Economic Status of the French Language and Francophones in Québec', in A-G. Gagnon, (ed), *Québec: State and Society*, Nelson Canada, Scarborough.

Valliéres, P. (1971), *White Niggers of America*, McClelland and Stewart Limited, Toronto.

Van Allen, J. (1976), ' "Aba Riots" or Igbo "Women's War"?' in N. J. Hafkin and E. G. Bay (eds), *Women in Africa*, Stanford University Press, Stanford.

van Wyk, D. (1995), 'Introduction to the South African Constitution', in D. van Wyk *et al* (eds), *Rights and Constitutionalism: The New South African Legal Order*, Clarendon Press, Oxford.

Vasak, K. (1963), 'The European Convention of Human Rights: Beyond the Frontiers of Europe', *International and Comparative Law Quarterly*, vol. 12, pp. 1206-31.

Von Eschen, P. M. (1997), *Race Against Empire: Black Americans and Anti-Colonialism, 1937-1957*, Cornell University Press, Ithaca.

Walker, R. B. J. (1993), *Inside Outside: International Relations as Political Theory*, Cambridge University Press, Cambridge.

Williams, M. S. (1995), 'Justice Towards Groups: Political Not Juridical', *Political Theory*, vol. 23, pp. 67-91.

Williams, M. S. (1998), *Voice, Trust, and Memory: Marginalized Groups and the Failings of Liberal Representation*, Princeton University Press, Princeton.

Williams, M. S. (forthcoming), 'The Uneasy Alliance of Group Representation and Deliberative Democracy', in W. Kymlicka and W. Norman (eds), *Citizenship in Diverse Societies*, Oxford University Press, Oxford.

Williams, S. (1990), 'Sovereignty and Accountability in the European Community', *The Political Quarterly*, vol. 61, pp. 299-317.

Wilson, W. J. (1978), *The Declining Significance of Race*, University of Chicago Press, Chicago.

Wollstonecraft, M. (1792/1982), *Vindication of the Rights of Woman*, Penguin, Harmondsworth.

Woodward, C. V. (1974), *The Strange Career of Jim Crow*, 3d ed., Oxford University Press, New York.

Wriston, W. B. (1992), *The Twilight of Sovereignity: How the Information Revolution Is Transforming Our World*, Scribner, New York.

Yahil, L. (1990), *The Holocaust: The Fate of European Jewry 1932-1945*, Oxford University Press, Oxford.

YIO (1997), *Yearbook of International Organizations 1997/98*, Volume 1, Saur, Munich.

Young, I. M. (1990), *Justice and the Politics of Difference*, Princeton University Press, Princeton.

Young, I. M. (1994), 'Justice and Communicative Democracy', in R. Gottlieb (ed), *Tradition, Counter-Tradition, Politics: Dimensions of Radical Democracy*, Temple University Press, Philadelphia.

Young, I. M. (1997), *Intersecting Voices: Dilemmas of Gender, Political Philosophy, and Policy*, Princeton University Press, Princeton.

Young, W. D. (1969), *The Anatomy of a Party: The National CCF 1932-1961*, University of Toronto Press, Toronto.

Zines, L. (1991), *Constitutional Change in the Commonwealth*, Cambridge University Press, Cambridge.

Index

For Product Safety Concerns and Information please contact our EU representative GPSR@taylorandfrancis.com Taylor & Francis Verlag GmbH, Kaufingerstraße 24, 80331 München, Germany

Batch number: 10782397

Printed by Printforce, the Netherlands